New Perspectives on

Microsoft® Office Word 2007

Brief

S. Scott Zimmerman
Brigham Young University

Beverly B. Zimmerman
Brigham Young University

Ann Shaffer

Katherine T. Pinard

THOMSON

COURSE TECHNOLOGY

Australia • Canada • Mexico • Singapore • Spain • United Kingdom • United States

THOMSON
―――――★――――― ™
COURSE TECHNOLOGY

New Perspectives on Microsoft Office Word 2007—Brief
is published by Thomson Course Technology.

Acquisitions Editor:
Kristina Matthews

Senior Product Manager:
Kathy Finnegan

Product Manager:
Erik Herman

Associate Product Manager:
Brandi Henson

Editorial Assistant:
Leigh Robbins

Senior Marketing Manager:
Joy Stark

Marketing Coordinator:
Jennifer Hankin

Developmental Editor:
Mary Kemper

Senior Content Project Manager:
Catherine G. DiMassa

Composition:
GEX Publishing Services

Text Designer:
Steve Deschene

Cover Designer:
Elizabeth Paquin

Cover Art:
Bill Brown

recording, taping, Web distribution, or information storage and retrieval systems—without the written permission of the publisher.

For permission to use material from this text or product, submit a request online at www.thomsonrights.com

Any additional questions about permissions can be submitted by e-mail to thomsonrights@thomson.com

Disclaimer
Thomson Course Technology reserves the right to revise this publication and make changes from time to time in its content without notice.

Some of the product names and company names used in this book have been used for identification purposes only and
may be trademarks or registered trademarks of their respective manufacturers and sellers.

Disclaimer: Any fictional URLs used throughout this book are intended for instructional purposes only. At the time this book was printed, any such URLs were fictional and not belonging to any real persons or companies.

Microsoft and the Office logo are either registered trademarks or trademarks of Microsoft Corporation in the United States and/or other countries. Thomson Course Technology is an independent entity from the Microsoft Corporation, and not affiliated with Microsoft in any manner.

ISBN-13: 978-1-4239-0580-6
ISBN-10: 1-4239-0580-6

Preface

The New Perspectives Series' critical-thinking, problem-solving approach is the ideal way to prepare students to transcend point-and-click skills and take advantage of all that Microsoft Office 2007 has to offer.

In developing the New Perspectives Series for Microsoft Office 2007, our goal was to create books that give students the software concepts and practical skills they need to succeed beyond the classroom. We've updated our proven case-based pedagogy with more practical content to make learning skills more meaningful to students.

With the New Perspectives Series, students understand *why* they are learning *what* they are learning, and are fully prepared to apply their skills to real-life situations.

"I really love the Margin Tips, which add 'tricks of the trade' to students' skills package. In addition, the Reality Check exercises provide for practical application of students' knowledge. I can't wait to use them in the classroom when we adopt Office 2007."

*—Terry Morse Colucci
Institute of Technology, Inc.*

About This Book

This book provides a thorough, hands-on introduction to the new Microsoft Office Word 2007 software, and includes the following:

- A new "Getting Started with Microsoft Office 2007" tutorial that familiarizes students with the new Office 2007 features and user interface
- Complete coverage of Word 2007 basics, including creating, editing, and formatting documents; working with multi-page documents; simple desktop publishing; and performing a mail merge
- Guidance in using themes and Quick Styles to create professional-looking documents quickly and easily, and in exploring styles for document elements using the new Live Preview feature
- Instruction in using the new SmartArt feature to create and modify diagrams that illustrate concepts, such as processes and organizational structures
- New business case scenarios throughout, which provide a rich and realistic context for students to apply the concepts and skills presented

System Requirements

This book assumes a typical installation of Microsoft Office Word 2007 and Microsoft Windows Vista Ultimate with the Aero feature turned off (or Windows Vista Home Premium or Business edition). Note that you can also complete the tutorials in this book using Windows XP; you will notice only minor differences if you are using Windows XP. Refer to the tutorial "Getting Started with Microsoft Office 2007" for Tips noting these differences. The browser used in this book for any steps that require a browser is Internet Explorer 7.

www.course.com/NewPerspectives

The New Perspectives Approach

"I appreciate the real-world approach that the New Perspective Series takes. It enables the transference of knowledge from step-by-step instructions to a far broader application of the software tools."

—Monique Sluymers
Kaplan University

Context

Each tutorial begins with a problem presented in a "real-world" case that is meaningful to students. The case sets the scene to help students understand what they will do in the tutorial.

Hands-on Approach

Each tutorial is divided into manageable sessions that combine reading and hands-on, step-by-step work. Colorful screenshots help guide students through the steps. **Trouble?** tips anticipate common mistakes or problems to help students stay on track and continue with the tutorial.

InSight

InSight Boxes

New for Office 2007! InSight boxes offer expert advice and best practices to help students better understand how to work with the software. With the information provided in the InSight boxes, students achieve a deeper understanding of the concepts behind the software features and skills.

Tip

Margin Tips

New for Office 2007! Margin Tips provide helpful hints and shortcuts for more efficient use of the software. The Tips appear in the margin at key points throughout each tutorial, giving students extra information when and where they need it.

Reality Check

Reality Checks

New for Office 2007! Comprehensive, open-ended Reality Check exercises give students the opportunity to practice skills by creating practical, real-world documents, such as resumes and budgets, which they are likely to use in their everyday lives at school, home, or work.

Review

In New Perspectives, retention is a key component to learning. At the end of each session, a series of Quick Check questions helps students test their understanding of the concepts before moving on. Each tutorial also contains an end-of-tutorial summary and a list of key terms for further reinforcement.

Apply

Assessment

Engaging and challenging Review Assignments and Case Problems have always been a hallmark feature of the New Perspectives Series. Colorful icons and brief descriptions accompany the exercises, making it easy to understand, at a glance, both the goal and level of challenge a particular assignment holds.

Reference Window

Task Reference

Reference

While contextual learning is excellent for retention, there are times when students will want a high-level understanding of how to accomplish a task. Within each tutorial, Reference Windows appear before a set of steps to provide a succinct summary and preview of how to perform a task. In addition, a complete Task Reference at the back of the book provides quick access to information on how to carry out common tasks. Finally, each book includes a combination Glossary/Index to promote easy reference of material.

www.course.com/NewPerspectives

Brief
Introductory
Comprehensive

Our Complete System of Instruction

Coverage To Meet Your Needs

Whether you're looking for just a small amount of coverage or enough to fill a semester-long class, we can provide you with a textbook that meets your needs.

- Brief books typically cover the essential skills in just 2 to 4 tutorials.
- Introductory books build and expand on those skills and contain an average of 5 to 8 tutorials.
- Comprehensive books are great for a full-semester class, and contain 9 to 12+ tutorials.

So if the book you're holding does not provide the right amount of coverage for you, there's probably another offering available. Go to our Web site or contact your Thomson Course Technology sales representative to find out what else we offer.

Student Online Companion

This book has an accompanying online companion Web site designed to enhance learning. This Web site includes:

- Internet Assignments for selected tutorials
- Student Data Files
- PowerPoint presentations

COURSECASTS

CourseCasts – Learning on the Go. Always available...always relevant.

Want to keep up with the latest technology trends relevant to you? Visit our site to find a library of podcasts, CourseCasts, featuring a "CourseCast of the Week," and download them to your mp3 player at http://coursecasts.course.com.

Our fast-paced world is driven by technology. You know because you're an active participant—always on the go, always keeping up with technological trends, and always learning new ways to embrace technology to power your life.

Ken Baldauf, host of CourseCasts, is a faculty member of the Florida State University Computer Science Department where he is responsible for teaching technology classes to thousands of FSU students each year. Ken is an expert in the latest technology trends; he gathers and sorts through the most pertinent news and information for CourseCasts so your students can spend their time enjoying technology, rather than trying to figure it out. Open or close your lecture with a discussion based on the latest CourseCast.

Visit us at http://coursecasts.course.com to learn on the go!

Instructor Resources

We offer more than just a book. We have all the tools you need to enhance your lectures, check students' work, and generate exams in a new, easier-to-use and completely revised package. This book's Instructor's Manual, ExamView testbank, PowerPoint presentations, data files, solution files, figure files, and a sample syllabus are all available on a single CD-ROM or for downloading at www.course.com.

Skills Assessment and Training

SAM 2007 helps bridge the gap between the classroom and the real world by allowing students to train and test on important computer skills in an active, hands-on environment.

SAM 2007's easy-to-use system includes powerful interactive exams, training or projects on critical applications such as Word, Excel, Access, PowerPoint, Outlook, Windows, the Internet, and much more. SAM simulates the application environment, allowing students to demonstrate their knowledge and think through the skills by performing real-world tasks.

Designed to be used with the New Perspectives Series, SAM 2007 includes built-in page references so students can print helpful study guides that match the New Perspectives textbooks used in class. Powerful administrative options allow instructors to schedule exams and assignments, secure tests, and run reports with almost limitless flexibility.

Blackboard

Online Content

Blackboard is the leading distance learning solution provider and class-management platform today. Thomson Course Technology has partnered with Blackboard to bring you premium online content. Content for use with *New Perspectives on Microsoft Office Word 2007, Brief* is available in a Blackboard Course Cartridge and may include topic reviews, case projects, review questions, test banks, practice tests, custom syllabi, and more.

Thomson Course Technology also has solutions for several other learning management systems. Please visit http://www.course.com today to see what's available for this title.

Acknowledgments

Thanks to Kristina Matthews, the fearless leader of the New Perspective Series. To Kathy Finnegan, amazing and resourceful project manager, thank you for the great ideas and much-needed encouragement. Thanks, also, to Brandi Henson, Associate Product Manager, and Leigh Robbins, Editorial Assistant, for their support during the development of this text. My thanks to Mary Kemper, Developmental Editor extraordinaire, who made this a far better book than it would have been without her careful edits. A special thanks to Kitty Pinard and Lisa Ruffolo for their patient advice and explanations at all hours of the day and night. Thank you to Cathie DiMassa, our hard-working Production Editor, who managed the million details involved in transforming the manuscript into a printed book. As always, I relied on the ace Manuscript Quality Assurance testers at Thomson Course Technology, who provided detailed comments on every tutorial, at several stages in the process. Many thanks to Christian Kunciw, MQA Project Leader, and to the following QA testers for their help and suggestions: John Freitas, Serge Palladino, Danielle Shaw, Marianne Snow, and Susan Whalen.

Finally, I'm extremely grateful to our reviewers, who provided valuable insights into the needs of their students: Carla Jones, Middle Tennessee State University; Pamela Silvers, Asheville-Buncombe Technical Community College; and Monique Sluymers, Kaplan University.

–Ann Shaffer

We likewise want to thank all those who made this book possible. We especially want to thank Ann Shaffer, our co-author, for her expertise, hard work, and creative talents. Special thanks also go to Mary Kemper for her dedication and expertise as Developmental Editor in bringing this new edition to fruition.

–Beverly and Scott Zimmerman
–Katherine T. Pinard

Table of Contents

Preface iii

Getting Started with Microsoft Office 2007
Preparing a Meeting Agenda .... OFF 1

Exploring Microsoft Office 2007 .... OFF 2
  Integrating Office Programs .... OFF 3
Starting Office Programs .... OFF 3
  Switching Between Open Programs and Files .... OFF 5
Exploring Common Window Elements .... OFF 6
  Resizing the Program Window and Workspace .... OFF 6
  Getting Information from the Status Bar .... OFF 7
  Switching Views .... OFF 8
  Zooming the Workspace .... OFF 8
Using the Ribbon .... OFF 10
  Clicking Button Icons .... OFF 10
  Using Galleries and Live Preview .... OFF 12
  Opening Dialog Boxes and Task Panes .... OFF 13
Using Contextual Tools .... OFF 15
  Displaying Contextual Tabs .... OFF 15
  Accessing the Mini Toolbar .... OFF 15
  Opening Shortcut Menus .... OFF 17
Working with Files .... OFF 18
  Saving a File .... OFF 18
  Closing a File .... OFF 21
  Opening a File .... OFF 21
Getting Help .... OFF 23
  Viewing ScreenTips .... OFF 23
  Using the Help Window .... OFF 23
Printing a File .... OFF 27
Exiting Programs .... OFF 28
Quick Check .... OFF 29
Tutorial Summary .... OFF 29
Key Terms .... OFF 29
Review Assignments .... OFF 30
SAM Assessment and Training .... OFF 30
Quick Check Answers .... OFF 31
Reality Check .... OFF 32

Tutorial 1 Creating a Document   WD 1
Writing a Business Letter .... WD 1

Session 1.1 .... WD 2
Four Steps to a Professional Document .... WD 2
Exploring the Word Window .... WD 3
Opening a New Document .... WD 5
Setting Up the Word Window .... WD 6
  Selecting Print Layout View .... WD 6
  Displaying the Rulers and Selecting the Home Tab ..... WD 7

Displaying Nonprinting Characters .... WD 8
  Checking the Font and Font Size .... WD 9
  Checking the Zoom Setting .... WD 9
Beginning a Letter .... WD 11
Entering Text .... WD 12
Session 1.1 Quick Check .... WD 15

Session 1.2 .... WD 16
Scrolling a Document .... WD 16
Moving the Insertion Point Around a Document .... WD 19
Using the Undo and Redo Commands .... WD 20
Correcting Errors .... WD 21
  Correcting Spelling Errors .... WD 23
  Proofreading the Letter .... WD 24
Inserting a Date with AutoComplete .... WD 25
Understanding Line and Paragraph Spacing .... WD 27
Selecting Parts of a Document .... WD 29
Adjusting Paragraph and Line Spacing .... WD 31
Previewing and Printing a Document .... WD 33
Creating an Envelope .... WD 35
Session 1.2 Quick Check .... WD 37
Tutorial Summary .... WD 37
Key Terms .... WD 37
Review Assignments .... WD 38
Case Problems .... WD 39
Internet Assignments .... WD 43
SAM Assessment and Training .... WD 44
Quick Check Answers .... WD 44

**Tutorial 2 Editing and Formatting
a Document   WD 45**
Preparing a Handout on Choosing a Design Style .... WD 45

Session 2.1 .... WD 46
Reviewing the Document .... WD 46
Using the Spelling and Grammar Checker .... WD 50
Deleting Text .... WD 52
Moving Text in a Document .... WD 54
  Dragging and Dropping Text .... WD 54
  Cutting or Copying and Pasting Text .... WD 57
Finding and Replacing Text .... WD 61
Session 2.1 Quick Check .... WD 64

Session 2.2 .... WD 64
Changing Margins .... WD 64
Aligning Text .... WD 69
Indenting a Paragraph .... WD 71
Using the Format Painter .... WD 72
Adding Bullets and Numbers .... WD 74

Emphasizing Text Using Bold and Italic ....WD 78

   Helpful Keyboard Shortcuts ....WD 79

Working with Themes and Fonts ....WD 80

   Applying a New Font and Font Size ....WD 80

Changing the Document's Theme ....WD 83

Previewing and Printing the Document ....WD 84

Session 2.2 Quick Check ....WD 85

Tutorial Summary ....WD 85

Key Terms ....WD 86

Review Assignments ....WD 87

Case Problems ....WD 90

Internet Assignments ....WD 95

SAM Assessment and Training ....WD 95

Quick Check Answers ....WD 95

Ending Data Files ....WD 96

Tutorial 3 Creating a Multiple-Page Report — WD 97
Writing a Recommendation ....WD 97

Session 3.1 ....**WD 98**

Planning the Document ....WD 98

Formatting Headings with Quick Styles ....WD 99

Inserting a Manual Page Break ....WD 102

Organizing Information in Tables ....WD 103

Inserting a Blank Table ....WD 103

Entering Data in a Table ....WD 105

Selecting Part of a Table ....WD 106

Sorting Rows in a Table ....WD 107

Inserting Rows and Columns in a Table ....WD 110

Deleting Rows and Columns ....WD 111

Changing Column Widths ....WD 111

Formatting Tables with Styles ....WD 112

Session 3.1 Quick Check ....WD 115

Session 3.2 ....**WD 115**

Setting Tab Stops ....WD 115

Creating Footnotes and Endnotes ....WD 119

Formatting a Document in Sections ....WD 122

Creating SmartArt ....WD 124

Adding Headers and Footers ....WD 128

Inserting a Cover Page ....WD 134

Session 3.2 Quick Check ....WD 137

Tutorial Summary ....WD 138

Review Assignments ....WD 139

Case Problems ....WD 140

Internet Assignments ....WD 145

SAM Assessment and Training ....WD 145

Quick Check Answers ....WD 145

Ending Data Files ....WD 146

Tutorial 4 Desktop Publishing and Mail Merge — WD 147
Creating a Newsletter, Cover Letter, and Blog Post ....WD 147

Session 4.1 ....**WD 148**

Elements of Desktop Publishing ....WD 148

Using WordArt to Create a Headline ....WD 149

   Editing a WordArt Object ....WD 152

   Changing the Shape of a WordArt Object ....WD 152

   Wrapping Text Below a WordArt Object ....WD 153

Positioning and Sizing the WordArt Object ....WD 155

Anchoring the WordArt Object to a Blank Paragraph ....WD 156

Formatting Text in Newspaper-Style Columns ....WD 158

Inserting Graphics ....WD 160

Resizing a Graphic ....WD 165

Cropping a Graphic ....WD 166

Session 4.1 Quick Check ....WD 167

Session 4.2 ....**WD 168**

Wrapping Text Around a Graphic ....WD 168

Moving and Aligning a Graphic ....WD 169

Inserting Drop Caps ....WD 170

Inserting Symbols and Special Characters ....WD 171

Balancing the Columns ....WD 173

Inserting a Border Around a Page ....WD 174

Performing a Simple Mail Merge ....WD 176

Selecting a Data Source ....WD 179

Inserting Merge Fields ....WD 180

Previewing the Merged Document ....WD 182

Merging the Main Document and Data Source ....WD 184

Creating a Blog Post ....WD 185

Session 4.2 Quick Check ....WD 187

Tutorial Summary ....WD 188

Review Assignments ....WD 189

Case Problems ....WD 190

Internet Assignments ....WD 197

SAM Assessment and Training ....WD 197

Quick Check Answers ....WD 198

Ending Data Files ....WD 199

Reality Check ....WD 200

Glossary/Index ....**REF 1**

Task Reference ....**REF 6**

Objectives

- Explore the programs that comprise Microsoft Office
- Start programs and switch between them
- Explore common window elements
- Minimize, maximize, and restore windows
- Use the Ribbon, tabs, and buttons
- Use the contextual tabs, Mini toolbar, and shortcut menus
- Save, close, and open a file
- Use the Help system
- Print a file
- Exit programs

Getting Started with Microsoft Office 2007

Preparing a Meeting Agenda

Case | Recycled Palette

Recycled Palette, a company in Oregon founded by Ean Nogella in 2006, sells 100 percent recycled latex paint to both individuals and businesses in the area. The high-quality recycled paint is filtered to industry standards and tested for performance and environmental safety. The paint is available in both 1 gallon cans and 5 gallon pails, and comes in colors ranging from white to shades of brown, blue, green, and red. The demand for affordable recycled paint has been growing each year. Ean and all his employees use Microsoft Office 2007, which provides everyone in the company with the power and flexibility to store a variety of information, create consistent files, and share data. In this tutorial, you'll review how the company's employees use Microsoft Office 2007.

Starting Data Files

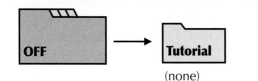

OFF → Tutorial
(none)

Review
Finances.xlsx
Letter.docx

Exploring Microsoft Office 2007

Microsoft Office 2007, or **Office**, is a collection of Microsoft programs. Office is available in many suites, each of which contains a different combination of these programs. For example, the Professional suite includes Word, Excel, PowerPoint, Access, Outlook, and Publisher. Other suites are available and can include more or fewer programs (for additional information about the available suites, go to the Microsoft Web site). Each Office program contains valuable tools to help you accomplish many tasks, such as composing reports, analyzing data, preparing presentations, compiling information, sending e-mail, and planning schedules.

Microsoft Office Word 2007, or **Word**, is a computer program you use to enter, edit, and format text. The files you create in Word are called **documents**, although many people use the term *document* to refer to any file created on a computer. Word, often called a word processing program, offers many special features that help you compose and update all types of documents, ranging from letters and newsletters to reports, brochures, faxes, and even books—all in attractive and readable formats. You can also use Word to create, insert, and position figures, tables, and other graphics to enhance the look of your documents. For example, the Recycled Palette employees create business letters using Word.

Microsoft Office Excel 2007, or **Excel**, is a computer program you use to enter, calculate, analyze, and present numerical data. You can do some of this in Word with tables, but Excel provides many more tools for recording and formatting numbers as well as performing calculations. The graphics capabilities in Excel also enable you to display data visually. You might, for example, generate a pie chart or a bar chart to help people quickly see the significance of and the connections between information. The files you create in Excel are called **workbooks** (commonly referred to as spreadsheets), and Excel is often called a spreadsheet program. The Recycled Palette accounting department uses a line chart in an Excel workbook to visually track the company's financial performance.

Microsoft Office Access 2007, or **Access**, is a computer program used to enter, maintain, and retrieve related information (or data) in a format known as a database. The files you create in Access are called **databases**, and Access is often referred to as a database or relational database program. With Access, you can create forms to make data entry easier, and you can create professional reports to improve the readability of your data. The Recycled Palette operations department tracks the company's inventory in a table in an Access database.

Microsoft Office PowerPoint 2007, or **PowerPoint**, is a computer program you use to create a collection of slides that can contain text, charts, pictures, sound, movies, multimedia, and so on. The files you create in PowerPoint are called **presentations**, and PowerPoint is often called a presentation graphics program. You can show these presentations on your computer monitor, project them onto a screen as a slide show, print them, share them over the Internet, or display them on the World Wide Web. You can also use PowerPoint to generate presentation-related documents such as audience handouts, outlines, and speakers' notes. The Recycled Palette marketing department has created an effective slide presentation with PowerPoint to promote its paints to a wider audience.

Microsoft Office Outlook 2007, or **Outlook**, is a computer program you use to send, receive, and organize e-mail; plan your schedule; arrange meetings; organize contacts; create a to-do list; and jot down notes. You can also use Outlook to print schedules, task lists, phone directories, and other documents. Outlook is often referred to as an information management program. The Recycled Palette staff use Outlook to send and receive e-mail, plan their schedules, and create to-do lists.

Although each Office program individually is a strong tool, their potential is even greater when used together.

Integrating Office Programs

One of the main advantages of Office is **integration**, the ability to share information between programs. Integration ensures consistency and accuracy, and it saves time because you don't have to reenter the same information in several Office programs. The staff at Recycled Palette uses the integration features of Office daily, including the following examples:

- The accounting department created an Excel bar chart on the previous two years' fourth-quarter results, which they inserted into the quarterly financial report created in Word. They included a hyperlink in the Word report that employees can click to open the Excel workbook and view the original data.
- The operations department included an Excel pie chart of sales percentages by paint colors on a PowerPoint slide, which is part of a presentation to stockholders.
- The marketing department produced a mailing to promote its recycled paints to local contractors and designers by combining a form letter created in Word with an Access database that stores the names and addresses of these potential customers.
- A sales representative wrote a letter in Word about an upcoming promotion for new customers and merged the letter with an Outlook contact list containing the names and addresses of prospective customers.

These are just a few examples of how you can take information from one Office program and integrate it with another.

Starting Office Programs

You can start any Office program by clicking the Start button on the Windows taskbar, and then selecting the program you want from the All Programs menu. As soon as the program starts, you can immediately begin to create new files or work with existing ones. If an Office program appears in the most frequently used programs list on the left side of the Start menu, you can click the program name to start the program.

Starting Office Programs | Reference Window

- Click the Start button on the taskbar.
- Click All Programs.
- Click Microsoft Office.
- Click the name of the program you want to start.

or

- Click the name of the program you want to start in the most frequently used programs list on the left side of the Start menu.

You'll start Excel using the Start button.

To start Excel and open a new, blank workbook:

▶ **1.** Make sure your computer is on and the Windows desktop appears on your screen.

  Trouble? If your screen varies slightly from those shown in the figures, your computer might be set up differently. The figures in this book were created while running Windows Vista with the Aero feature turned off, but how your screen looks depends on the version of Windows you are using, the background settings, and so forth.

▶ **2.** Click the **Start** button ⊛ on the taskbar, and then click **All Programs** to display the All Programs menu.

▶ **3.** Click **Microsoft Office** on the All Programs list, and then point to **Microsoft Office Excel 2007**. Depending on how your computer is set up, your desktop and menu might contain different icons and commands.

  Trouble? If you don't see Microsoft Office on the All Programs list, click Microsoft Office Excel 2007 on the All Programs list. If you still don't see Microsoft Office Excel 2007, ask your instructor or technical support person for help.

▶ **4.** Click **Microsoft Office Excel 2007**. Excel starts, and a new, blank workbook opens. See Figure 1.

Figure 1	New, blank Excel workbook

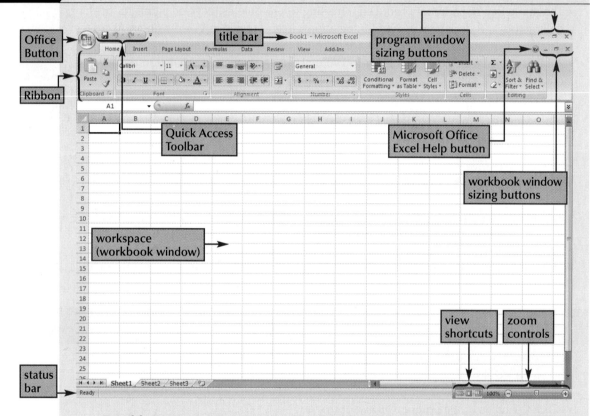

  Trouble? If the Excel window doesn't fill your entire screen, the window is not maximized, or expanded to its full size. You'll maximize the window shortly.

You can have more than one Office program open at once. You'll use this same method to start Word and open a new, blank document.

To start Word and open a new, blank document:

▶ **1.** Click the **Start** button ⊛ on the taskbar, click **All Programs** to display the All Programs list, and then click **Microsoft Office**.

  Trouble? If you don't see Microsoft Office on the All Programs list, click Microsoft Office Word 2007 on the All Programs list. If you still don't see Microsoft Office Word 2007, ask your instructor or technical support person for help.

▶ **2.** Click **Microsoft Office Word 2007**. Word starts, and a new, blank document opens. See Figure 2.

New, blank document in Word | Figure 2

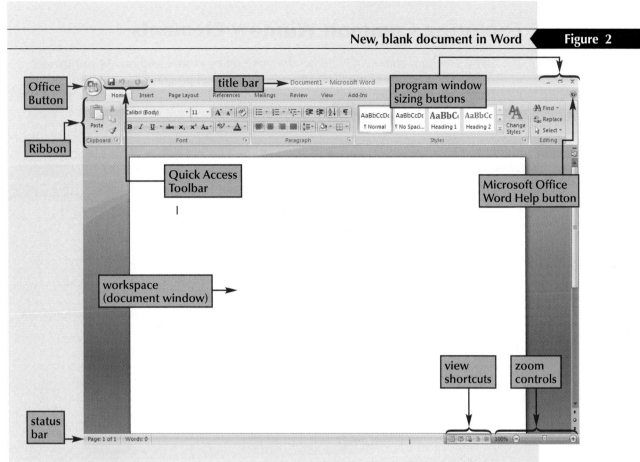

Trouble? If the Word window doesn't fill your entire screen, the window is not maximized. You'll maximize the window shortly.

Switching Between Open Programs and Files

Two programs are running at the same time—Excel and Word. The taskbar contains buttons for both programs. When you have two or more programs running or two files within the same program open, you can use the taskbar buttons to switch from one program or file to another. The button for the active program or file is darker. The employees at Recycled Palette often work in several programs at once.

To switch between Word and Excel files:

▶ 1. Click the **Microsoft Excel – Book1** button on the taskbar. The active program switches from Word to Excel. See Figure 3.

Excel and Word programs opened simultaneously | Figure 3

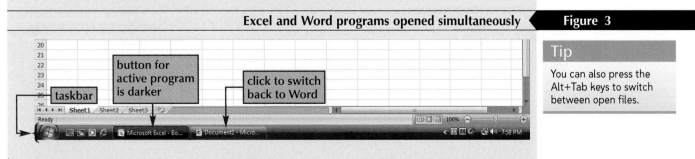

Tip

You can also press the Alt+Tab keys to switch between open files.

▶ 2. Click the **Document1 – Microsoft Word** button on the taskbar to return to Word.

Exploring Common Window Elements

The Office programs consist of windows that have many similar features. As you can see in Figures 1 and 2, many of the elements in both the Excel program window and the Word program window are the same. In fact, all the Office programs have these same elements. Figure 4 describes some of the most common window elements.

Figure 4 | **Common window elements**

Element	Description
Office Button	Provides access to document-level features and program settings
Quick Access Toolbar	Provides one-click access to commonly used commands, such as Save, Undo, and Repeat
Title bar	Contains the name of the open file, the program name, and the sizing buttons
Sizing buttons	Resize and close the program window or the workspace
Ribbon	Provides access to the main set of commands organized by task into tabs and groups
Microsoft Office Help button	Opens the Help window for that program
Workspace	Displays the file you are working on (Word document, Excel workbook, Access database, or PowerPoint slide)
Status bar	Provides information about the program, open file, or current task as well as the view shortcuts and zoom controls
View shortcuts	Change how a file is displayed in the workspace
Zoom controls	Magnify or shrink the content displayed in the workspace

Because these elements are the same in each program, after you've learned one program, it's easy to learn the others. The next sections explore these common features.

Resizing the Program Window and Workspace

There are three different sizing buttons. The Minimize button ⊟ , which is the left button, hides a window so that only its program button is visible on the taskbar. The middle button changes name and function depending on the status of the window—the Maximize button ⊡ expands the window to the full screen size or to the program window size, and the Restore Down button ⧉ returns the window to a predefined size. The Close button ☒ , on the right, exits the program or closes the file. Excel has two sets of sizing buttons. The top set controls the program window and the lower set controls the workspace. The workspace sizing buttons look and function in exactly the same way as the program window sizing buttons, except the button names change to Minimize Window and Restore Window when the workspace is maximized.

Most often, you'll want to maximize the program window and workspace to take advantage of the full screen size you have available. If you have several files open, you might want to restore down their windows so that you can see more than one window at a time, or you might want to minimize programs or files you are not working on at the moment. You'll try minimizing, maximizing, and restoring down windows and workspaces now.

To resize windows and workspaces:

▶ **1.** Click the **Minimize** button ─ on the Word title bar. The Word program window reduces to a taskbar button. The Excel program window is visible again.

▶ **2.** If necessary, click the **Maximize** button on the Excel title bar. The Excel program window expands to fill the screen.

▶ **3.** Click the **Restore Window** button in the lower set of Excel sizing buttons. The workspace is resized and is now smaller than the full program window. See Figure 5.

Resized Excel window and workspace | **Figure 5**

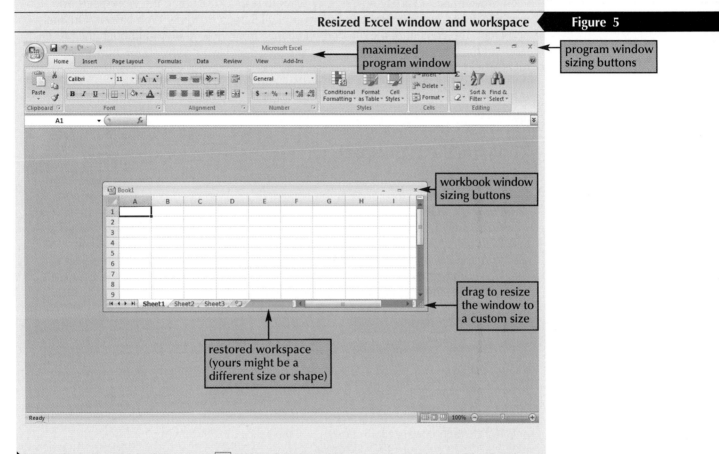

maximized program window

program window sizing buttons

workbook window sizing buttons

drag to resize the window to a custom size

restored workspace (yours might be a different size or shape)

▶ **4.** Click the **Maximize** button on the Excel workbook window title bar. The Excel workspace expands to fill the program window.

▶ **5.** Click the **Document1 - Microsoft Word** button on the taskbar. The Word program window returns to its previous size.

▶ **6.** If necessary, click the **Maximize** button on the Word title bar. The Word program window expands to fill the screen.

The sizing buttons give you the flexibility to arrange the program and file windows on your screen to best fit your needs.

Getting Information from the Status Bar

The **status bar** at the bottom of the program window provides information about the open file and current task or selection. It also has buttons and other controls for working with the file and its content. The status bar buttons and information displays are specific to the individual programs. For example, the Excel status bar displays summary information about a selected range of numbers (such as their sum or average), whereas the Word status bar shows the current page number and total number of words in a document. The right side of the status bar includes buttons that enable you to switch the workspace view in Word, Excel, PowerPoint, and Access as well as zoom the workspace in Word, Excel, and PowerPoint. You can customize the status bar to display other information or hide the **default** (original or preset) information.

Switching Views

Each program has a variety of views, or ways to display the file in the workspace. For example, Word has five views: Print Layout, Full Screen Reading, Web Layout, Outline, and Draft. The content of the file doesn't change from view to view, although the presentation of the content will. In Word, for example, Page Layout view shows how a document would appear as the printed page, whereas Web Layout view shows how the document would appear as a Web page. You can quickly switch between views using the shortcuts at the right side of the status bar. You can also change the view from the View tab on the Ribbon. You'll change views in later tutorials.

Zooming the Workspace

Zooming is a way to magnify or shrink the file content displayed in the workspace. You can zoom in to get a closer look at the content of an open document, worksheet, or slide, or you can zoom out to see more of the content at a smaller size. There are several ways to change the zoom percentage. You can use the Zoom slider at the right of the status bar to quickly change the zoom percentage. You can click the Zoom level button to the left of the Zoom slider in the status bar to open the Zoom dialog box and select a specific zoom percentage or size based on your file. You can also change the zoom settings using the Zoom group in the View tab on the Ribbon.

Reference Window | Zooming the Workspace

- Click the Zoom Out or Zoom In button on the status bar (or drag the Zoom slider button left or right) to the desired zoom percentage.
or
- Click the Zoom level button on the status bar.
- Select the appropriate zoom setting, and then click the OK button.
or
- Click the View tab on the Ribbon, and then in the Zoom group, click the zoom setting you want.

The figures shown in these tutorials are zoomed to enhance readability. You'll zoom the Word and Excel workspaces.

To zoom the Word and Excel workspaces:

▶ 1. On the Zoom slider on the Word status bar, drag the **slider button** to the left until the Zoom percentage is **10%**. The document reduces to its smallest size, which makes the entire page visible but unreadable. See Figure 6.

Word document zoomed to 10% ◄ Figure 6

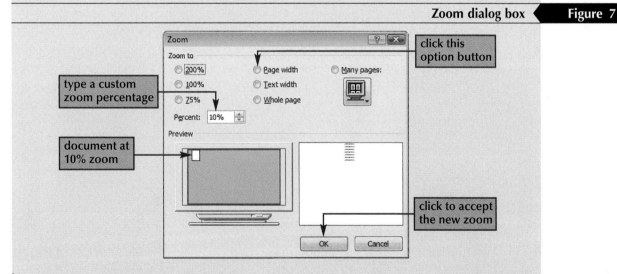

You'll zoom the document so its page width fills the workspace.

▶ **2.** Click the **Zoom level** button `10%` on the Word status bar. The Zoom dialog box opens. See Figure 7.

Zoom dialog box ◄ Figure 7

▶ **3.** Click the **Page width** option button, and then click the **OK** button. The Word document magnifies to its page width to match the rest of the Word figures shown in these tutorials.

Now, you'll zoom the workbook to 120%.

▶ **4.** Click the **Microsoft Excel – Book1** button on the taskbar. The Excel program window is displayed.

▶ **5.** Click the **Zoom In** button ⊕ on the status bar two times. The workspace magnifies to 120%. This is the zoom percentage that matches the rest of the Excel figures shown in these tutorials.

▶ **6.** Click the **Document1 – Microsoft Word** button on the taskbar. The Word program window is displayed.

Using the Ribbon

The **Ribbon** at the top of the program window just below the title bar is the main set of commands that you click to execute tasks. The Ribbon is organized into tabs. Each **tab** has commands related to particular activities. For example, in Word, the Insert tab on the Ribbon provides access to all the commands for adding objects such as shapes, pages, tables, illustrations, text, and symbols to a document. Although the tabs differ from program to program, the first tab in each program, called the Home tab, contains the commands for the most frequently performed activities, including cutting and pasting, changing fonts, and using editing tools. In addition, the Insert, Review, View, and Add-Ins tabs appear on the Ribbon in all the Office programs except Access, although the commands they include might differ from program to program. Other tabs are program specific, such as the Design tab in PowerPoint and the Datasheet tab in Access.

To use the Ribbon tabs:

▶ **1.** In Word, point to the **Insert** tab on the Ribbon. The Insert tab is highlighted, though the Home tab with the options for using the Clipboard and formatting text remains visible.

▶ **2.** Click the **Insert** tab. The Ribbon displays the Insert tab, which provides access to all the options for adding objects such as shapes, pages, tables, illustrations, text, and symbols to a document. See Figure 8.

| Figure 8 | Insert tab on the Ribbon |

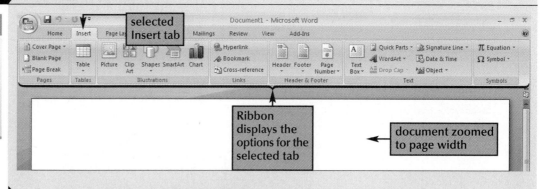

▶ **3.** Click the **Home** tab on the Ribbon. The Ribbon displays the Home options.

Clicking Button Icons

Each **button**, or icon, on the tabs provides one-click access to a command. Most buttons are labeled so that you can easily find the command you need. For the most part, when you click a button, something happens in your file. If you want to repeat that action, you click the button again. Buttons for related commands are organized on a tab in **groups**. For example, the Clipboard group on the Home tab includes the Cut, Copy, Paste, and Format Painter buttons—the commands for moving or copying text, objects, and formatting.

Buttons can be toggle switches: one click turns on the feature and the next click turns off the feature. While the feature is on, the button remains colored or highlighted to remind you that it is active. For example, in Word, the Show/Hide button on the Home tab in the Paragraph group displays the nonprinting screen characters when toggled on and hides them when toggled off.

Some buttons have two parts: a button that accesses a command and an arrow that opens a menu of all the commands available for that task. For example, the Paste button on the Home tab includes the default Paste command and an arrow that opens the menu of all the Paste commands—Paste, Paste Special, and Paste as Hyperlink. To select a command on the menu, you click the button arrow and then click the command on the menu.

The buttons and groups change based on your monitor size, your screen resolution, and the size of the program window. With smaller monitors, lower screen resolutions, and reduced program windows, buttons can appear as icons without labels and a group can be condensed into a button that you click to display the group options. The figures in these tutorials were created using a screen resolution of 1024 × 768 and, unless otherwise specified, the program and workspace windows are maximized. If you are using a different screen resolution or window size, the button icons on the Ribbon might show more or fewer button names, and some groups might be condensed into buttons.

You'll type text in the Word document, and then use the buttons on the Ribbon.

To use buttons on the Ribbon:

▶ **1.** Type **Recycled Palette**, and then press the **Enter** key. The text appears in the first line of the document and the insertion point moves to the second line.

Trouble? If you make a typing error, press the Backspace key to delete the incorrect letters, and then retype the text.

▶ **2.** In the Paragraph group on the Home tab, click the **Show/Hide** button ¶ . The nonprinting screen characters appear in the document, and the Show/Hide button remains toggled on. See Figure 9.

Trouble? If the nonprinting characters are removed from your screen, the Show/Hide button ¶ was already selected. Repeat Step 2 to show the nonprinting screen characters.

Button toggled on ◀ Figure 9

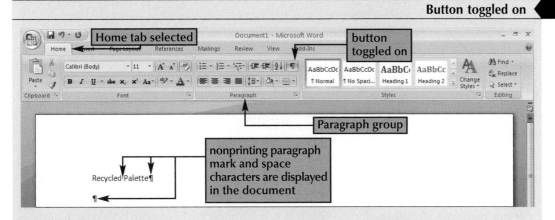

▶ **3.** Drag to select all the text in the first line of the document (but not the paragraph mark).

▶ **4.** In the Clipboard group on the Home tab, click the **Copy** button . The selected text is copied to the Clipboard.

▶ **5.** Press the ↓ key. The text is deselected and the insertion point moves to the second line in the document.

▶ **6.** In the Clipboard group on the Home tab, point to the top part of the **Paste** button. Both parts of the Paste button are highlighted, but the icon at top is darker to indicate it will be clicked if you press the mouse button.

▶ **7.** Point to the **Paste button arrow**. The button arrow is now darker.

▶ **8.** Click the **Paste button arrow**. A menu of paste commands opens. See Figure 10. To select one of the commands on the list, you click it.

| Figure 10 | Two-part Paste button |

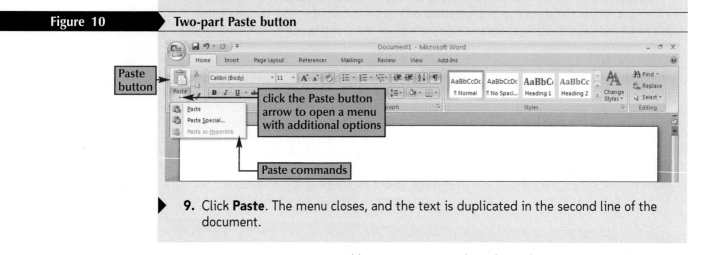

▶ **9.** Click **Paste**. The menu closes, and the text is duplicated in the second line of the document.

As you can see, you can quickly access commands and turn features on and off with the buttons on the Ribbon.

Using Galleries and Live Preview

A button can also open a **gallery**, which is a grid or menu that shows a visual representation of the options available for that command. For example, the Bullet Library gallery in Word shows an icon of each bullet style you can select. Some galleries include a More button that you click to expand the gallery to see all the options in it. When you hover the pointer over an option in a gallery, **Live Preview** shows the results you would achieve in your file if you clicked that option. To continue the bullets example, when you hover over a bullet style in the Bullet Library gallery, the current paragraph or selected text previews that bullet style. By moving the pointer from option to option, you can quickly see the text set with different bullet styles; you can then select the style that works best for your needs.

To use a gallery and Live Preview:

▶ **1.** In the Paragraph group on the Home tab, click the **Bullets button arrow** 📋 ▼. The Bullet Library gallery opens.

▶ **2.** Point to the **check mark bullet** style. Live Preview shows the selected bullet style in your document, so you can determine if you like that bullet style. See Figure 11.

Live Preview of bullet style ◀ **Figure 11**

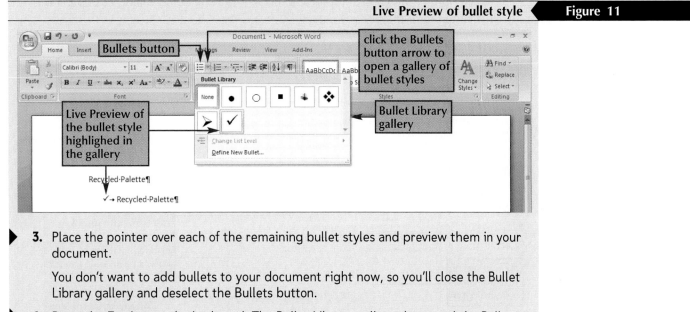

▶ **3.** Place the pointer over each of the remaining bullet styles and preview them in your document.

   You don't want to add bullets to your document right now, so you'll close the Bullet Library gallery and deselect the Bullets button.

▶ **4.** Press the **Esc** key on the keyboard. The Bullet Library gallery closes and the Bullets button is deselected.

▶ **5.** Press the **Backspace** key on the keyboard to delete the text "Recycled Palette" on the second line.

Galleries and Live Preview let you quickly see how your file will be affected by a selection.

Opening Dialog Boxes and Task Panes

The button to the right of the group names is the **Dialog Box Launcher**, which you click to open a task pane or dialog box that provides more advanced functionality for that group of tasks. A **task pane** is a window that helps you navigate through a complex task or feature. For example, the Clipboard task pane allows you to paste some or all of the items that have been cut or copied from any Office program during the current work session and the Research task pane allows you to search a variety of reference resources from within a file. A **dialog box** is a window from which you enter or choose settings for how you want to perform a task. For example, the Page Setup dialog box in Word contains options for how you want a document to look. Some dialog boxes organize related information into tabs, and related options and settings are organized into groups, just as they are on the Ribbon. You select settings in a dialog box using option buttons, check boxes, text boxes, lists, and other controls to collect information about how you want to perform a task.

In Excel, you'll use the Dialog Box Launcher for the Page Setup group to open the Page Setup dialog box.

To open the Page Setup dialog box using the Dialog Box Launcher:

▶ **1.** Click the **Microsoft Excel – Book1** button on the taskbar to switch from Word to Excel.

▶ **2.** Click the **Page Layout** tab on the Ribbon.

▶ **3.** In the Page Setup group, click the **Dialog Box Launcher**, which is the small button to the right of the Page Setup group name. The Page Setup dialog box opens with the Page tab displayed. See Figure 12.

Figure 12 ▶ Page tab in the Page Setup dialog box

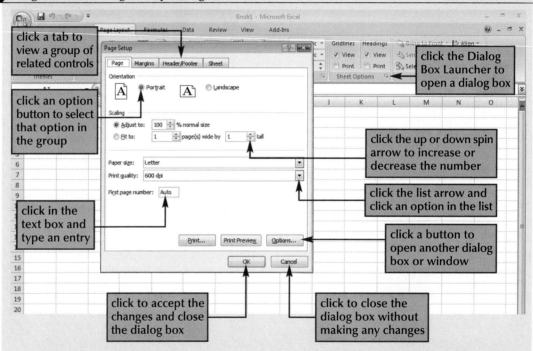

click a tab to view a group of related controls

click an option button to select that option in the group

click in the text box and type an entry

click the Dialog Box Launcher to open a dialog box

click the up or down spin arrow to increase or decrease the number

click the list arrow and click an option in the list

click a button to open another dialog box or window

click to accept the changes and close the dialog box

click to close the dialog box without making any changes

▶ **4.** Click the **Landscape** option button. The workbook's page orientation changes to a page wider than it is long.

▶ **5.** Click the **Sheet** tab. The dialog box displays options related to the worksheet. You can click a check box to turn an option on (checked) or off (unchecked). You can check more than one check box in a group, whereas you can select only one option button in a group.

▶ **6.** In the Print group, click the **Gridlines** check box and the **Row and column headings** check box. Check marks appear in both check boxes, indicating that these options are selected.

You don't want to change the page setup right now, so you'll close the dialog box.

▶ **7.** Click the **Cancel** button. The dialog box closes without making any changes to the page setup.

Using Contextual Tools

Some tabs, toolbars, and menus come into view as you work. Because these tools become available only as you might need them, the workspace on your screen remains more open and less cluttered. However, tools that appear and disappear as you work can be distracting and take some getting used to.

Displaying Contextual Tabs

Any object that you can select in a file has a related contextual tab. An **object** is anything that appears on your screen that can be selected and manipulated as a whole, such as a table, a picture, a text box, a shape, a chart, WordArt, an equation, a diagram, a header, or a footer. A **contextual tab** is a Ribbon tab that contains commands related to the selected object so you can manipulate, edit, and format that object. Contextual tabs appear to the right of the standard Ribbon tabs just below a title label. For example, Figure 13 shows the Table Tools contextual tabs that appear when you select a table in a Word document. Although the contextual tabs appear only when you select an object, they function in the same way as standard tabs on the Ribbon. Contextual tabs disappear when you click elsewhere on the screen and deselect the object. Contextual tabs can also appear as you switch views. You'll use contextual tabs in later tutorials.

Table Tools contextual tabs   **Figure 13**

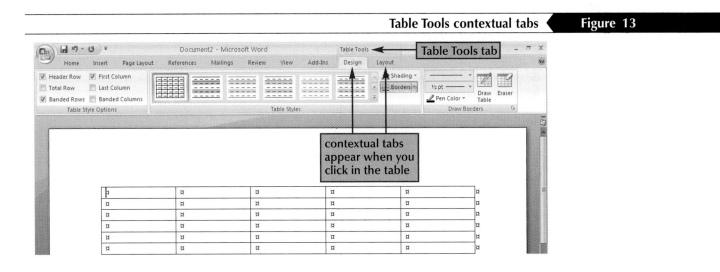

Accessing the Mini Toolbar

The **Mini toolbar** is a toolbar that appears next to the pointer whenever you select text, and it contains buttons for the most commonly used formatting commands, such as font, font size, styles, color, alignment, and indents that may appear in different groups or tabs on the Ribbon. The Mini toolbar buttons differ in each program. A transparent version of the Mini toolbar appears immediately after you select text. When you move the pointer over the Mini toolbar, it comes into full view so you can click the appropriate formatting button or buttons. The Mini toolbar disappears if you move the pointer away from the toolbar, press a key, or press a mouse button. The Mini toolbar can help you format your text faster, but initially you might find that the toolbar disappears unexpectedly. All the commands on the Mini toolbar are also available on the Ribbon. Be aware that Live Preview of selected styles does not work in the Mini toolbar.

You'll use the Mini toolbar to format text you enter in the workbook.

Tip

You can turn off the Mini toolbar and Live Preview in Word, Excel, and PowerPoint. Click the Office Button, click the Options button at the bottom of the Office menu, uncheck the first two check boxes in the Popular category, and then click the OK button.

To use the Mini toolbar to format text:

1. If necessary, click cell **A1** (the rectangle in the upper-left corner of the worksheet).

2. Type **Budget**. The text appears in the cell.

3. Press the **Enter** key. The text is entered in cell A1 and cell A2 is selected.

4. Type **2008**, and then press the **Enter** key. The year is entered in cell A2 and cell A3 is selected.

   You'll use the Mini toolbar to make the word in cell A1 boldface.

5. Double-click cell **A1** to place the insertion point in the cell. Now you can select the text you typed.

6. Double-click **Budget** in cell A1. The selected text appears white in a black background, and the transparent Mini toolbar appears directly above the selected text. See Figure 14.

Figure 14	Transparent Mini toolbar

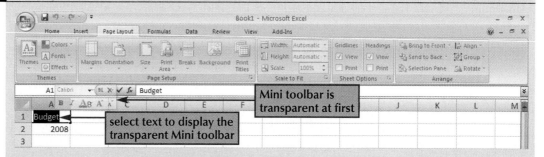

7. Move the pointer over the Mini toolbar. The Mini toolbar is now completely visible, and you can click buttons.

   Trouble? If the Mini toolbar disappears, you probably moved the pointer to another area of the worksheet. To redisplay the Mini toolbar, repeat Steps 5 through 7, being careful to move the pointer directly over the Mini toolbar in Step 7.

8. Click the **Bold** button **B** on the Mini toolbar. The text in cell A1 is bold and the Mini toolbar remains visible so you can continue formatting the selected text. See Figure 15.

Tip

You can redisplay the Mini toolbar if it disappears by right-clicking the selected text.

Figure 15	Mini toolbar with the Bold button selected

You don't want to make any other changes, so you'll close the Mini toolbar.

9. Press the **Enter** key. The Mini toolbar disappears and cell A2 is selected.

Opening Shortcut Menus

A **shortcut menu** is a list of commands related to a selection that opens when you click the right mouse button. Each shortcut menu provides access to the commands you'll most likely want to use with the object or selection you right-click. The shortcut menu includes commands that perform actions, commands that open dialog boxes, and galleries of options that provide Live Preview. The Mini toolbar also opens when you right-click. If you click a button on the Mini toolbar, the rest of the shortcut menu closes while the Mini toolbar remains open so you can continue formatting the selection. Using a shortcut menu provides quick access to the commands you need without having to access the tabs on the Ribbon. For example, you can right-click selected text to open a shortcut menu with a Mini toolbar, text-related commands, such as Cut, Copy, and Paste, as well as other program-specific commands.

You'll use a shortcut menu in Excel to delete the content you entered in cell A1.

To use a shortcut menu to delete content:

▶ 1. Right-click cell **A1**. A shortcut menu opens, listing commands related to common tasks you'd perform in a cell, along with a Mini toolbar. See Figure 16.

Shortcut menu with Mini toolbar ◀ Figure 16

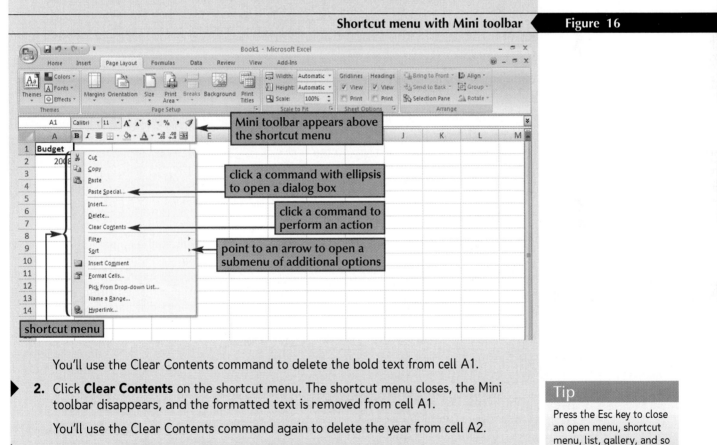

Mini toolbar appears above the shortcut menu

click a command with ellipsis to open a dialog box

click a command to perform an action

point to an arrow to open a submenu of additional options

shortcut menu

You'll use the Clear Contents command to delete the bold text from cell A1.

▶ 2. Click **Clear Contents** on the shortcut menu. The shortcut menu closes, the Mini toolbar disappears, and the formatted text is removed from cell A1.

You'll use the Clear Contents command again to delete the year from cell A2.

▶ 3. Right-click cell **A2**, and then click **Clear Contents** on the shortcut menu. The year is removed from cell A2.

Shortcut menus enable you to quickly access commands that you're most likely to need in the context of the task you're performing.

Tip

Press the Esc key to close an open menu, shortcut menu, list, gallery, and so forth without selecting an option.

Working with Files

The most common tasks you perform in any Office program are to create, open, save, and close files. The processes for these tasks are basically the same in all the Office programs. In addition, there are several methods for performing most tasks in Office. This flexibility enables you to use Office in a way that best fits how you like to work.

The **Office Button** provides access to document-level features, such as creating new files, opening existing files, saving files, printing files, and closing files, as well as the most common program options, called **application settings**. The **Quick Access Toolbar** is a collection of buttons that provide one-click access to commonly used commands, such as Save, Undo, and Repeat.

To begin working in a program, you need to create a new file or open an existing file. When you start Word, Excel, or PowerPoint, the program opens along with a blank file—ready for you to begin working on a new document, workbook, or presentation. When you start Access, the Getting Started with Microsoft Access window opens, displaying options for creating a new database or opening an existing one.

Ean has asked you to continue working on the agenda for the stockholder meeting. You already started typing in the document that opened when you started Word. Next, you will enter more text in the Word document.

To enter text in the Word document:

▶ 1. Click the **Document1 – Microsoft Word** button on the taskbar to activate the Word program window.

▶ 2. Type **Meeting Agenda** on the second line of the document, and then press the **Enter** key. The text you typed appears in the document.

Trouble? If you make a typing error, press the Backspace key to delete the incorrect letters, and then retype the text.

Saving a File

As you create and modify Office files, your work is stored only in the computer's temporary memory, not on a hard disk. If you were to exit the programs without saving, turn off your computer, or experience a power failure, your work would be lost. To prevent losing work, save your file to a disk frequently—at least every 10 minutes. You can save files to the hard disk located inside your computer, a floppy disk, an external hard drive, a network storage drive, or a portable storage disk, such as a USB flash drive.

Reference Window | **Saving a File**

To save a file the first time or with a new name or location:
- Click the Office Button, and then click Save As (or for an unnamed file, click the Save button on the Quick Access Toolbar or click the Office Button, and then click Save).
- In the Save As dialog box, navigate to the location where you want to save the file.
- Type a descriptive title in the File name box, and then click the Save button.

To resave a named file to the same location:
- Click the Save button on the Quick Access Toolbar (or click the Office Button, and then click Save).

The first time you save a file, you need to name it. This **filename** includes a descriptive title you select and a file extension assigned by Office. You should choose a descriptive title that accurately reflects the content of the document, workbook, presentation, or database, such as "Shipping Options Letter" or "Fourth Quarter Financial Analysis." Your descriptive title can include uppercase and lowercase letters, numbers, hyphens, and spaces in any combination, but not the following special characters: ? " / \ < > * | and :. Each filename ends with a **file extension**, a period followed by several characters that Office adds to your descriptive title to identify the program in which that file was created. The default file extensions for Office 2007 are .docx for Word, .xlsx for Excel, .pptx for PowerPoint, and .accdb for Access. Filenames (the descriptive title and the file extension) can include a maximum of 255 characters. You might see file extensions depending on how Windows is set up on your computer. The figures in these tutorials do not show file extensions.

You also need to decide where to save the file—on which disk and in what folder. A **folder** is a container for your files. Just as you organize paper documents within folders stored in a filing cabinet, you can organize your files within folders stored on your computer's hard disk or a removable disk, such as a USB flash drive. Store each file in a logical location that you will remember whenever you want to use the file again. The default storage location for Office files is the Documents folder; you can create additional storage folders within that folder or navigate to a new storage location.

You can navigate the Save As dialog box by clicking a folder or location on your computer in the Navigation pane along the left side of the dialog box, and then double-clicking folders in the file list until you display the storage location you want. You can also navigate to a storage location with the Address bar, which displays the current file path. Each location in the file path has a corresponding arrow that you can click to quickly select a folder within that location. For example, you can click the Documents arrow in the Address bar to open a list of all the folders in the Documents folder, and then click the folder you want to open. If you want to return to a specific spot in the file hierarchy, you click that folder name in the Address bar. The Back and Forward buttons let you quickly move between folders.

Tip

Office adds the correct file extension when you save a file. Do not type one in the descriptive title, or you will create a duplicate (such as Meeting Agenda. docx.docx).

Windows XP Tip

The default storage location for Office files is the My Documents folder.

Saving and Using Files with Earlier Versions of Office | InSight

The default file types in Office 2007 are different from those used in earlier versions. This means that someone using Office 2003 or earlier cannot open files created in Office 2007. Files you want to share with earlier Office users must be saved in the earlier formats, which use the following extensions: .doc for Word, .xls for Excel, .mdb for Access, and .ppt for PowerPoint. To save a file in an earlier format, open the Save As dialog box, click the Save as type list arrow, and then click the appropriate 97-2003 format. A compatibility checker reports which Office 2007 features or elements are not supported by the earlier version of Office, and you can choose to remove them before saving. You can use Office 2007 to open and work with files created in earlier versions of Office. You can then save the file in its current format or update it to the Office 2007 format.

The lines of text you typed are not yet saved on disk. You'll do that now.

To save a file for the first time:

Windows XP Tip

To navigate to a location in the Save As dialog box, you use the Save in arrow.

▶ **1.** Click the **Save** button 💾 on the Quick Access Toolbar. The Save As dialog box opens because you have not yet saved the file and need to specify a storage location and filename. The default location is set to the Documents folder, and the first few words of the first line appear in the File name box as a suggested title.

▶ **2.** In the Navigation pane, click the link for the location that contains your Data Files, if necessary.

Trouble? If you don't have the starting Data Files, you need to get them before you can proceed. Your instructor will either give you the Data Files or ask you to obtain them from a specified location (such as a network drive). In either case, make a backup copy of the Data Files before you start so that you will have the original files available in case you need to start over. If you have any questions about the Data Files, see your instructor or technical support person for assistance.

▶ **3.** Double-click the **OFF** folder in the file list, and then double-click the **Tutorial** folder. This is the location where you want to save the document.

Next, you'll enter a more descriptive title for the filename.

▶ **4.** Type **Meeting Agenda** in the File name box. See Figure 17.

Figure 17 ▶ Completed Save As dialog box

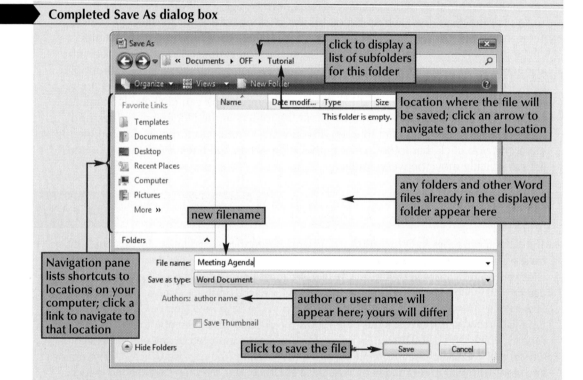

Trouble? If the .docx file extension appears after the filename, your computer is configured to show file extensions. Continue with Step 5.

▶ **5.** Click the **Save** button. The Save As dialog box closes, and the name of your file appears in the title bar.

The saved file includes everything in the document at the time you last saved it. Any new edits or additions you make to the document exist only in the computer's memory and are not saved in the file on the disk. As you work, remember to save frequently so that the file is updated to reflect the latest content of the document.

Because you already named the document and selected a storage location, the Save As dialog box doesn't open whenever you save the document again. If you want to save a copy of the file with a different filename or to a different location, you reopen the Save As dialog box by clicking the Office Button, and then clicking Save As. The previous version of the file remains on your disk as well.

You need to add your name to the agenda. Then, you'll save your changes.

To modify and save the Word document:

▶ **1.** Type your name, and then press the **Enter** key. The text you typed appears on the next line.

▶ **2.** Click the **Save** button 🖫 on the Quick Access Toolbar to save your changes.

Closing a File

Although you can keep multiple files open at one time, you should close any file you are no longer working on to conserve system resources as well as to ensure that you don't inadvertently make changes to the file. You can close a file by clicking the Office Button and then clicking the Close command. If that's the only file open for the program, the program window remains open and no file appears in the window. You can also close a file by clicking the Close button in the upper-right corner of the title bar or double-clicking the Office Button. If that's the only file open for the program, the program also closes.

As a standard practice, you should save your file before closing it. However, Office has an added safeguard: If you attempt to close a file without saving your changes, a dialog box opens, asking whether you want to save the file. Click the Yes button to save the changes to the file before closing the file and program. Click the No button to close the file and program without saving changes. Click the Cancel button to return to the program window without saving changes or closing the file and program. This feature helps to ensure that you always save the most current version of any file.

You'll add the date to the agenda. Then, you'll attempt to close it without saving.

To modify and close the Word document:

▶ **1.** Type today's date, and then press the **Enter** key. The text you typed appears below your name in the document.

▶ **2.** In the upper-left corner of the program window, click the **Office Button** 🏢. A menu opens with commands for creating new files, opening existing files, saving files, printing files, and closing files.

▶ **3.** Click **Close**. A dialog box opens, asking whether you want to save the changes you made to the document.

▶ **4.** Click the **Yes** button. The current version of the document is saved to the file, and then the document closes. Word is still running.

After you have a program open, you can create additional new files for the open program or you can open previously created and saved files.

Opening a File

When you want to open a blank document, workbook, presentation, or database, you create a new file. When you want to work on a previously created file, you must first open it. Opening a file transfers a copy of the file from the storage disk (either a hard disk or a portable disk) to the computer's memory and displays it on your screen. The file is then in your computer's memory and on the disk.

Reference Window | **Opening an Existing File or Creating a New File**

- Click the Office Button, and then click Open.
- In the Open dialog box, navigate to the storage location of the file you want to open.
- Click the filename of the file you want to open.
- Click the Open button.

or

- Click the Office Button, and then click a filename in the Recent Documents list.

or

- Click the Office Button, and then click New.
- In the New dialog box, click Blank Document, Blank Workbook, Blank Presentation, or Blank Database (depending on the program).
- Click the Create button.

Ean asks you to print the agenda. To do that, you'll reopen the file.

To open the existing Word document:

▶ **1.** Click the **Office Button** 🔘, and then click **Open**. The Open dialog box, which works similarly to the Save As dialog box, opens.

Windows XP Tip

To navigate to a location in the Open dialog box, you use the Look in arrow.

▶ **2.** Use the Navigation pane or the Address bar to navigate to the **OFF\Tutorial** folder included with your Data Files. This is the location where you saved the agenda document.

▶ **3.** Click **Meeting Agenda** in the file list. See Figure 18.

Figure 18 ▶ **Open dialog box**

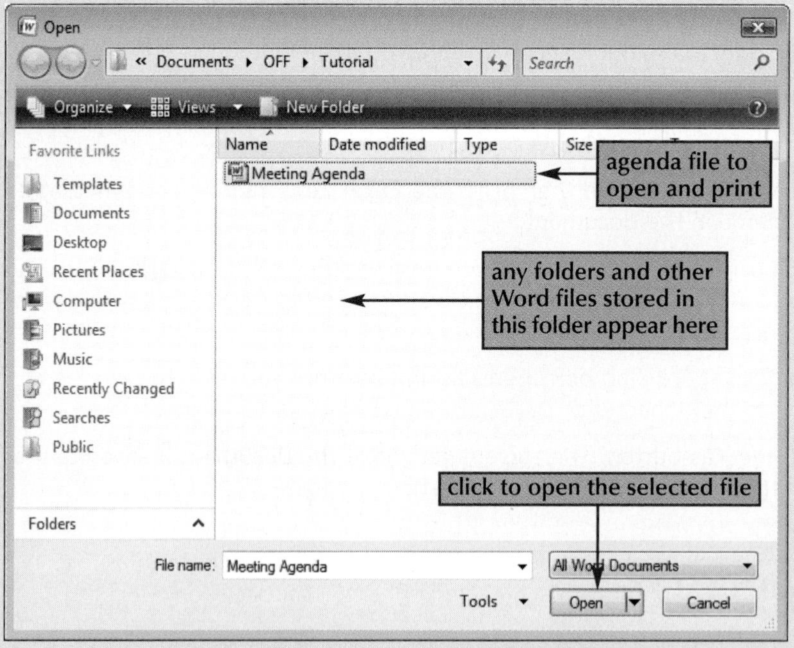

agenda file to open and print

any folders and other Word files stored in this folder appear here

click to open the selected file

▶ **4.** Click the **Open** button. The agenda file opens in the Word program window.

Next, you'll use Help to get information about printing files in Word.

Getting Help

If you don't know how to perform a task or want more information about a feature, you can turn to Office itself for information on how to use it. This information, referred to simply as **Help**, is like a huge encyclopedia available from your desktop. You can get Help in ScreenTips, from the Help window, and in Microsoft Office Online.

Viewing ScreenTips

ScreenTips are a fast and simple method you can use to get help about objects you see on the screen. A **ScreenTip** is a box with the button's name, its keyboard shortcut if it has one, a description of the command's function, and, in some cases, a link to more information. Just position the mouse pointer over a button or object to view its ScreenTip. If a link to more information appears in the ScreenTip, press the F1 key while the Screen-Tip is displayed to open the Help window with the appropriate topic displayed.

To view ScreenTips:

▶ 1. Point to the **Microsoft Office Word Help** button 🔘. The ScreenTip shows the button's name, its keyboard shortcut, and a brief explanation of the button. See Figure 19.

ScreenTip for the Help button ◀ **Figure 19**

button's name | button's keyboard shortcut | description of the button's function

▶ 2. Point to other buttons on the Ribbon to display their ScreenTips.

Using the Help Window

For more detailed information, you can use the **Help window** to access all the Help topics, templates, and training installed on your computer with Office and available on Microsoft Office Online. **Microsoft Office Online** is a Web site maintained by Microsoft that provides access to the latest information and additional Help resources. For example, you can access current Help topics, templates of predesigned files, and training for Office. To connect to Microsoft Office Online, you need Internet access on your computer. Otherwise, you see only those topics stored locally.

Reference Window | **Getting Help**

- Click the Microsoft Office Help button (the button name depends on the Office program).
- Type a keyword or phrase in the "Type words to search for" box, and then click the Search button.
- Click a Help topic in the search results list.
- Read the information in the Help window. For more information, click other topics or links.
- Click the Close button on the Help window title bar.

You open the Help window by clicking the Microsoft Office Help button 🔘 located below the sizing buttons in every Office program. Each program has its own Help window from which you can find information about all the Office commands and features as well as step-by-step instructions for using them. You can search for information in the Help window using the "Type words to search for" box and the Table of Contents pane.

The "Type words to search for" box enables you to search the Help system using keywords or phrases. You type a specific word or phrase about a task you want to perform or a topic you need help with, and then click the Search button to search the Help system. A list of Help topics related to the keyword or phrase you entered appears in the Help window. If your computer is connected to the Internet, your search results come from Microsoft Office Online rather than only the Help topics stored locally on your computer. You can click a link to open a Help topic with step-by-step instructions that will guide you through a specific procedure and/or provide explanations of difficult concepts in clear, easy-to-understand language. For example, if you type "format cell" in the Excel Help window, a list of Help topics related to the words you typed appears in the Help window. You can navigate through the topics you've viewed using the buttons on the Help window toolbar. These buttons—including Back, Forward, Stop, Refresh, Home, and Print—are the same as those in the Microsoft Internet Explorer Web browser.

You'll use the "Type words to search for" box in the Help window to obtain more information about printing a document in Word.

To use the "Type words to search for" box:

▶ 1. Click the **Microsoft Office Word Help** button 🔘 . The Word Help window opens.

▶ 2. Click the **Type words to search for** box, if necessary, and then type **print document**. You can set where you want to search.

▶ 3. Click the **Search button arrow**. The Search menu shows the online and local content available.

▶ 4. If your computer is connected to the Internet, click **All Word** in the Content from Office Online list. If your computer is not connected to the Internet, click **Word Help** in the Content from this computer list.

▶ 5. Click the **Search** button. The Help window displays a list of topics related to your keywords. See Figure 20.

Search results displaying Help topics ◀ **Figure 20**

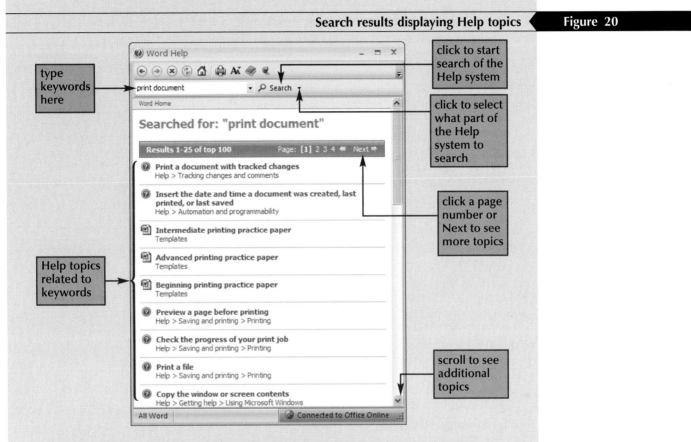

Trouble? If your search results list differs from the one shown in Figure 20, your computer is not connected to the Internet or Microsoft has updated the list of available Help topics since this book was published. Continue with Step 6.

▶ 6. Scroll through the list to review the Help topics.

▶ 7. Click **Print a file**. The Help topic is displayed in the Help window so you can learn more about how to print a document. See Figure 21.

Figure 21	Print a file Help topic

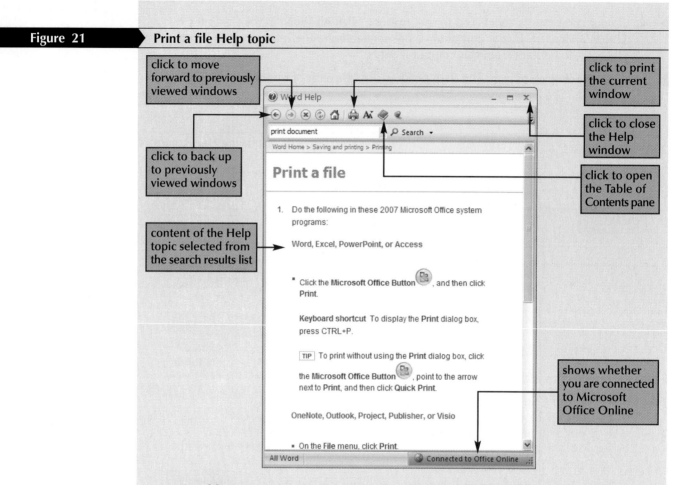

Trouble? If you don't see the Print a file Help topic on page 1, its current location might be on another page. Click the Next link to move to the next page, and then scroll down to find the Print a file topic, repeating to search additional pages until you locate the topic.

▶ **8.** Read the information.

Another way to find information in the Help system is to use the Table of Contents pane. The Show Table of Contents button on the Help window toolbar opens a pane that displays a list of the Help system content organized by subjects and topics, similar to a book's table of contents. You click main subject links to display related topic links. You click a topic link to display that Help topic in the Help window. You'll use the Table of Contents to find information about getting help in Office.

To use the Help window table of contents:

▶ **1.** Click the **Show Table of Contents** button ◈ on the Help window toolbar. The Table of Contents pane opens on the left side of the Help window.

▶ **2.** Click **Getting help** in the Table of Contents pane, scrolling up if necessary. The Getting help "book" opens, listing the topics related to that subject.

▶ **3.** Click the **Work with the Help window** topic, and then click the **Maximize** button ▢ on the title bar. The Help topic is displayed in the maximized Help window, and you can read the text to learn more about the various ways to obtain help in Word. See Figure 22.

Table of Contents pane in the Help window ◂ **Figure 22**

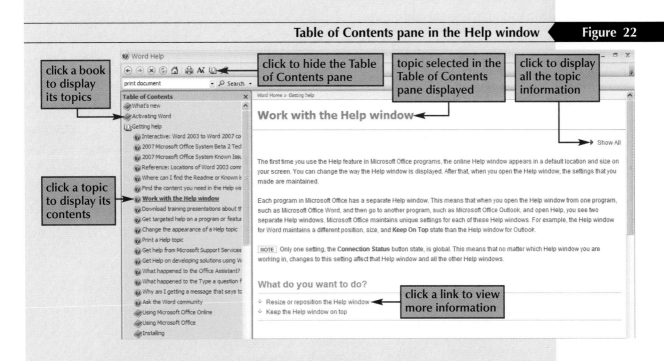

Trouble? If your search results list differs from the one shown in Figure 22, your computer is not connected to the Internet or Microsoft has updated the list of available Help topics since this book was published. Continue with Step 4.

▶ **4.** Click **Using Microsoft Office Online** in the Table of Contents pane, click the **Get online Help, templates, training, and additional content** topic to display information about that topic, and then read the information.

▶ **5.** Click the links within this topic and read the information.

▶ **6.** Click the **Close** button ⊠ on the Help window title bar to close the window.

Printing a File

At times, you'll want a paper copy of your Office file. The first time you print during each session at the computer, you should use the Print command to open the Print dialog box so you can verify or adjust the printing settings. You can select a printer, the number of copies to print, the portion of the file to print, and so forth; the printing settings vary slightly from program to program. If you want to use the same default settings for subsequent print jobs, you can use the Quick Print button to print without opening the dialog box.

Printing a File | Reference Window

- Click the Office Button, and then click Print.
- Verify the print settings in the Print dialog box.
- Click the OK button.

or

- Click the Office Button, point to Print, and then click Quick Print.

Now that you know how to print, you'll print the agenda for Ean.

To print the Word document:

▶ **1.** Make sure your printer is turned on and contains paper.

▶ **2.** Click the **Office Button** (⊞), and then click **Print**. The Print dialog box opens. See Figure 23.

Figure 23 ▶ Print dialog box

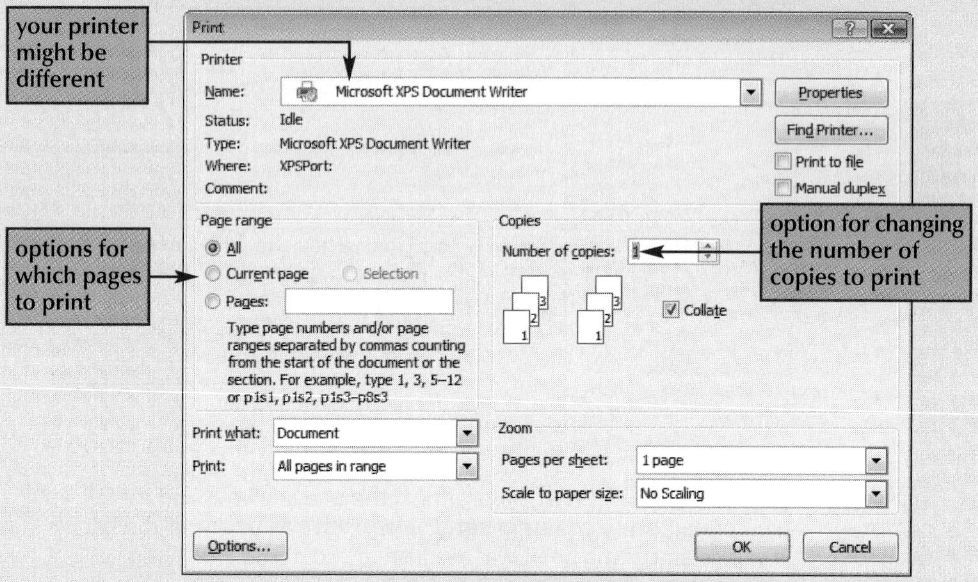

Trouble? If a menu of Print commands opens, you clicked the Print button arrow on the two-part Print button. Click Print on the menu to open the Print dialog box.

▶ **3.** Verify that the correct printer appears in the Name box in the Printer group. If necessary, click the **Name** arrow, and then click the correct printer from the list of available printers.

▶ **4.** Verify that **1** appears in the Number of copies box.

▶ **5.** Click the **OK** button to print the document.

Trouble? If the document does not print, see your instructor or technical support person for help.

Exiting Programs

When you finish working with a program, you should exit it. As with many other aspects of Office, you can exit programs with a button or a command. You'll use both methods to exit Word and Excel. You can use the Exit command to exit a program and close an open file in one step. If you haven't saved the final version of the open file, a dialog box opens, asking whether you want to save your changes. Clicking the Yes button saves the open file, closes the file, and then exits the program.

To exit the Word and Excel programs:

▶ **1.** Click the **Close** button ☒ on the Word title bar to exit Word. The Word document closes and the Word program exits. The Excel window is visible again.

> **Trouble?** If a dialog box opens, asking if you want to save the document, you might have inadvertently made a change to the document. Click the No button.
>
> ▶ **2.** Click the **Office Button** (🔘), and then click **Exit Excel**. A dialog box opens, asking whether you want to save the changes you made to the workbook. If you click the Yes button, the Save As dialog box opens and Excel exits after you finish saving the workbook. This time, you don't want to save the workbook.
>
> ▶ **3.** Click the **No** button. The workbook closes without saving a copy, and the Excel program exits.

Exiting programs after you are done using them keeps your Windows desktop uncluttered for the next person using the computer, frees up your system's resources, and prevents data from being lost accidentally.

Quick Check | Review

1. What Office program would be best to use to create a budget?
2. How do you start an Office program?
3. Explain the difference between Save and Save As.
4. How do you open an existing Office file?
5. What happens if you open a file, make edits, and then attempt to close the file or exit the program without saving the current version of the file?
6. What are two ways to get Help in Office?

Tutorial Summary | Review

You have learned how to use features common to all the programs included in Microsoft Office 2007, including starting and exiting programs; resizing windows; using the Ribbon, dialog boxes, shortcut menus, and the Mini toolbar; opening, closing, and printing files; and getting Help.

Key Terms

Access	Help window	Office Button
application settings	integration	Outlook
button	keyboard shortcut	PowerPoint
contextual tab	Live Preview	presentation
database	Microsoft Office 2007	Quick Access Toolbar
default	Microsoft Office Access 2007	Ribbon
dialog box	Microsoft Office Excel 2007	ScreenTip
Dialog Box Launcher	Microsoft Office Online	shortcut menu
document	Microsoft Office	status bar
Excel	Outlook 2007	tab
file extension	Microsoft Office	task pane
filename	PowerPoint 2007	Word
folder	Microsoft Office Word 2007	workbook
gallery	Mini toolbar	zoom
group	object	
Help	Office	

| Practice | **Review Assignments** |

Practice the skills you learned in the tutorial.

Data Files needed for the Review Assignments: Finances.xlsx, Letter.docx

You need to prepare for an upcoming meeting at Recycled Palette. You'll open and print documents for the presentation. Complete the following:

1. Start PowerPoint.
2. Use the Help window to search Office Online for the PowerPoint demo "Demo: Up to Speed with PowerPoint 2007." (*Hint*: Use "demo" as the keyword to search for, and make sure you search All PowerPoint in the Content from Office Online list. If you are not connected to the Internet, continue with Step 3.) Open the Demo topic, and then click the Play Demo link to view it. Close Internet Explorer and the Help window when you're done.
3. Start Excel.
4. Switch to the PowerPoint window using the taskbar, and then close the presentation but leave open the PowerPoint program. (*Hint:* Click the Office Button and then click Close.)
5. Open a new, blank PowerPoint presentation from the New Presentation dialog box.
6. Close the PowerPoint presentation and program using the Close button on the PowerPoint title bar; do not save changes if asked.
7. Open the **Finances** workbook located in the OFF\Review folder included with your Data Files.
8. Use the Save As command to save the workbook as **Recycled Palette Finances** in the OFF\Review folder.
9. Type your name, press the Enter key to insert your name at the top of the worksheet, and then save the workbook.
10. Print one copy of the worksheet using the Print button on the Office Button menu.
11. Exit Excel using the Office Button.
12. Start Word, and then open the **Letter** document located in the OFF\Review folder included with your Data Files.
13. Use the Save As command to save the document with the filename **Recycled Palette Letter** in the OFF\Review folder.
14. Press and hold the Ctrl key, press the End key, and then release both keys to move the insertion point to the end of the letter, and then type your name.
15. Use the Save button on the Quick Access Toolbar to save the change to the Recycled Palette Letter document.
16. Print one copy of the document, and then close the document.
17. Exit the Word program using the Close button on the title bar.

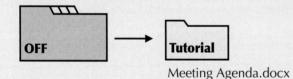

Review | **Quick Check Answers**

1. Excel
2. Click the Start button on the taskbar, click All Programs, click Microsoft Office, and then click the name of the program you want to open.
3. Save updates a file to reflect its latest contents using its current filename and location. Save As enables you to change the filename and storage location of a file.
4. Click the Office Button, and then click Open.
5. A dialog box opens asking whether you want to save the changes to the file.
6. Two of the following: ScreenTips, Help window, Microsoft Office Online

Ending Data Files

OFF → **Tutorial**   **Review**

Meeting Agenda.docx   Recycled Palette Finances.xlsx
Recycled Palette Letter.docx

Reality Check

At home, school, or work, you probably complete many types of tasks, such as writing letters and balancing a checkbook, on a regular basis. You can use Microsoft Office to streamline many of these tasks.

Note: Please be sure *not* to include any personal information of a sensitive nature in the documents you create to be submitted to your instructor for this exercise. Later on, you can update the documents with such information for your own personal use.

1. Start Word, and open a new document, if necessary.
2. In the document, type a list of all the personal, work, and/or school tasks you do on a regular basis.
3. For each task, identify the type of Office file (document, workbook, presentation, or database) you would create to complete that task. For example, you would create a Word document to write a letter.
4. For each file, identify the Office program you would use to create that file, and explain why you would use that program. For example, Word is the best program to use to create a document for a letter.
5. Save the document with an appropriate filename in an appropriate folder location.
6. Use a Web browser to visit the Microsoft Web site at *www.microsoft.com* and research the different Office 2007 suites available. Determine which suite includes all the programs you need to complete the tasks on your list.
7. At the end of the task list you created in your Word document, type which Office suite you decided on and a brief explanation of why you chose that suite. Then save the document.
8. Double-click the Home tab on the Ribbon to minimize the Ribbon to show only the tab names and extend the workspace area. At the end of the Word document, type your opinion of whether minimizing the Ribbon is a helpful feature. When you're done, double-click the Home tab to display the full Ribbon.
9. Print the finished document, and then submit it to your instructor.

Objectives

Session 1.1
- Plan a document
- Identify the components of the Word window
- Set up the Word window
- Create a new document

Session 1.2
- Scroll a document and move the insertion point
- Correct errors and undo and redo changes
- Enter the date with AutoComplete
- Change a document's line and paragraph spacing
- Save, preview, and print a document
- Create an envelope

Creating a Document

Writing a Business Letter

Case | Carlyle University Press

Carlyle University Press is a nonprofit book publisher associated with Carlyle State University in Albany, New York. The Press, as it is referred to by both editors and authors, publishes scholarly books, with an emphasis on history and literature. When a new author signs a contract for a book, he or she receives the *Author's Guide*, a handbook describing the process of creating a manuscript. In this tutorial, you will help one of the editors, Andrew Suri, create a cover letter to accompany a copy of the *Author's Guide*.

You will create the letter using **Microsoft Office Word 2007** (or simply **Word**), a popular word-processing program. Before you begin typing the letter, you will learn how to start the Word program, identify and use the elements of the Word window, and adjust some Word settings. Next, you will create a new Word document, type the text of the cover letter, save the letter, and then print the letter. In the process of entering the text, you'll learn several ways to correct typing errors. Finally, you will create an envelope for the letter.

Starting Data Files

There are no starting Data Files needed for this tutorial.

Session 1.1

Four Steps to a Professional Document

With Word, you can create polished, professional documents in a minimal amount of time. You can type a document in Word, adjust margins and spacing, create columns and tables, add graphics, and then quickly make revisions and corrections. The most efficient way to produce a document is to follow these four steps: (1) planning, (2) creating and editing, (3) formatting, and (4) printing or distributing online.

In the long run, planning saves time and effort. First, you should determine what you want to say. State your purpose clearly and include enough information to achieve that purpose without overwhelming or boring your reader. Be sure to organize your ideas logically. Decide how you want your document to look as well. In this case, your letter will take the form of a standard business letter, in the block style.

Figure 1-1 shows what the completed, block style letter will look like when it is printed on Carlyle University Press letterhead. You will create the letter in this tutorial by following detailed steps. Throughout the tutorial, you might want to refer back to Figure 1-1 for help locating the various parts of a block style letter.

Figure 1-1 | Completed block style letter

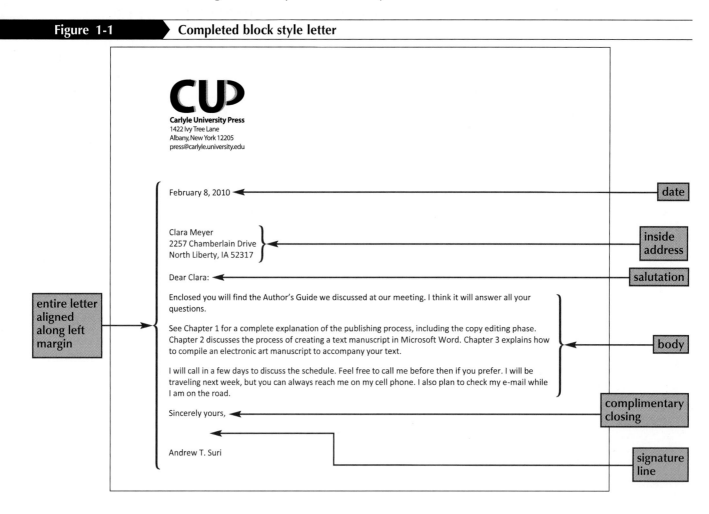

Writing a Business Letter | InSight

There are several accepted styles for business letters. The main differences among them have to do with how parts of the letter are indented from the left margin. In the block style, which you will use to create the letter in this tutorial, each line of text starts at the left margin. In other words, nothing is indented. Another style is to indent the first line of each paragraph. The choice of style is largely a matter of personal preference, or it can be determined by the standards used in a particular business or organization.

After you plan your document, you can create and edit it using Word. Creating the document generally means typing the text of your document. Editing consists of reading the document you've created; correcting, adding, deleting, or moving text to make the document easy to read; and finally, correcting your errors.

To make your document visually appealing, you need to format it. Formatting—for example, adjusting margins, setting line spacing, and using bold and italic—can help make your document easier to read.

Finally, you will usually want to print your document so that you can give it to other people, or you might want to distribute it via e-mail. Whether you print the document yourself or e-mail it to others, it is important to preview it first to make sure it is suitable for printing.

Exploring the Word Window

Before you can apply these four steps to produce a letter in Word, you need to start Word and learn about the general organization of the Word window. You'll do that now.

To start Microsoft Word:

▶ **1.** Click the **Start** button 🌐 on the taskbar, click **All Programs**, click **Microsoft Office**, and then click **Microsoft Office Word 2007**. The Word window opens. See Figure 1-2.

Figure 1-2 | Maximized Word window

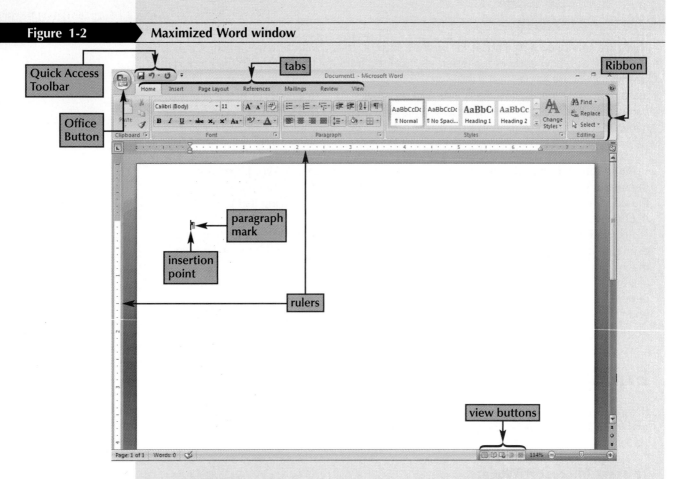

Trouble? If you don't see the Microsoft Office Word 2007 option on the Microsoft Office submenu, look for it in a different submenu or as an option on the All Programs menu. If you still can't find the Microsoft Office Word 2007 option, ask your instructor or technical support person for help.

2. If the Word window does not fill the entire screen, click the **Maximize** button ▣ in the upper-right corner of the Word window. Your screen should now resemble Figure 1-2.

Trouble? If your screen looks slightly different from Figure 1-2, just continue with the steps. You will learn how to change the appearance of the Word window shortly.

Word is now running and ready to use. Don't be concerned if you don't see everything shown in Figure 1-2. You'll learn how to adjust the appearance of the Word window soon.

The Word window is made up of a number of elements, which are described in Figure 1-3. You might be familiar with some of these elements, such as the Office Button and the Ribbon, because they are common to all Microsoft Office 2007 programs.

Parts of the Word window ◀ Figure 1-3

Window Element	Description
Office Button	Provides access to the Word Options dialog box and to commands that control what you can do with a document that you have created, such as saving, printing, and so on
Ribbon	Provides access to commands that are grouped according to the tasks you perform in Word
Tabs	Provide one-click access to the groups of commands on the Ribbon; the tabs you see change depending on the task you are currently performing
Quick Access Toolbar	Provides access to common commands you use frequently, such as Save
Rulers	Show page margins, tab stops, row heights, and column widths
Insertion point	Shows where characters will appear when you start typing
Paragraph mark	Marks the end of a paragraph
View buttons	Allow you to change the way the document is displayed

If at any time you would like to learn more about an item on the Ribbon, position your mouse pointer over the item without clicking anything. A **ScreenTip**, a small box with information about the item, will appear.

Opening a New Document

You'll begin by opening a new blank document (in case you accidentally typed something in the current page while you were examining the Word window).

To open a new document:

▶ **1.** Click the **Office Button** 🔘 in the upper-left corner of the Word window and view the menu of commands that opens. These commands are all related to working with Word documents. See Figure 1-4.

Microsoft Office menu ◀ Figure 1-4

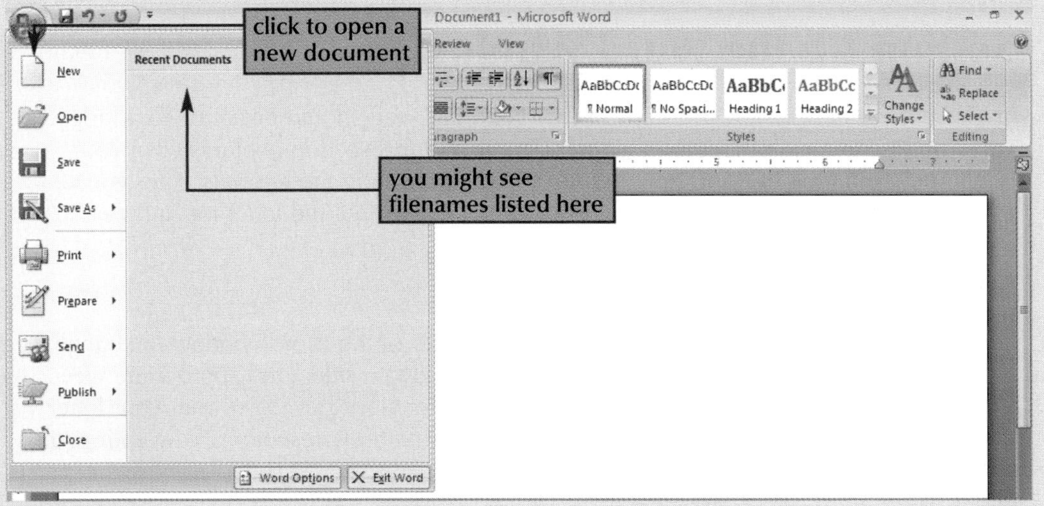

▶ **2.** Click **New**. The New Document dialog box opens. See Figure 1-5. In this dialog box, you can choose from several different types of documents. In this case, you simply want a new, blank document, which is already selected for you, as in Figure 1-5.

| Figure 1-5 | New Document dialog box |

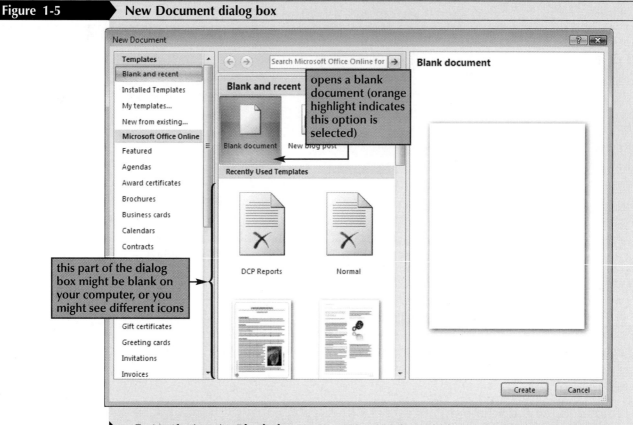

▶ **3.** Verify that the **Blank document** option is selected (that is, highlighted in orange), and then click the **Create** button at the bottom of the dialog box. The New Document dialog box closes and a new document (named Document2) opens. Later in this tutorial, you'll choose a more descriptive name for this document.

Setting Up the Word Window

To make it easier to follow the steps in these tutorials, you should take care to arrange your window to match the tutorial figures. The rest of this section explains what your window should look like and how to make it match those in the tutorials. After you've set up your window to match the figures, you'll begin writing the letter for Andrew.

Selecting Print Layout View

You can use the View buttons in the lower-right corner of the Word window to change the way your document is displayed. You will learn how to select the appropriate view for a document as you gain more experience with Word. For now, you want your letter displayed in Print Layout view because this view most closely resembles how your letter will look when you print it.

To make sure Print Layout view is selected:

▶ **1.** Click the **Print Layout** button 📄 , as shown in Figure 1-6. If your window was not in Print Layout view, it changes to Print Layout view now. The Print Layout button is now highlighted in orange, indicating that it is selected. See Figure 1-6.

Selecting Print Layout view ◀ **Figure 1-6**

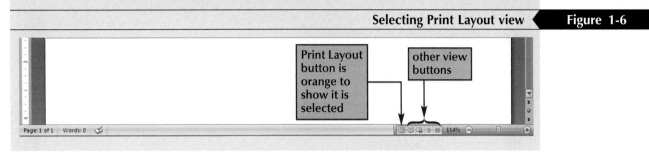

Displaying the Rulers and Selecting the Home Tab

Depending on the choices made by the last person to use your computer, you might not see the rulers. The options controlling the rulers are located on the Ribbon's View tab. When Word opens, the Home tab is typically displayed, so to display the rulers, you need to switch to the View tab. Even if the rulers are currently displayed on your computer, perform the following steps to get some practice moving among the tabs on the Ribbon.

Displaying the Rulers | Reference Window

- Click the View tab.
- In the Show/Hide group, click the Ruler check box to display a check mark.

To display the rulers:

▶ **1.** At the top of the Word window, click the **View** tab. This tab contains buttons and commands related to displaying the document.

▶ **2.** In the Show/Hide group on the View tab, locate the Ruler check box. If it already contains a check mark, the rulers are already displayed on your screen. If the Ruler check box is empty, click it to insert a check mark. You should now see a vertical ruler on the left side of the document and a horizontal ruler below the Ribbon. See Figure 1-7.

Figure 1-7 ▶ **Displaying the rulers**

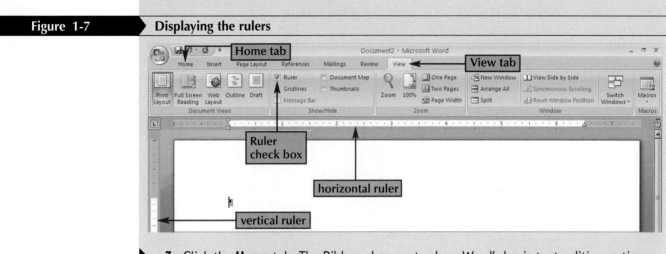

3. Click the **Home** tab. The Ribbon changes to show Word's basic text-editing options, as shown earlier in Figure 1-2.

Displaying Nonprinting Characters

Tip

The Show/Hide ¶ button is an example of a toggle button. Clicking it toggles the nonprinting characters on or off, just as flipping a toggle light switch turns a lamp on or off.

Nonprinting characters are symbols that appear on the screen but are not visible on the printed page; they help you see details that you might otherwise miss. For example, one nonprinting character (¶) marks the end of a paragraph, and another (•) marks the space between words. It is helpful to display nonprinting characters so you can see whether you've typed an extra space, ended a paragraph, and so on.

Depending on how your computer is set up, nonprinting characters might be displayed automatically when you start Word. In Figure 1-8, you can see the paragraph symbol (¶) in the blank document window. Also, the Show/Hide ¶ button is highlighted on the Ribbon. Both of these indicate that nonprinting characters are displayed. If they are not displayed on your screen, you need to perform the following step.

To display nonprinting characters:

1. In the Paragraph group on the Home tab, click the **Show/Hide ¶** button ¶ if it is not already selected. A paragraph mark (¶) appears at the top of the document window. Your screen should match Figure 1-8.

Figure 1-8 ▶ **Nonprinting characters displayed**

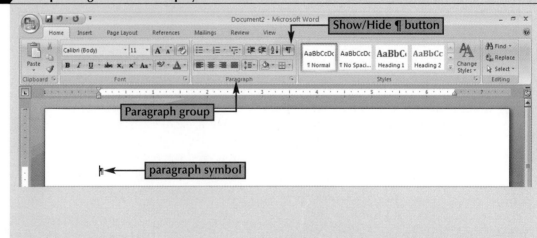

Trouble? If the Show/Hide ¶ button was already highlighted before you clicked it, you turned off nonprinting characters instead of turning them on. Click the Show/Hide ¶ button a second time to select it.

Checking the Font and Font Size

Next, you need to make sure the correct font and font size are selected. The term **font** refers to the shape of the characters in a document. **Font size** refers to the size of the characters. You'll learn more about fonts in Tutorial 2. For now, you just need to make sure that the font and font size selected on your computer match those selected in the figures in this book. The figures in this book were created using the default font and font size. (The term **default** refers to settings that are automatically selected.)

To verify that the correct font is selected:

▶ 1. In the Font group on the Home tab, locate the **Font** and **Font Size** boxes. See Figure 1-9.

Font settings ◀ **Figure 1-9**

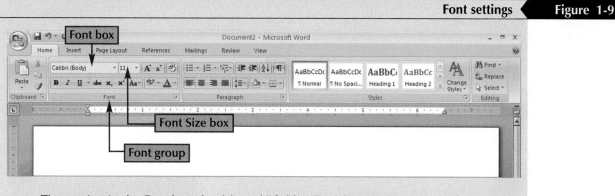

The setting in the Font box should read "Calibri (Body)" as in Figure 1-9. If you see something else in your Font box, click the **Font** list arrow, and then click **Calibri (Body)**.

Trouble? If you see just "Calibri" in your font box instead of "Calibri (Body)" you should still perform Step 1.

▶ 2. The setting in your Font Size box should read "11." If you see something else in your Font size box, click the **Font Size** list arrow, and then click **11**.

Checking the Zoom Setting

Next, you'll take care of the document **Zoom level**, which controls the document's on-screen magnification. A Zoom level of 100% shows the document as if it were printed on paper. It is often helpful to increase the Zoom level to more than 100% (zoom in) to make the text easier to read. Other times, you may want to decrease the Zoom level to less than 100% (zoom out) so that you can see more of the document at a glance. To make your screen match the figures in this tutorial, you need to set the Zoom level to **Page width**, a setting that shows the entire width of the document on your screen. You can change the Zoom level by using the Zoom buttons in the lower-right corner of the Word window.

Tip

Changing the zoom affects only the way the document is displayed on the screen; it does not affect the document itself.

To check your Zoom setting:

▶ **1.** In the lower-right corner of the Word window, locate the current Zoom level, the Zoom Out button, the Zoom In button, and the Zoom slider. In Figure 1-10, the current Zoom setting is 114%, but yours might be higher or lower. In the next two steps you'll practice zooming in and zooming out. Then you will select the Page width setting.

Figure 1-10	Options for changing the Zoom setting

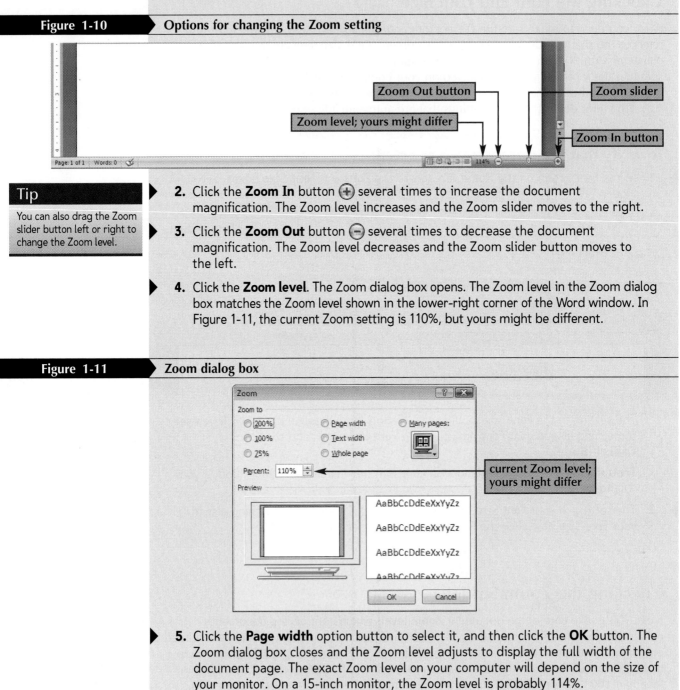

Tip

You can also drag the Zoom slider button left or right to change the Zoom level.

▶ **2.** Click the **Zoom In** button ⊕ several times to increase the document magnification. The Zoom level increases and the Zoom slider moves to the right.

▶ **3.** Click the **Zoom Out** button ⊖ several times to decrease the document magnification. The Zoom level decreases and the Zoom slider button moves to the left.

▶ **4.** Click the **Zoom level**. The Zoom dialog box opens. The Zoom level in the Zoom dialog box matches the Zoom level shown in the lower-right corner of the Word window. In Figure 1-11, the current Zoom setting is 110%, but yours might be different.

Figure 1-11	Zoom dialog box

▶ **5.** Click the **Page width** option button to select it, and then click the **OK** button. The Zoom dialog box closes and the Zoom level adjusts to display the full width of the document page. The exact Zoom level on your computer will depend on the size of your monitor. On a 15-inch monitor, the Zoom level is probably 114%.

To make sure your window always matches the figures in these tutorials, remember to complete the checklist in Figure 1-12 each time you are working in this book.

Window Element	Setting
Document view	Print Layout
Nonprinting characters	Displayed
Rulers	Displayed
Word window	Maximized
Zoom	Page width
Font	Identical to setting shown in figures
Font size	Identical to setting shown in figures

Now that you have planned your letter, opened Word, identified screen elements, and adjusted settings, you are ready to begin your letter to Clara Meyer, Carlyle Press's new author.

Beginning a Letter

Before you begin writing, you should insert some blank lines to ensure that you leave enough room for the Carlyle University Press letterhead. The amount of space you leave at the top of a letter depends on the size of the letterhead. In this case, pressing Enter four times should add enough space.

Adjusting Margins vs. Inserting Blank Lines | InSight

As you gain experience with Word, you'll learn how to adjust a document's margin to add blank space at the beginning of a document. (The term **margin** refers to the blank space around the top, bottom, and sides of document.) Adjusting margins is a better method than inserting blank lines, because it ensures that you won't accidentally delete a blank line as you edit the document. However, until you learn more about margins, inserting blank lines is a useful shortcut that enables you to jump right into the task of typing your letter.

To insert blank lines in the document:

▶ 1. Press the **Enter** key four times. Each time you press the Enter key, a nonprinting paragraph mark appears, and the insertion point moves down to the next line. By default, Word inserts some space between each paragraph mark. You'll learn how to change this setting later in this tutorial. For now, you can ignore this space. On the vertical ruler, you can see that the insertion point is about 1.5 inches from the top margin. Although you might find it hard to see on the ruler, the top margin itself is 1 inch. This means the insertion point is now located a total of 2.5 inches from the top of the page. See Figure 1-13.

Figure 1-13 **Document window after inserting blank lines**

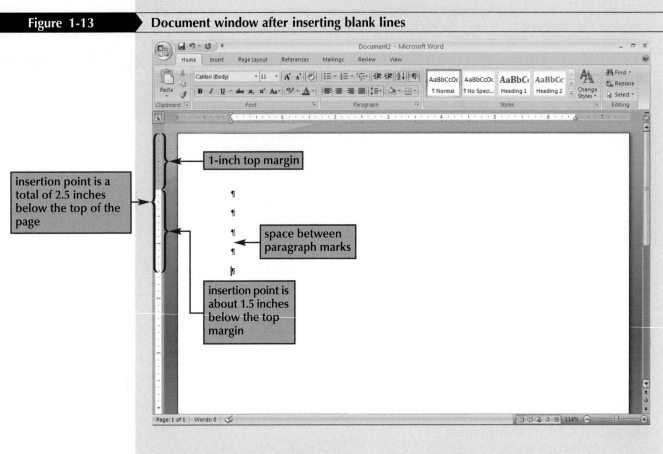

insertion point is a total of 2.5 inches below the top of the page

1-inch top margin

space between paragraph marks

insertion point is about 1.5 inches below the top margin

Trouble? If your insertion point is higher or lower on the vertical ruler than in Figure 1-13, don't worry. Different monitors produce slightly different measurements when you press the Enter key.

The insertion point is now low enough in your document to allow room for the letterhead when you print the document. You are ready to start typing.

Entering Text

Normally, you begin a letter by typing the date followed by the inside address. However, typing these two items involves using some specialized Word features. To give you some experience with simply typing text, you'll start with the salutation and the body of the letter. Then you'll go back later to add the date and the inside address.

You'll start by typing the salutation (the "Dear Clara:" text, shown earlier in Figure 1-1). If you make a mistake while typing, press the Backspace key to delete the incorrect character and then type the correct character.

To type the salutation:

► 1. Type **Dear Clara:** and then pause to notice the nonprinting character (•) that appears to indicate a space between the two words.

2. Press the **Enter** key to start a new paragraph for the body of the letter. If you have typed a block style business letter before, you might be accustomed to pressing Enter twice between paragraphs. However, because Word is set up to insert extra space between paragraphs by default, you need to press the Enter key only once to start a new paragraph. See Figure 1-14.

Letter with salutation | Figure 1-14

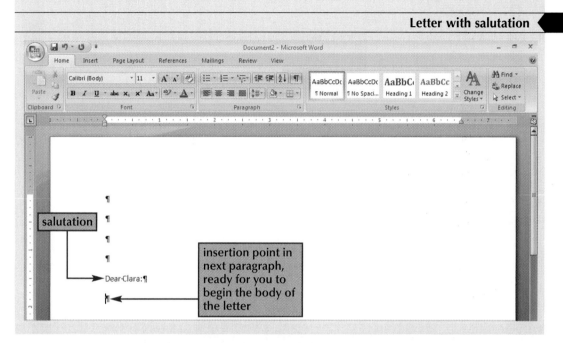

Now you are ready to begin typing the body of the letter (shown earlier in Figure 1-1). As you do, notice that when you reach the end of a line, you can keep typing; the insertion point just moves down to the next line. Depending on the length of the word you are typing when you reach the end of the line, the word will either stay on that line, or if it is long, it will move to the next line. This automatic line breaking is called **word wrap**. You'll see how word wrap works as you begin typing the body of the letter.

To begin typing the body of the letter:

1. Type the following sentence, including the period: **Enclosed you will find the Author's Guide we discussed at our meeting.**

2. Press the **spacebar**.

3. Type the following sentence: **I think it will answer all your questions.**

Notice how Word moves the insertion point to a new line when the preceding line is full.

4. Press the **Enter** key to end the first paragraph. When you are finished, your screen should look similar to Figure 1-15. Notice that, in addition to inserting space between paragraphs, Word also inserts a smaller amount of space between lines within a paragraph.

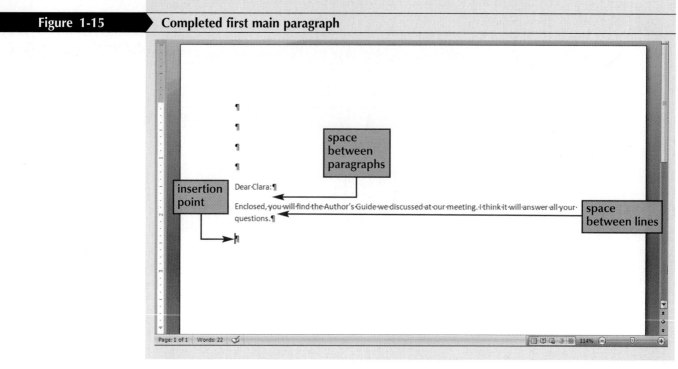

Figure 1-15 Completed first main paragraph

Before you continue with the rest of the letter, you should save what you have typed so far.

Reference Window | **Saving a Document for the First Time**

- Click the Save button on the Quick Access Toolbar.
- Type a name in the File name text box.
- Select the location where you want to save the file.
- Click the Save button at the bottom of the Save As dialog box.

To save the document:

▶ **1.** On the Quick Access Toolbar, click the **Save** button 💾 . The Save As dialog box opens. Note that Word suggests using the first line you typed ("Dear Clara") as the filename. You will replace the suggested filename with something more descriptive.

▶ **2.** Type **Meyer Letter** in the File name text box, replacing the suggested filename.

Next, you need to tell Word where you want to save the document. In this case, you want to use the Tutorial subfolder in the Tutorial.01 folder provided with your Data Files.

Trouble? The Tutorial.01 folder is included with the Data Files for this text. If you don't have the Word Data Files, you need to get them before you can proceed. Your instructor will either give you the Data Files or ask you to obtain them from a specified location (such as a network drive). In either case, be sure that you make a backup copy of your Data Files before you start using them, so that the original files will be available on your copied disk in case you need to start over because of an error or problem. If you have any questions about the Data Files, see your instructor or technical support person for assistance.

▶ **3.** Use the options in the Save As dialog box to select the Tutorial subfolder within the Tutorial.01 folder. See Figure 1-16.

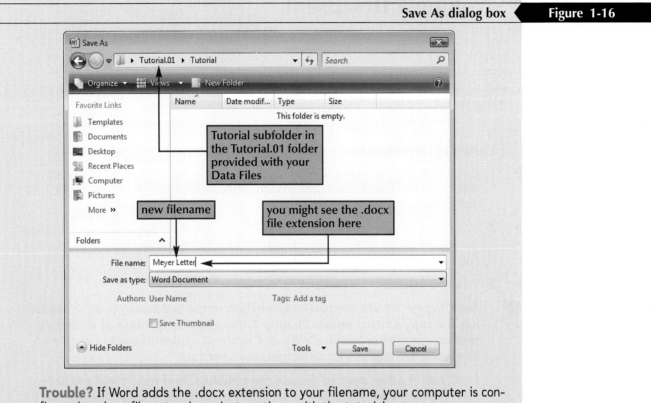

Trouble? If Word adds the .docx extension to your filename, your computer is configured to show file extensions. Just continue with the tutorial.

▶ **4.** Click the **Save** button in the Save As dialog box. The dialog box closes, and you return to the document window. The new document name (Meyer Letter) appears in the title bar.

Note that Word adds the .docx extension to document filenames to identify them as Microsoft Word 2007 documents, whether your computer is set up to display them or not. These tutorials assume that file extensions are hidden, but it is okay if they are displayed.

You've made a good start on the letter, and you've saved your work so far. In the next session, you'll finish typing the letter, and then you'll print it.

Session 1.1 Quick Check | Review

1. In your own words, explain the importance of planning a document.
2. On what tab is the Ruler check box located?
3. Explain how to change the document view to Print Layout.
4. True or False: Nonprinting characters are symbols that can appear on the screen but are not visible on the printed page.
5. True or False: Pressing the Enter key is the only way to insert blank space at the top of a document.
6. What is the file extension for Microsoft Word 2007 documents?

Session 1.2

Scrolling a Document

At this point, unless you are working on a large monitor, your screen probably looks as if it doesn't have enough room to type the rest of Andrew's letter—but of course there is room. As you continue to add text to your document, the text at the top will **scroll** (or shift up) and disappear from the top of the document window. You'll see how scrolling works as you type the second paragraph in the body of the letter.

To observe scrolling while you're typing text:

1. If you took a break after the previous session, make sure that Word is running and that the Meyer Letter document is open. Also, review the checklist in Figure 1-12 and verify that your screen is set up to match the figures in this tutorial.

2. Make sure the insertion point is positioned to the left of the paragraph symbol below the first paragraph in the body of the letter (as shown earlier in Figure 1-15). If it is not, move the insertion point by clicking in that location now.

3. Type the following two paragraphs:

   See Chapter 1 for a complete explanation of the publishing process, including the copy editing phase. Chapter 2 discusses the process of creating a text manuscript in Microsoft Word. Chapter 3 explains how to compile an electronic art manuscript to accompany your text.

   I will call in a few days to discuss the schedule. Feel free to call me before then if you prefer. I will be traveling next week, but you can always reach me on my cell phone. I also plan to check my e-mail while I am on the road.

   Trouble? If you make a mistake while typing, press the Backspace key or the Delete key to delete any incorrect characters, and then type the correct characters.

4. Press the **Enter** key.

5. Type **Sincerely yours,** (including the comma) to enter the complimentary closing.

6. Press the **Enter** key 10 times so you can see the document scroll up to accommodate the blank paragraphs. You're doing this only to demonstrate how a document scrolls up. You'll delete the extra blank paragraphs shortly.

   As you pressed the Enter key repeatedly, the upper part of the document probably scrolled off the top of the document window. Exactly when this happens depends on the size of your monitor. See Figure 1-17.

Part of the document scrolled off the window | Figure 1-17

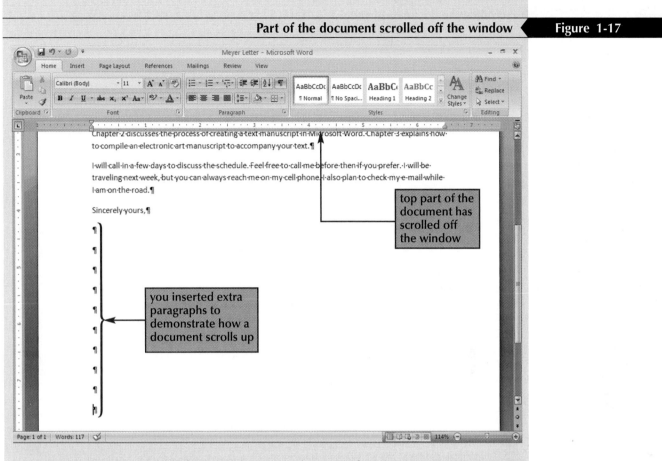

You don't really want all those blank paragraph marks after the complimentary closing, so you need to delete them.

▶ **7.** Press the **Backspace** key eight times. When you finish, you should see two paragraph marks below the complimentary closing, with the insertion point blinking to the left of the bottom one. This allows enough space for a signature.

▶ **8.** Type **Andrew Suri**, and then press the **Enter** key. A wavy red line appears below "Suri." In Word, such lines indicate possible spelling errors. Because Andrew's last name is not in the Word dictionary, Word suggests that it might be spelled incorrectly. You'll learn more about Word's error-checking features in a moment. For now, you can ignore the wavy red line.

You've completed most of the letter, so you should save your work.

▶ **9.** On the Quick Access Toolbar, click the **Save** button 🖫 . Word saves your letter with the same name and in the same location you specified earlier. Don't be concerned about any typing errors. You'll learn how to correct them later in this tutorial.

In the previous set of steps, you watched paragraph marks and text at the top of your document move off the window. Anytime you need to see the beginning of the letter, you can scroll this hidden text back into view. When you do, the text at the bottom of the window will scroll out of view. There are three ways to scroll the document window: click the up or down arrows in the vertical scroll bar, click anywhere in the vertical scroll bar, or drag the scroll box. See Figure 1-18.

Figure 1-18 ▶ **Scrolling the document window**

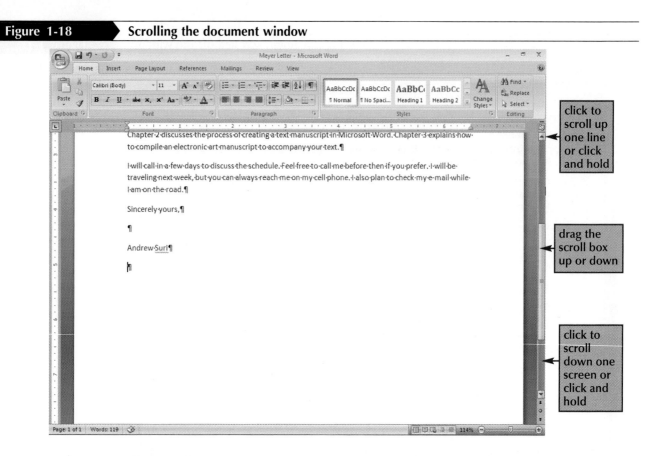

To practice scrolling the document using the vertical scroll bar:

▶ **1.** Position the mouse pointer over the arrow at the top of the vertical scroll bar. Press and hold the mouse button to scroll the text. When the text stops scrolling, you have reached the top of the document and can see the beginning of the letter. Note that scrolling does not change the location of the insertion point in the document.

▶ **2.** Click the down arrow on the vertical scroll bar several times. The document scrolls down one line at a time.

▶ **3.** Click anywhere in the vertical scroll bar below the scroll box. The document scrolls down one full screen.

▶ **4.** Drag the scroll box up to the top of the scroll bar, so you can see the beginning of the letter.

▶ **5.** Continue practicing these steps until you feel comfortable scrolling up and down. When you are finished, scroll the document so you can see the complimentary closing at the end of the letter.

Andrew asks you to include his middle initial in the signature line. Performing this task will give you a chance to practice moving the insertion point around the document.

Moving the Insertion Point Around a Document

When you scroll a document, you change the part of the document that is displayed on the screen. But to change the location in the document where new text will appear when you type, you need to move the insertion point. One way to move the insertion point is to scroll up or down and then click where you want to insert new text. However, it is often more efficient to use the keyboard so you don't have to move your hand to the mouse, move the insertion point, and then move your hand back to the keyboard to type. You can use the arrow keys, ←, ↑, →, and ↓, to move the insertion point one character at a time to the left or right or one line at a time up or down. In addition, you can press a variety of key combinations to move the insertion point from one paragraph to another, to the beginning or end of the document, and so on. As you become more experienced with Word, you'll learn which methods you prefer.

Before you add Andrew's middle initial to the signature line, you'll take some time to practice moving the insertion point around the document.

To move the insertion point with keystrokes:

▶ **1.** Press the **Ctrl+Home** keys (that is, press the Ctrl key and hold it down while you press the Home key). The insertion point moves to the beginning of the document.

▶ **2.** Press the **Page Down** key to move the insertion point down to the next screen.

▶ **3.** Press the ↑ key several times to move the insertion point up one line at a time, and then press the → key several times to move the insertion point to the right one character at a time.

▶ **4.** Press the **Ctrl+End** keys. The insertion point moves to the end of the document.

▶ **5.** Use the arrow keys to position the insertion point to the right of the "w" in "Andrew." Now you can add Andrew's middle initial.

▶ **6.** Press the **spacebar**, and then type the letter **T** followed by a period so that the signature line reads "Andrew T. Suri."

Figure 1-19 summarizes the keystrokes you can use to move the insertion point around a document.

Keystrokes for moving the insertion point ◀ **Figure 1-19**

To move the insertion point	Press
Left or right one character at a time	← or →
Up or down one line at a time	↑ or ↓
Left or right one word at a time	Ctrl+ ← or Ctrl+ →
Up or down one paragraph at a time	Ctrl+ ↑ or Ctrl+ ↓
To the beginning or to the end of the current line	Home or End
To the beginning or to the end of the document	Ctrl+Home or Ctrl+End
To the previous screen or to the next screen	Page Up or Page Down
To the top or to the bottom of the document window	Alt+Ctrl+Page Up or Alt+Ctrl+Page Down

Using the Undo and Redo Commands

To undo (or reverse) the last thing you did in a document, you can click the **Undo button** on the Quick Access Toolbar. If you want to restore your original change, the **Redo button** reverses the action of the Undo button (or redoes the undo). To undo more than your last action, you can click the Undo button arrow on the Quick Access Toolbar. A list will open that shows your most recent actions.

Andrew asks you to undo the addition of his middle initial, to see how the signature line looks without it.

To undo the addition of the "T.":

▶ 1. On the Quick Access Toolbar, place the mouse pointer over the **Undo** button , but don't click it. The ScreenTip "Undo Typing (Ctrl + Z)" appears, indicating that your most recent action involved typing. The item in parentheses is the keyboard shortcut for the Undo command. See Figure 1-20.

Figure 1-20 | **Using the Undo button**

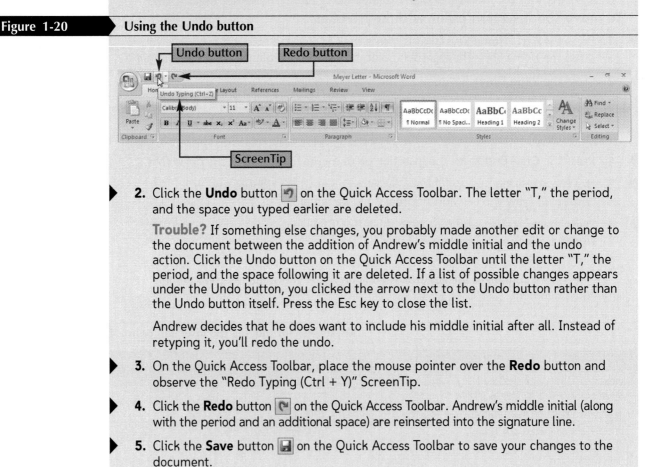

▶ 2. Click the **Undo** button on the Quick Access Toolbar. The letter "T," the period, and the space you typed earlier are deleted.

Trouble? If something else changes, you probably made another edit or change to the document between the addition of Andrew's middle initial and the undo action. Click the Undo button on the Quick Access Toolbar until the letter "T," the period, and the space following it are deleted. If a list of possible changes appears under the Undo button, you clicked the arrow next to the Undo button rather than the Undo button itself. Press the Esc key to close the list.

Andrew decides that he does want to include his middle initial after all. Instead of retyping it, you'll redo the undo.

▶ 3. On the Quick Access Toolbar, place the mouse pointer over the **Redo** button and observe the "Redo Typing (Ctrl + Y)" ScreenTip.

▶ 4. Click the **Redo** button on the Quick Access Toolbar. Andrew's middle initial (along with the period and an additional space) are reinserted into the signature line.

▶ 5. Click the **Save** button on the Quick Access Toolbar to save your changes to the document.

Correcting Errors

If you notice a typing error as soon as you make it, you can press the Backspace key, which deletes the characters and spaces to the left of the insertion point one at a time. Backspacing erases both printing and nonprinting characters. After you erase the error, you can type the correct character(s). You can also press the Delete key, which deletes characters to the right of the insertion point one at a time.

In many cases, however, Word's **AutoCorrect** feature will do the work for you. Among other things, AutoCorrect automatically corrects common typing errors, such as typing "adn" for "and." For example, you might have noticed AutoCorrect at work if you forgot to capitalize the first letter in a sentence as you typed the letter. AutoCorrect can automatically correct this error as you type the rest of the sentence. You'll learn more about using AutoCorrect as you become a more experienced Word user. For now, just keep in mind that AutoCorrect corrects certain typing errors automatically. Depending on how your computer is set up, some or all AutoCorrect features might be turned off. You'll learn how to turn AutoCorrect on in the following steps.

Whether or not AutoCorrect is turned on, you can always rely on Word's **spelling checker**. By default, this feature continually checks your document against Word's built-in dictionary. If you type a word that doesn't match the correct spelling in Word's dictionary, or if a word is not in the dictionary at all (as is the case with Andrew's last name, Suri), a wavy red line appears beneath the word. A wavy red line also appears if you type duplicate words (such as "the the"). Word also includes a grammar checker, which is turned off by default. You will learn how to use the grammar checker in Tutorial 2.

Before you can practice using AutoCorrect and the spelling checker, you need to verify that you have the correct settings in the Word Options dialog box.

To verify the spelling checker and AutoCorrect settings:

▶ **1.** Click the **Office Button** 🔘, and then (at the bottom of the Office menu) click the **Word Options** button. The Word Options dialog box opens.

▶ **2.** In the left pane, click **Proofing**. Options related to proofing a document are displayed in the right pane.

▶ **3.** Verify that the **Check spelling as you type** check box contains a check mark.

▶ **4.** Verify that the **Mark grammar errors as you type** check box does *not* contain a check mark. (This option is typically turned off by default.)

▶ **5.** Near the top of the right pane, click the **AutoCorrect Options** button. The AutoCorrect: English (United States) dialog box opens.

▶ **6.** Locate the **Capitalize first letter of sentences** check box and the **Replace text as you type** check box. If they are not already checked, click them to insert check marks now. (It is okay if other check boxes have check marks.) See Figure 1-21.

Figure 1-21 ▶ **Selecting AutoCorrect options**

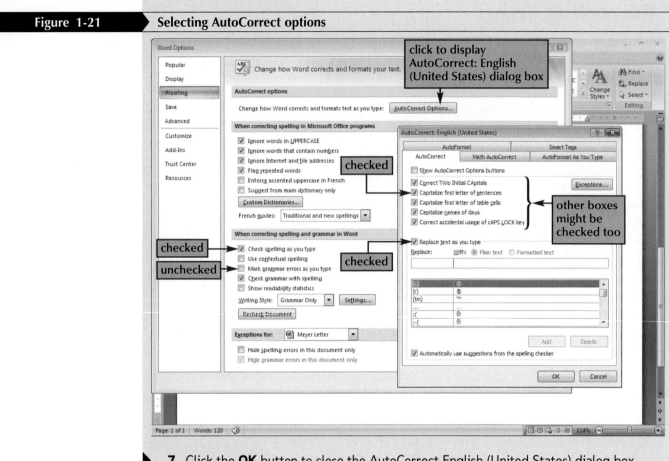

▶ **7.** Click the **OK** button to close the AutoCorrect English (United States) dialog box, and then click the **OK** button again to close the Word Options dialog box.

The easiest way to see how these features work is to make some intentional typing errors.

To correct intentional typing errors:

▶ **1.** Use the arrow keys to move the insertion point to the left of the last paragraph mark in the document.

▶ **2.** Carefully and slowly type the following sentence exactly as it is shown, including the spelling errors: **notice how microsoft Word corects teh commen typing misTakes you make**. See Figure 1-22.

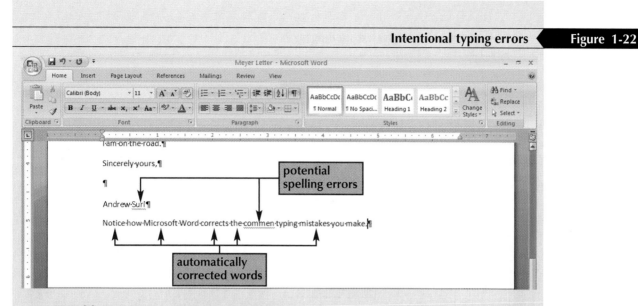

Intentional typing errors ◄ **Figure 1-22**

Trouble? If you see wavy green underlines, the grammar checker is turned on and you made a mistake not included in Step 2. Delete the text you just typed, repeat Steps 1–4 in the preceding set of steps to turn the grammar checker off, click the OK button to close the Word Options dialog box, and then begin these steps again with Step 1.

When you pressed the spacebar after the word "commen," a wavy red line appeared beneath it, indicating that the word might be misspelled. Also, Word automatically capitalized the word "Notice" (because it is the first word in the sentence) and "Microsoft" (because it is a proper noun). And, when you pressed the spacebar after the words "corects," "teh," and "misTakes," Word automatically corrected the typing errors.

Correcting Spelling Errors

After you verify that AutoCorrect made the changes you want, you should review your document for red wavy underlines, which indicate potential spelling errors. In the following steps, you will learn a quick way to correct such errors.

To correct spelling and grammar errors:

► **1.** Position the I-beam pointer over the word "commen," and then click the right mouse button. A shortcut menu appears with suggested spellings. You also see the Mini toolbar, which provides easy access to some of the most commonly used options in the Home tab for the object you've right-clicked. You'll learn more about the Mini toolbar as you gain more experience with Word. See Figure 1-23.

Figure 1-23 ▶ **Shortcut menu with suggested spellings**

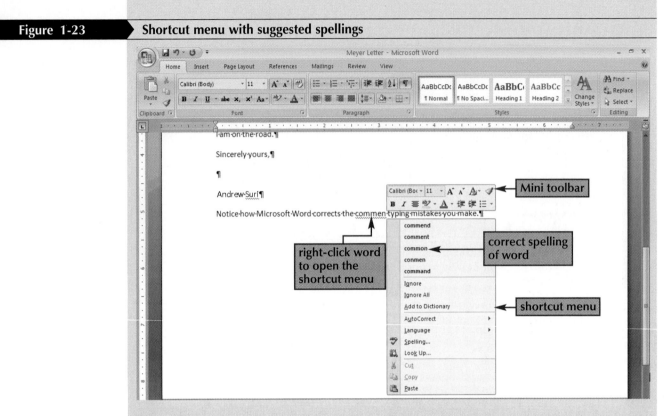

Trouble? If the shortcut menu doesn't appear, repeat Step 1, making sure you click the right mouse button, not the left one. If you see a different menu from the one shown in Figure 1-23, you didn't right-click exactly on the word "commen." Press the Esc key to close the menu, and then repeat Step 1.

▶ **2.** Click **common** in the shortcut menu. The menu closes (along with the Mini toolbar), and the correct spelling appears in your document. Notice that the wavy red line disappears after you correct the error.

Proofreading the Letter

You can see how quick and easy it is to correct common typing errors with AutoCorrect and the spelling checker. Remember, however, to proofread each document you create thoroughly. AutoCorrect will not catch words that are spelled correctly but used improperly (such as "your" for "you're"). Before you can proofread your letter, you need to delete the practice sentence.

To delete the practice sentence:

▶ **1.** Make sure the insertion point is to the right of "common" in the sentence you just typed, and then press the **Delete** key repeatedly to delete any spaces and characters to the right of the insertion point.

▶ **2.** Press the **Backspace** key repeatedly until the insertion point is located just left of the paragraph mark below Andrew's name. There should only be one paragraph mark below his name. If you accidentally delete part of the letter, retype it, using Figure 1-1 as a guide.

Now you can proofread the letter for any typos. You can also get rid of the wavy red underline below Andrew's last name.

To proofread the document:

▶ **1.** Be sure the signature line is visible. Because Word doesn't recognize "Suri" as a word, it is marked as a potential error. You need to tell Word to ignore this name wherever it occurs in the letter.

▶ **2.** Right-click **Suri**. A shortcut menu and the Mini toolbar open.

▶ **3.** Click **Ignore All** on the shortcut menu. This tells Word to ignore the word "Suri" each time it occurs in this document. The wavy red underline disappears from below Andrew's last name.

▶ **4.** Scroll up to the beginning of the letter and proofread it for typing errors. If a word has a wavy red underline, right-click it and choose an option on the shortcut menu. To correct other errors, click to the right or left of the error, use the Backspace or Delete key to remove it, and then type a correction.

▶ **5.** On the Quick Access Toolbar, click the **Save** button 🔲 . Word saves your letter with the same name and to the same location you specified earlier.

Next, you need to return to the beginning of the document and insert the date. In the process, you'll learn how to use Word's AutoComplete feature.

Inserting a Date with AutoComplete

The advantage of using a word-processing program such as Microsoft Word is that you can easily make changes to text you have already typed. In this case, you need to insert the current date at the beginning of the letter. Andrew tells you that he wants to send the *Author's Guide* to Clara Meyer on February 8, so you need to insert that date into the letter now.

Before you can enter the date, you need to move the insertion point to the correct location.

To move the insertion point and add some blank lines:

▶ **1.** Scroll up to display the top of the document.

▶ **2.** Click to the left of the "D" in "Dear Clara" in the salutation, press the **Enter** key twice, then press the ↑ key twice to move the insertion point up to two paragraphs above the salutation. There are now six blank paragraphs before the salutation. The insertion point is located in the second blank paragraph above the salutation. The vertical ruler tells you that the insertion point is located about 1.5 inches from the top margin (that is, the insertion point is now located where the salutation used to be). As you'll recall, the top margin is one inch deep, so the insertion point is now approximately 2.5 inches from the top of the page. This is where you will insert the date. See Figure 1-24.

Figure 1-24 ▶ **Insertion point positioned for adding date**

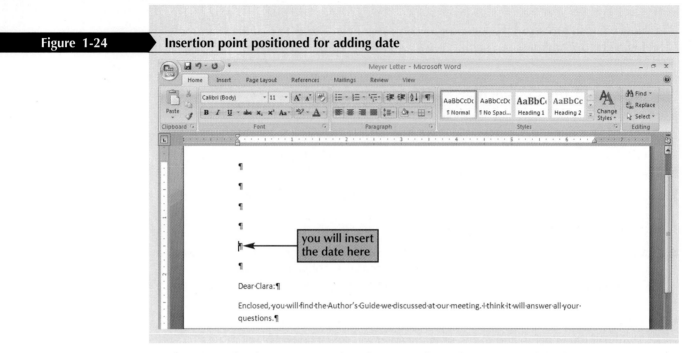

To insert the date, you can take advantage of Word's **AutoComplete** feature, which automatically inserts dates and other regularly used items for you. In this case, you can type the first few characters of the month, and let Word insert the rest.

To insert the date:

▶ 1. Type **Febr** (the first four letters of February). A rectangular box appears above the line, as shown in Figure 1-25. If you wanted to type something other than February, you could continue typing to complete the word. In this case, though, you want to accept the AutoComplete suggestion.

Figure 1-25 ▶ **AutoComplete suggestion**

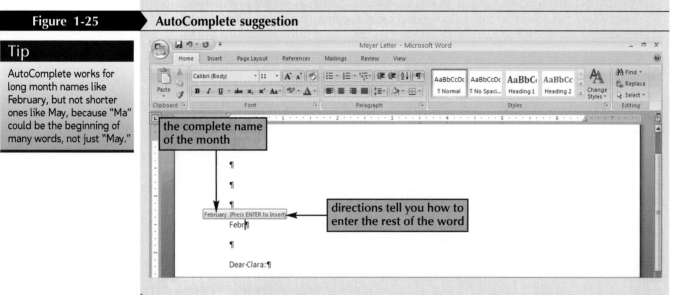

▶ 2. Press the **Enter** key. The rest of the word "February" is inserted in the document.

▶ **3.** Press the **spacebar**, type **8, 2010**, and then press the **Enter** key twice. The date is finished, and the insertion point is now located where you want to begin typing the inside address.

Trouble? If February happens to be the current month, you will see a second AutoComplete suggestion displaying the current date after you press the spacebar. To ignore that AutoComplete suggestion, continue typing the rest of the date as instructed in Step 3.

You're ready to type the inside address. But first, you need to learn a little more about paragraph and line spacing in Microsoft Word.

Understanding Line and Paragraph Spacing

In Word, any text that ends with a paragraph mark symbol (¶) is a paragraph. A **paragraph** can be a group of words that is many lines long, a single word, or even a blank line, in which case you see a paragraph mark alone on a single line. (Recall that the letter to Clara Meyer includes several blank paragraphs at the beginning of the document.) As you work with paragraphs in a document, you need to be concerned with two types of spacing—line spacing and paragraph spacing.

Line spacing determines the amount of space between lines of text within a paragraph. Lines that are closely positioned one on top of another are said to be single spaced. Technically speaking, single spacing allows for the tallest character in a line of text. All other line spacing options are measured as multiples of single spacing. For example, 1.5 line spacing allows for one and one-half times the space of single spacing. Likewise, double spacing allows for twice the space of single spacing. By default, the line spacing in Word 2007 documents is set to 1.15 times the space allowed in single spacing. This allows for the largest character in a particular line as well as a small amount of extra space.

The other type of spacing you need to be concerned with, **paragraph spacing**, determines the amount of space before and after a paragraph. Paragraph spacing is measured in points; a **point** is approximately $1/72$ of an inch. The default setting for paragraph spacing in Word is 0 points before each paragraph and 10 points after each paragraph.

Although line spacing and paragraph spacing are two different things, it is common to refer to paragraph spacing with the same terms used to refer to line spacing. So, paragraphs that appear very close together, with no space for text in between, are often referred to as single spaced. Paragraphs that have space enough for a single line of text between them are said to be double spaced. The default paragraph spacing in Word (10 points after each paragraph) is designed to look like double spacing (although it is slightly tighter than true double spacing). Figure 1-26 shows the Meyer Letter document zoomed to 90%, so you can see its spacing at a glance.

Figure 1-26 **Line and paragraph spacing in the letter to Clara Meyer**

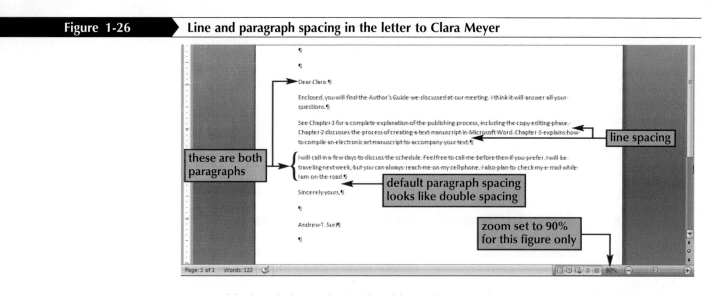

In a block style letter, the inside address (shown earlier in Figure 1-1) should be single spaced. However, with Word's default paragraph spacing, when you press the Enter key to move from the name line in the inside address, to the street address line, and then to the city and state line, Word inserts extra space after each paragraph. This results in an inside address that is double spaced. You'll see how this works in the following steps. Then you'll learn how to correct the problem.

To type the inside address:

1. Type the following: **Clara Meyer**, press the **Enter** key, type **2257 Chamberlain Drive**, press the **Enter** key, and then type **North Liberty, IA 52317**. Do not press the Enter key after typing the zip code; you should already see one blank paragraph before and after the inside address. See Figure 1-27.

Letter with inside address | Figure 1-27

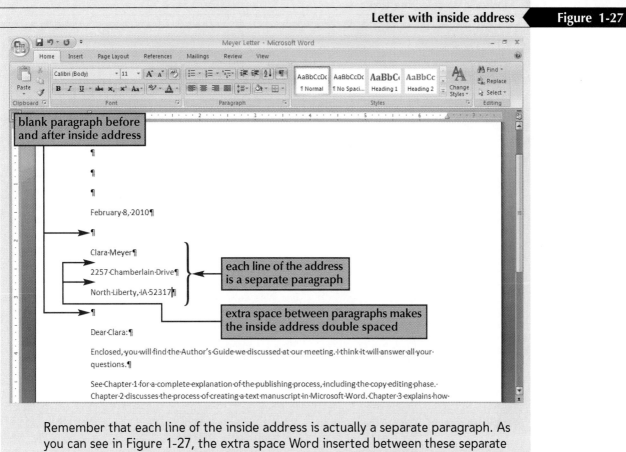

Remember that each line of the inside address is actually a separate paragraph. As you can see in Figure 1-27, the extra space Word inserted between these separate paragraphs results in an inside address that appears to be double spaced.

To correct this problem, you need to **select**, or highlight, the inside address and then change the paragraph spacing. Andrew is also concerned about the document's line spacing. He doesn't really like the extra space between lines, so he asks you to remove it. To change this, you need to select the entire document and then change the line spacing.

Selecting Parts of a Document

You can select one or more paragraphs, one or more words, any other part of a document, or even the entire document, by using the mouse or the keyboard. However, most people find that the mouse is easier and more efficient to use. With the mouse you can quickly select a line or paragraph by clicking the **selection bar** (the blank space in the left margin area of the document window). You can also select text using various combinations of keys. Figure 1-28 summarizes methods for selecting text with the mouse and the keyboard. A notation such as "Ctrl+Shift" means you press and hold the two keys at the same time.

Figure 1-28 ▷ **Methods for selecting text**

To Select	Mouse	Keyboard	Mouse and Keyboard
A word	Double-click the word	Move the insertion point to the beginning of the word, hold down Ctrl+Shift, and then press →	
A line	Click in the selection bar next to the line	Move the insertion point to the beginning of the line, hold down Shift, and then press ↓	
A sentence	Click at the beginning of the sentence, then drag the pointer until the sentence is selected		Press and hold down Ctrl, and then click within the sentence
Multiple lines	Click and drag in the selection bar next to the lines	Move the insertion point to the beginning of the first line, hold down Shift, and then press ↓ until all the lines are selected	
A paragraph	Double-click in the selection bar next to the paragraph, or triple-click within the paragraph	Move the insertion point to the beginning of the paragraph, hold down Ctrl+Shift, and then press ↓	
Multiple paragraphs	Click in the selection bar next to the first paragraph in the group, and then drag in the selection bar to select the paragraphs	Move the insertion point to the beginning of the first paragraph, hold down Ctrl+Shift, and then press ↓ until all the para-graphs are selected	
An entire document	Triple-click in the selection bar	Press Ctrl+A	Press and hold down Ctrl, and then click in the selection bar
A block of text	Click at the beginning of the block, and then drag the pointer until the entire block is selected		Click at the beginning of the block, press and hold down Shift, and then click at the end of the block
Nonadjacent blocks of text	Press and hold down Ctrl, and then drag the mouse pointer to select multiple blocks of nonadjacent text		

You'll practice many of these selection methods in Tutorial 2. For now, you will focus on selecting the multiple paragraphs of the inside address and the entire document. You'll start by selecting the inside address.

To select the inside address:

▷ **1.** Click to the left of the "C" in "Clara Meyer" in the inside address, and then drag the mouse right and down until the entire inside address is selected. Make sure the paragraph mark to the right of the zip code is also selected. See Figure 1-29.

Selected inside address | Figure 1-29

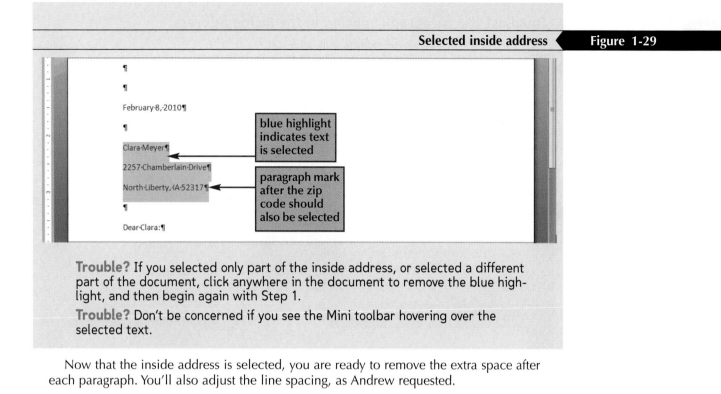

Trouble? If you selected only part of the inside address, or selected a different part of the document, click anywhere in the document to remove the blue highlight, and then begin again with Step 1.

Trouble? Don't be concerned if you see the Mini toolbar hovering over the selected text.

Now that the inside address is selected, you are ready to remove the extra space after each paragraph. You'll also adjust the line spacing, as Andrew requested.

Adjusting Paragraph and Line Spacing

There are several ways to adjust paragraph and line spacing in Word. The quickest method, which you'll use in this tutorial, is to click the Line spacing button in the Paragraph group on the Home tab. (In Tutorial 2, you'll learn another technique that offers more options.)

Clicking the Line spacing button opens a menu with some commonly used line spacing options: single spacing (listed on the Line spacing menu as 1.0), double spacing (listed as 2.0), and so on. The paragraph spacing options offered by the Line spacing button are more streamlined: you can choose to add or remove a default amount of extra space before or after each paragraph. You cannot specify a particular amount of space.

Understanding Spacing Between Paragraphs | InSight

To many people, "to single space between paragraphs" means pressing the Enter key once after each paragraph. Likewise, "to double space between paragraphs" means pressing the Enter key twice after each paragraph. With the default paragraph spacing in Word 2007, however, you only need to press the Enter key once to insert a double space after a paragraph. Keep this in mind if you're used to pressing the Enter key twice; otherwise, you could end up with more space than you want between paragraphs.

Andrew asks you to remove the extra space between the lines within paragraphs. This means you need to change the line spacing from 1.15 to 1.0 (that is, to single spacing). You'll start by adjusting the paragraph spacing in the inside address, and then turn your attention to the line spacing for the entire document.

To adjust the paragraph spacing in the inside address:

▶ **1.** Verify that the inside address is still selected.

▶ **2.** In the Paragraph group on the Home tab, click the **Line spacing** button. A menu of line spacing options appears, with two paragraph spacing options at the bottom. The current line spacing setting for the selected text (1.15) is indicated by a check mark. Because the line spacing is the same throughout the document, this is also the current line spacing setting for the entire document. At the moment, you are more interested in the paragraph spacing options. Your goal is to remove the extra space after each paragraph in the inside address, so you need to use the last option on the menu, Remove Space After Paragraph. See Figure 1-30.

Figure 1-30 ▶ **Line and paragraph spacing options**

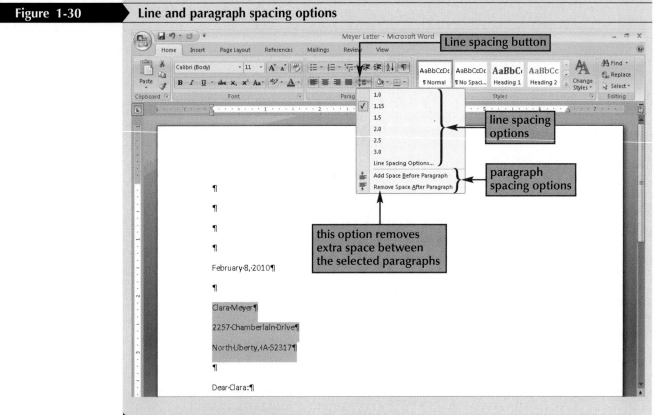

▶ **3.** Click **Remove Space After Paragraph**. The menu closes, and the extra space after each of the three paragraphs of the inside address is removed. The paragraphs are now closer together.

▶ **4.** Click anywhere in the document to deselect the inside address. Notice that the change in paragraph spacing in the inside address did not affect the rest of the document because you had selected only the inside address. The paragraphs in the body of the letter are still separated by extra space, so that they appear to be double spaced.

The three paragraphs of the inside address are closer together, but they don't exactly look single spaced. That's because the default line spacing setting (which you'll recall adds a small amount of space below each line) remains in effect, adding a small amount of extra space below the single line of text in each of the three inside address paragraphs. When you change the line spacing for the entire document to single spaced in the next set of steps, the inside address will finally look single spaced.

To adjust the line spacing for the entire document:

▶ 1. Press the **Ctrl + A** keys. The entire document is selected, as indicated by the blue highlight.

▶ 2. In the Paragraph group on the Home tab, click the **Line spacing** button 📄. The Line spacing menu opens. As you saw earlier, the default line spacing setting of 1.15 is currently selected, as indicated by the check mark. You want to change the setting to single spacing, or 1.0.

▶ 3. Click **1.0**. The Line spacing menu closes.

▶ 4. Click anywhere in the document to deselect it. The lines of the entire document move closer together, and the inside address is now single spaced. The lines within the paragraphs in the rest of the document are also single spaced. The double spacing between paragraphs everywhere in the letter except the inside address remains unchanged. See Figure 1-31.

Tip

A line spacing setting of 1.15 is fine for most documents. However, some people prefer a setting of 1.0.

New line spacing in the document | Figure 1-31

Previewing and Printing a Document

Do you think the letter is ready to print? If you print too soon, you risk wasting paper and printer time. For example, if you failed to insert enough space for the company letterhead, you would have to add more space, and then print the letter again. To avoid wasting paper and time, you should first display the document in the **Print Preview window**. By default, the Print Preview window shows you the full page; there's no need to scroll through the document.

To preview the document:

▶ **1.** Proof the document one last time and correct any new errors. Always remember to proof your document immediately before printing it.

▶ **2.** Click to the left of the last paragraph mark in the document (just below Andrew's name), press the **Enter** key and type your first, middle, and last initials in lowercase. In a block style letter, it is customary for the typist to include his or her initials below the signature line. In this case, adding your initials also ensures that you will be able to identify your copy of the letter when you retrieve it from the printer.

▶ **3.** Click the **Office Button** 🏢 , point to **Print**, and then click **Print Preview**. The Print Preview window opens and displays a full-page version of your letter, as shown in Figure 1-32. This shows how the letter will fit on the printed page. The Ribbon in Print Preview includes a number of useful options for changing the way the printed page will look.

Figure 1-32 | **Full page displayed in the Print Preview window**

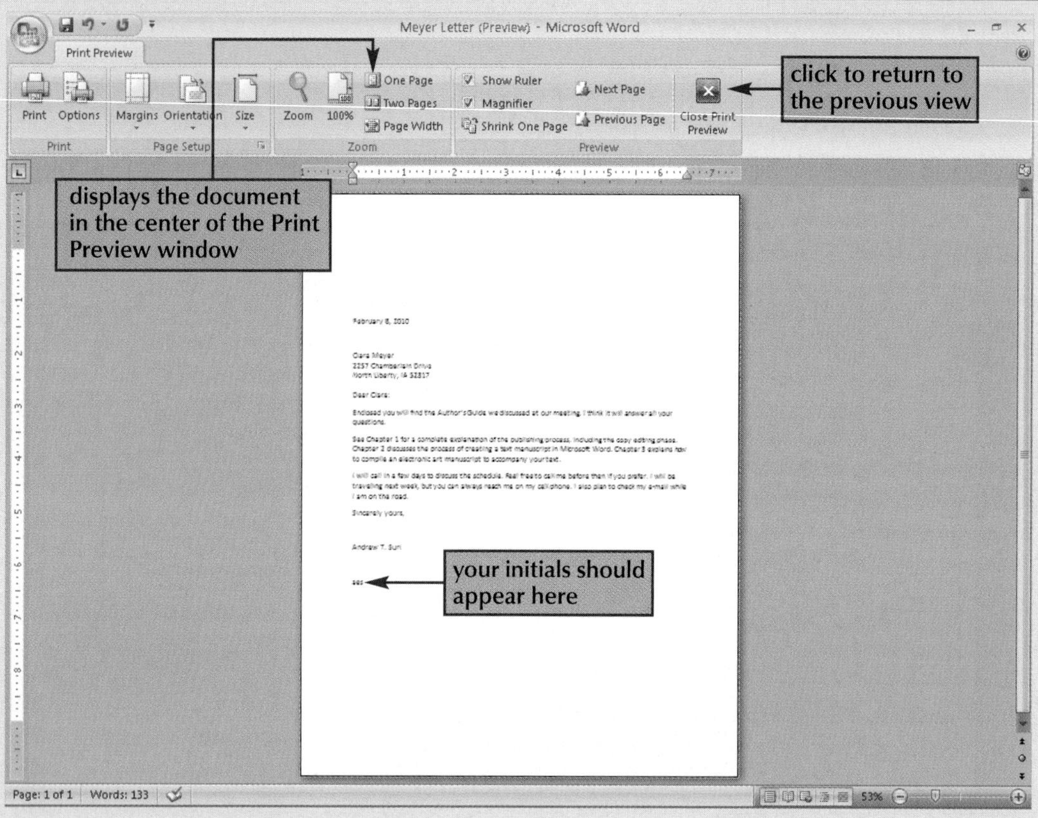

Trouble? If your letter is not centered in the Print Preview window, click the One Page button in the Zoom group on the Print Preview tab.

Trouble? If you don't see a ruler above the document, click the Show Ruler check box in the Preview group on the Print Preview tab to insert a check mark and display the ruler.

▶ **4.** Review your document and make sure its overall layout matches the document in Figure 1-32. If you notice a problem with paragraph breaks or spacing, click the Close Print Preview button in the Preview group on the Print Preview tab, edit the document, and then open the Print Preview window again and check your work.

▶ **5.** In the Preview group on the Print Preview tab, click the **Close Print Preview** button to return to Print Layout view.

▶ **6.** Click the **Save** button 🖫 on the Quick Access Toolbar to save the letter with your newly added initials.

In Andrew's letter, the text looks well spaced, and the letterhead will fit at the top of the page. You are ready to print the letter.

To print a document, click the Office Button, and then click Print. This opens the Print dialog box, where you can adjust various printer settings. Or, if you prefer, you can click the Office Button, point to Print, and then click Quick Print. This prints the document using default settings, without opening a dialog box. In these tutorials, the first time you print, you should check the settings in the Print dialog box and make sure the number of copies is set to 1. After that, you can use the Quick Print command.

To print the letter document:

▶ **1.** Make sure your printer is turned on and contains paper.

▶ **2.** Click the **Office Button** 🔘 , and then click **Print**. The Print dialog box opens.

▶ **3.** Make sure the Printer section of the dialog box shows the correct printer. Also, make sure the number of copies is set to 1.

   Trouble? If the Name list box in the Print dialog box shows the wrong printer, click the Name list arrow, and then select the correct printer from the list of available printers. If you're not sure what the correct printer is, check with your instructor or technical support person.

▶ **4.** Click the **OK** button. Assuming your computer is attached to a printer, the letter prints.

Your printed letter should look similar to Figure 1-1, but without the Carlyle University letterhead. Also, your initials should appear below Andrew's name, on the last line of the letter.

Printing Documents on a Shared Printer		InSight

If your computer is connected to a network, be sure to print only those documents that you need in hard copy format. You should avoid tying up a shared printer with unnecessary printing.

Creating an Envelope

After you print the letter, Andrew asks you to create an envelope in which to mail the *Author's Guide*. Creating an envelope is a simple process because Word automatically uses the inside address from the letter as the address on the envelope. By default, Word does not add extra space between the paragraphs on an envelope, and the line spacing is set to 1.0. As a result, addresses on an envelope are single spaced.

Reference Window | **Creating an Envelope**

- Click the Mailings tab on the Ribbon.
- In the Create group, click the Envelopes button to open the Envelopes and Labels dialog box.
- Verify that the Delivery address box contains the correct address. If necessary, type a new address or edit the existing one.
- If necessary, type a return address. If you are using preprinted stationery that already includes a return address, click the Omit check box to insert a check mark.
- To print the envelope immediately, insert an envelope in your printer, and then click the Print button.
- To store the envelope along with the rest of the document, click the Add to Document button.
- To print the envelope after you have added it to the document, insert an envelope in your printer, open the Print dialog box, and print the page containing the envelope.

Andrew tells you that your printer is not currently stocked with envelopes. He asks you to create the envelope and add it to the document. Then he will print the envelope later, when he is ready to mail the *Author's Guide* to Clara.

To create an envelope:

▶ **1.** Click the **Mailings** tab on the Ribbon.

▶ **2.** In the Create group on the Mailings tab, click the **Envelopes** button. The Envelopes and Labels dialog box opens, as shown in Figure 1-33. By default, Word uses the inside address from the letter as the delivery address. Depending on how your computer is set up, you might see an address in the Return address box. Because Andrew will be using his company's printed envelopes, you don't need to print a return address on this envelope.

Figure 1-33 ▶ **Envelopes and Labels dialog box**

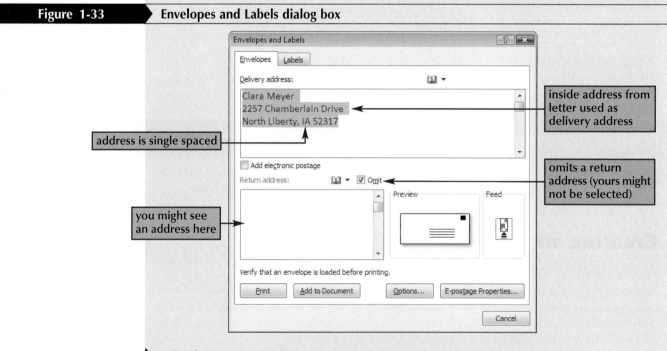

address is single spaced

inside address from letter used as delivery address

you might see an address here

omits a return address (yours might not be selected)

▶ **3.** If necessary, click the **Omit** check box to insert a check mark.

▶ **4.** Click the **Add to Document** button. The dialog box closes, and you return to the document window. The envelope is inserted at the top of the document, with the address single spaced. The double line with the words "Section Break (Next Page)" indicate how the envelope is formatted, and will not be visible when you print the envelope. The envelope will print in the standard business envelope format. (You'll have a chance to print an envelope in the exercises at the end of this tutorial.)

▶ **5.** Save your changes to the document. You are finished with the letter and the envelope, so you can close the document.

▶ **6.** Click the **Close** button ⊠ on the Word program title bar. The Meyer Letter document closes. If you have no other documents open, Word closes also.

Trouble? If you see a dialog box with the message "Do you want to save the changes to 'Meyer Letter?'" click the Yes button.

Congratulations on creating your first letter in Microsoft Word 2007. You'll be able to use the skills you learned in this tutorial to create a variety of professional documents.

Session 1.2 Quick Check | Review

1. True or False: The spelling checker is turned off by default.
2. True or False: To accept an AutoComplete suggestion, such as the name of a month, you need to click a button on the Ribbon.
3. Explain how to correct a misspelled word using a shortcut menu.
4. What's the difference between paragraph spacing and line spacing?
5. Explain how to preview a document before you print it.
6. What tab on the Ribbon do you use to create an envelope?

Tutorial Summary | Review

In this tutorial, you learned how to set up your Word window to match the figures in this book, create a new document from scratch, and type a professional-looking letter. You practiced correcting errors and moving the insertion point around a document. You learned how to undo and redo changes and how to insert a date with AutoComplete. You adjusted paragraph and line spacing, and then you previewed and printed a document. Finally, you created an envelope.

Key Terms

AutoComplete	nonprinting characters	scroll
AutoCorrect	Page width	select
default	paragraph	selection bar
font	paragraph spacing	spelling checker
font size	point	Undo button
line spacing	Print Preview window	Word
margin	Redo button	word wrap
Microsoft Office Word	ScreenTip	Zoom level

Practice the skills you learned in the tutorial using the same case scenario.

There are no Data Files needed for the Review Assignments.

Andrew asks you to write a letter to a local author, Philippa Gallatin, inviting her to an upcoming convention. He also asks you to create an envelope for the letter. You'll create the letter and envelope by completing the following steps. (Note: Text you need to type is shown in bold for ease of reference only; do not bold the text unless otherwise instructed.)

1. Open a new blank document.
2. Compare your screen to the checklist in Figure 1-12, and change any settings if necessary. In particular, make sure that nonprinting characters are displayed.
3. Press the Enter key four times to insert enough space for the company letterhead.
4. Type the date **November 25, 2010** using AutoComplete for "November."
5. Press the Enter key twice, then type the following inside address, using the default paragraph spacing for now:
   Philippa Gallatin
   787 First Street
   Albany, NY 12205
6. Press the Enter key twice, then type the letter's salutation, body, complimentary closing, and signature line, as shown in Figure 1-34. Accept any relevant AutoCorrect suggestions. Use the default line and paragraph spacing; do not insert any extra blank paragraphs.

Figure 1-34

Dear Philippa:

The Albany Visitors Bureau will be hosting the 2011 convention for the National Editorial Association. The convention is scheduled for the first week in March. As a major publishing force in the Albany area, we'd like to make a strong showing at the convention. In particular, we'd like to invite you to attend the opening banquet as our guest. Our own editor-in-chief, Sally Ann Hamilton, will be the keynote speaker.

The complete convention schedule will be posted on the National Editorial Association's Web site after the New Year. I'll e-mail you shortly afterward to confirm your reservation for the opening banquet. At that time, you can tell me if you'll be available to attend any of the afternoon seminars.

Sincerely,

Andrew T. Suri

7. Save your work as **Gallatin Letter** in the Tutorial.01\Review folder provided with your Data Files.
8. Practice using the keyboard to move the insertion point around the document. Use the arrow keys so the insertion point is positioned immediately to the right of the "a" in "Philippa" in the inside address.

9. Press the spacebar and then type **M.**, so the first line of the inside address reads "Philippa M. Gallatin." (Don't forget the period after the middle initial.)

10. Undo the change and then redo it.

11. Scroll to the beginning of the document and proofread your work.

12. Correct any misspelled words marked by wavy red lines. If the correct spelling of a word does not appear in the shortcut menu, close the list, and then make the correction yourself. Remove any red wavy lines below words that are spelled correctly.

13. Click at the end of Andrew's name in the signature line, press the Enter key twice, and type your initials in lowercase.

14. Select the inside address and remove the extra paragraph spacing from the selected paragraphs.

15. Select the entire document and change the line spacing to single spacing.

16. Save your changes to the letter, and then preview and print it.

17. Add an envelope to the document. Use your own address as the delivery address. Do not include a return address.

18. Save your changes and close the document.

| Apply | | **Case Problem 1** |

Apply the skills you learned to create a letter about a health-care lecture.

There are no Data Files needed for this Case Problem.

Wingra Family Practice Clinic You are a nurse at Wingra Family Practice Clinic. You have organized a lunchtime lecture series for the clinic staff in which regional medical professionals will discuss topics related to pediatric health care. You have hired your first speaker and need to write a letter confirming your agreement and asking a few questions. Create the letter by completing the following steps. As you type the document, accept the default paragraph and line spacing until you are asked to change them. Because the clinic is currently out of letterhead, you will start the letter by typing a return address. (Note: Text you need to type is shown in bold for ease of reference only; do not bold the text unless otherwise instructed.)

1. Open a new blank document. Compare your screen to the checklist in Figure 1-12, and change any settings if necessary. In particular, make sure that nonprinting characters are displayed.

2. Type your name, press the Enter key, and then type the following return address:
   Wingra Family Practice Clinic
   2278 Norwood Place
   Middleton, WI 52247

3. Press the Enter key twice, and then type **May 8, 2010** as the date.

4. Press the Enter key twice, and then type this inside address:
   Dr. Susanna Trevay
   James Madison Medical Center
   56 Ingersoll Drive
   Madison, WI 53788

5. Press the Enter key twice, type the salutation **Dear Dr. Trevay:** (don't forget the colon), and then press the Enter key once.

6. Type the following paragraph: **Thank you so much for agreeing to lecture about early childhood vaccinations on Friday, May 21. Before I can publicize your talk, I need some information. Please call by Tuesday with your answers to these questions:**

7. Press the Enter key, and then type the following questions as separate paragraphs, using the default paragraph spacing:
   Which vaccines will you cover in detail?
   Will you discuss common immune responses to vaccine antigens?
   Will you provide hand-outs with suggested vaccination schedules?
8. Save the document as **Lecture Series Letter** in the Tutorial.01\Case1 folder provided with your Data Files.
9. Move the insertion point to the beginning of the third question (which begins "Will you provide..."). Insert a new paragraph, and add the following as the new third question in the list: **Would you be willing to take questions from the audience?**
10. Correct any spelling errors indicated by red wavy lines. Because "Wingra" is spelled correctly, use the shortcut menu to remove the wavy red line under the word "Wingra" and prevent Word from marking the word as a misspelling. Repeat this to ignore "Trevay," "Ingersoll," and any other words that are spelled correctly but are marked as misspellings.
11. Insert a new paragraph after the last question, and then type the complimentary closing **Sincerely,** (including the comma).
12. Press the Enter key twice to leave room for your signature, and then type your full name. Press the Enter key and type **Wingra Family Practice Clinic**. Notice that "Wingra" is not marked as a spelling error this time.
13. Select the return address and remove the extra paragraph spacing. Do the same for the inside address. Do not attempt to change them both at the same time by selecting the return address, the date, and the inside address all at once, or you will end up with too little space before and after the date.
14. Select the entire document and change the line spacing to single spacing.
15. Save the document, preview and print it, and then close it.

Apply | **Case Problem 2**

Apply the skills you learned to create a letter informing a client about a new investment program.

There are no Data Files needed for this Case Problem.

Pear Tree Investment Services As a financial planner at Pear Tree Investment Services, you are responsible for keeping your clients informed about new investment options. You have just learned about a program called HigherEdVest, which encourages parents to save for their children's college educations. You'll write a letter to Joseph Robbins, a client of yours, in which you introduce the program and ask him to call for more information. Create the letter by completing the following steps. (Note: Text you need to type is shown in bold for ease of reference only; do not bold the text unless otherwise instructed.)

1. Open a new blank document. Compare your screen to the checklist in Figure 1-12, and change any settings if necessary. In particular, make sure that nonprinting characters are displayed.
2. To leave room for the company letterhead, press the Enter key until the insertion point is positioned about three inches from the top of the page. (Remember that you can see the exact position of the insertion point, in inches, on the vertical ruler.)

⊕ EXPLORE

3. Type the current date, accepting any AutoComplete suggestions that appear.

4. Press the Enter key twice and type the inside address: **Joseph Robbins, 5788 Rugby Road, Hillsborough, CO 80732**.

5. Press the Enter key twice, type the salutation **Dear Joseph:**, and then press the Enter key once.

6. Write one paragraph introducing the HigherEdVest program, explaining that you think the client might be interested, and asking him to call your office at (555) 555-5555 for more details.

7. In the next paragraph, type the complimentary closing **Sincerely,**.

8. Press the Enter key twice to leave room for your signature, and then type your name and title.

9. Save the letter as **EdVest Letter** in the Tutorial.01\Case2 folder provided with your Data Files.

10. Reread your letter carefully and correct any errors. Use the keyboard to move the insertion point as necessary.

11. Remove the extra paragraph spacing in the inside address, and then change the entire document to single spacing.

12. Save your changes, and then preview and print the letter.

⊕ EXPLORE

13. Create an envelope for the letter. Click the Omit check box to deselect it (if necessary), and then, for the return address, type your own address. Add the envelope to the document. If you are asked if you want to save the return address as the new default return address, answer No. If your computer is connected to a printer that is stocked with envelopes, click the Office Button, click Print, click the Pages option button, type **1** in the Pages text box, and then click the OK button.

14. Save and close the document.

| Create | **Case Problem 3** |

Use your skills to create the letter of recommendation shown in Figure 1-35.

There are no Data Files needed for this Case Problem.

Monterrey Mountain Bike Tours   You are the owner of Monterrey Mountain Bike Tours, located in Eugene, Oregon. One of your tour guides, Melissa Coia, has decided to move to the Midwest to be closer to her family. She has applied for a job as a tour guide at Horicon Marsh in Wisconsin, and has asked you to write a letter of recommendation. To create the letter, complete the following steps:

1. Open a new blank document. Compare your screen to the checklist in Figure 1-12, and change any settings if necessary. In particular, make sure that nonprinting characters are displayed.

2. Type the letter shown in Figure 1-35. Assume that you will print the letter on the company's letterhead, with the date positioned about 2.5 inches from the top of the page. Replace "Your Name" with your first and last name.

Figure 1-35

June 27, 2010

Peter Roundtree
Horicon Marsh Ranger Station
9875 Scales Bend Road
Horicon, Wisconsin 57338

Dear Mr. Roundtree:

I am writing on behalf of Melissa Coia, who has applied for a job as a tour guide at Horicon Marsh. I highly recommend that you hire Melissa. She is enthusiastic, energetic, and extremely well organized.

I would be glad to tell you more about Melissa over the phone. You can reach me during business hours at (555) 555-5555.

Sincerely,

Your Name

3. Save the document as **Melissa** in the Tutorial.01\Case3 folder provided with your Data Files.
4. Correct any typing errors.
5. Change the paragraph and line spacing so that the entire letter is single spaced, including the inside address.
6. Preview and print the letter.
7. Create an envelope for the letter. Click the Omit check box to deselect it (if necessary), and then, for the return address, type your own address. Add the envelope to the document. If you are asked if you want to save the return address as the new default return address, answer No. If your computer is connected to a printer that is stocked with envelopes, click the Office Button, click Print, click the Pages option button, type **1** in the Pages text box, and then click the OK button.
8. Save the document and close it.

| Challenge | **Case Problem 4** |

Go beyond what you've learned to write a fax coversheet for a small engineering company.

There are no Data Files needed for this Case Problem.

Gladstone Engineering   As the office manager for Gladstone Engineering, you are responsible for faxing technical drawings to clients. Along with each set of drawings, you need to include a coversheet that explains what you are faxing, lists the total number of pages, and provides the name and cell phone number of the engineer who created the drawings. The fastest way to create a professional-looking coversheet is to use a template—a special Word document that comes with predefined headings, line and paragraph spacing, and other types of formatting. To create the fax coversheet, perform the following steps. (Note: Text you need to type is shown in bold for ease of reference only; do not bold the text unless otherwise instructed.)

 EXPLORE

1. Click the Microsoft Office Button, and then click New. The New Document dialog box opens. In the Template list (on the left), click Installed Templates.

⊕ EXPLORE

2. In the Installed Templates pane (on the right), click Equity Fax, and then click Create. A fax template opens, containing generic text called placeholders that you replace with your own information. (You should always take care to remove any placeholders you don't replace with other text.)

3. Compare your screen to the checklist in Figure 1-12 and change any settings if necessary. In particular, make sure that nonprinting characters are displayed.

⊕ EXPLORE

4. Click the text "[Type the recipient name]." The placeholder text appears in a blue box with blue highlighting. The box containing the highlighted text (with the small rectangle attached) is called a document control, or a content control. You can enter text in this document control just as you enter text in a dialog box. You'll learn more about document controls in Tutorial 3.

5. Type **Robert Mason**, and then press the Tab key twice. A document control is now visible to the right of the word "From." If you see a name here, click in the document control (if necessary) and delete the name.

6. Type your first and last name in the document control, and then press the Tab key to highlight the placeholder text "[Type the recipient fax number]."

7. Type **(555) 555-5555**, and then continue using the Tab key as necessary to enter **4** as the number of pages and **(333) 333-3333** as the phone number. If you press the Tab key too many times and skip past a document control, you can click the document control to highlight it. If you make a typing mistake, use the Undo button to reverse the error.

⊕ EXPLORE

8. Use the Tab key to select the placeholder text "[Pick the date]," click the list arrow on the document control, click the right facing arrow above the calendar as necessary until you see the calendar for December 2010, and then click 10 in the calendar. The date 12.10.2010 appears in the Date document control.

9. Use the Tab key to select the placeholder text in the "Re:" section, and then press the Delete key to delete the placeholder text. Delete the "CC:" placeholder text as well.

10. Click the box to the left of "Please Reply," and then type an uppercase **X**.

11. Click the placeholder text "[Type comments]," and then type the following message: **Here are the latest drawings, created for you by Matt Xio. After you review them, please call Matt on his cell phone to discuss the next phase of this project. Thank you very much**.

12. Save the coversheet as **Mason Fax** in the Tutorial.01\Case4 folder provided with your Data Files.

⊕ EXPLORE

13. Zoom the document out until you can see the entire page on the screen. When you are finished reviewing the document, zoom the document until it returns to its original zoom setting.

14. Review the coversheet and correct any typos. Save the coversheet again, preview it, and then print it.

15. Close the document.

| Research | **Internet Assignments** |

Go to the Web to find information you can use to create documents.

The purpose of the Internet Assignments is to challenge you to find information on the Internet that you can use to work effectively with this software. The actual assignments are updated and maintained on the Course Technology Web site. Log on to the Internet and use your Web browser to go to the Student Online Companion for New Perspectives Office 2007 at **www.course.com/np/office2007**. Then navigate to the Internet Assignments for this tutorial.

Review | **Quick Check Answers**

Session 1.1

1. Planning a document saves time and effort. It ensures that you include enough information to achieve the document's purpose without overwhelming or boring the reader. It also ensures that the document is organized logically and has the appearance you want.
2. View tab
3. Click the Print Layout button on the bottom-right area of the window.
4. True
5. False
6. .docx

Session 1.2

1. False
2. False
3. Right-click the word, and then click the correct spelling in the shortcut menu.
4. Paragraph spacing controls the amount of space inserted between paragraphs. Line spacing controls the amount of space inserted between lines within a paragraph.
5. Click the Office Button, point to Print, and then click Print Preview. In the Preview group on the Print Preview tab, click the Close Print Preview button to return to the previous view.
6. Mailings tab

Ending Data Files

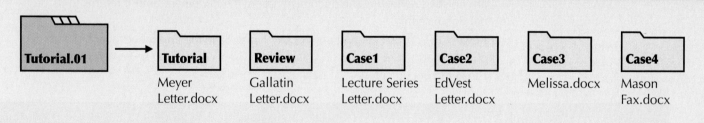

Tutorial.01 → Tutorial — Meyer Letter.docx

Review — Gallatin Letter.docx

Case1 — Lecture Series Letter.docx

Case2 — EdVest Letter.docx

Case3 — Melissa.docx

Case4 — Mason Fax.docx

Objectives

Session 2.1
• Check spelling and grammar
• Select and delete text
• Move text within a document
• Find and replace text

Session 2.2
• Change margins
• Change alignment and paragraph indents
• Copy formatting with the Format Painter
• Emphasize points with bullets, numbering, bold, and italic
• Change fonts and adjust font sizes
• Change the document theme
• Preview and print a document

Editing and Formatting a Document

Preparing a Handout on Choosing a Design Style

Case | Pemberly Furniture and Interiors

Natalie Lanci is the lead designer at Pemberly Furniture and Interiors, a design and furniture firm. Over the years, she has found that new customers are often intimidated by the prospect of decorating their homes. To make things easier, she has decided to create a series of handouts about interior styles and furniture. She's just finished a draft of her first handout, "Getting the Look You Want." She has marked up a printed copy of the document with notes about what she wants changed. As her assistant, it's your job to make the necessary changes and reprint the document.

In this tutorial, you will edit the handout according to Natalie's comments. You will open a draft of the document, save it with a different name, and then make the changes Natalie requested. First, you will check the document's grammar and spelling, and then you'll move text using two different methods. You will also use Word's Find and Replace feature to replace one version of the company name with another.

Next, you will change the overall look of the document by changing margins, indenting and justifying paragraphs, and copying the formatting from one paragraph to another. You'll create two bulleted lists and one numbered list. Then you'll make the title and subtitle more prominent by centering them, changing their font, and enlarging them. You'll also change the font of the company name in the body of the document, and you'll add bold to the headings to set them off from the rest of the text. You will experiment with changing the document's theme, and finally, you will preview and print the formatted document.

Starting Data Files

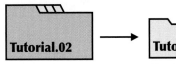
Tutorial.02

Tutorial
Design.docx

Review
Getting.docx
Staff.docx

Case1
New.docx

Case2
Moth.docx

Case3
Resume.docx

Case4
Flour.docx

Session 2.1

Reviewing the Document

You'll begin by opening Natalie's first draft of the document, which has the filename Design.

To open the document:

▶ **1.** Start Word.

▶ **2.** On the Quick Access Toolbar, click the **Office Button** 🔘, and then click **Open**. The Open dialog box opens.

▶ **3.** Use the options in the Open dialog box to open the **Tutorial** subfolder within the **Tutorial.02** folder included with your Data Files.

▶ **4.** Click **Design** to select the file, if necessary. The name of the selected file appears in the File name text box. See Figure 2-1.

Figure 2-1 | **Open dialog box**

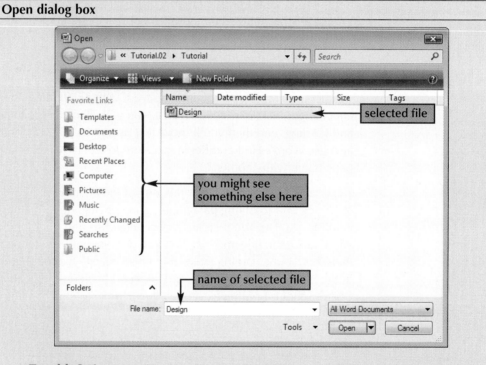

Trouble? If you see "Design.docx" in the folder, it's okay; click Design.docx and continue with Step 5. This just means that Windows is configured to display file extensions. If you can't find the file with or without the file extension, make sure you're looking in the Tutorial subfolder within the Tutorial.02 folder included with your Data Files, and check to make sure the list box next to the File name text box displays All Word Documents or All Files. If you still can't locate the file, ask your instructor or technical support person for help.

▶ **5.** Click the **Open** button. The document opens with the insertion point at the beginning.

Before revising a document for someone else, it's a good idea to familiarize yourself with its overall structure. You'll do that now, and in the process make sure the document is displayed in a way that makes editing it as easy as possible.

To review the document:

▸ **1.** Verify that the document is displayed in Print Layout view, and if necessary, in the Paragraph group, click the **Show/Hide ¶** button ¶ to display nonprinting characters. If the rulers are not visible, switch to the **View** tab, and then click the **Ruler** check box to display the rulers.

▸ **2.** Take a moment to read the document. It consists of a series of headings, with explanatory text below each heading. Right now, the headings (such as "Ask Yourself Some Questions" and "Pick a Style") are hard to spot because they don't look any different from the surrounding text. You'll change that when you format the document. The document also includes some lists; you will format these later in this tutorial to make them easier to read. Natalie used the default font size, 11-point, and the default font, Calibri (Body), for the entire document. She relied on Word's default paragraph spacing to provide a visual separation between paragraphs.

▸ **3.** Scroll down until you can see the line "Stay True to Your Style." The white space after this line is the page's bottom margin. The blue space below the margin indicates a page break. This tells you that the line "Stay True to Your Style" appears on the last line of the first page. Word starts a new page whenever your text fills up a page. The Page box in the lower-left corner of the document window tells you the total number of pages in the document and which page currently contains the insertion point.

Figure 2-2 shows the page break, along with other important elements of the document. Note that in Figure 2-2 the Word window has been zoomed to 80%; this is to make it easy to see several parts of the document at once. At this point, your Zoom setting is probably 100%. To make sure you can see the entire width of the page, you'll select Page width in the Zoom dialog box in the next step.

Document with two pages ◀ **Figure 2-2**

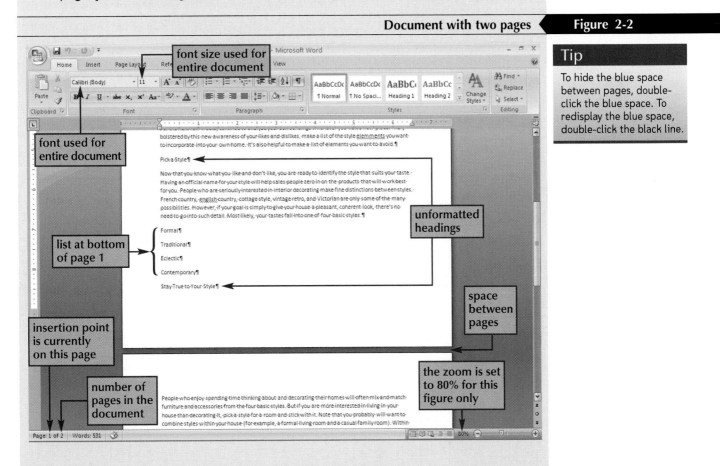

Tip

To hide the blue space between pages, double-click the blue space. To redisplay the blue space, double-click the black line.

▶ **4.** In the bottom-right corner of the Word window, click the current Zoom setting to open the Zoom dialog box, click **Page width**, and then click the **OK** button to close the Zoom dialog box. Word displays the full width of the document.

Now that you are familiar with Natalie's document, you can turn your attention to the edits she has requested. Natalie's editing marks and notes on the first draft are shown in Figure 2-3.

Figure 2-3 ▶ **Draft of handout with Natalie's edits (page 1)**

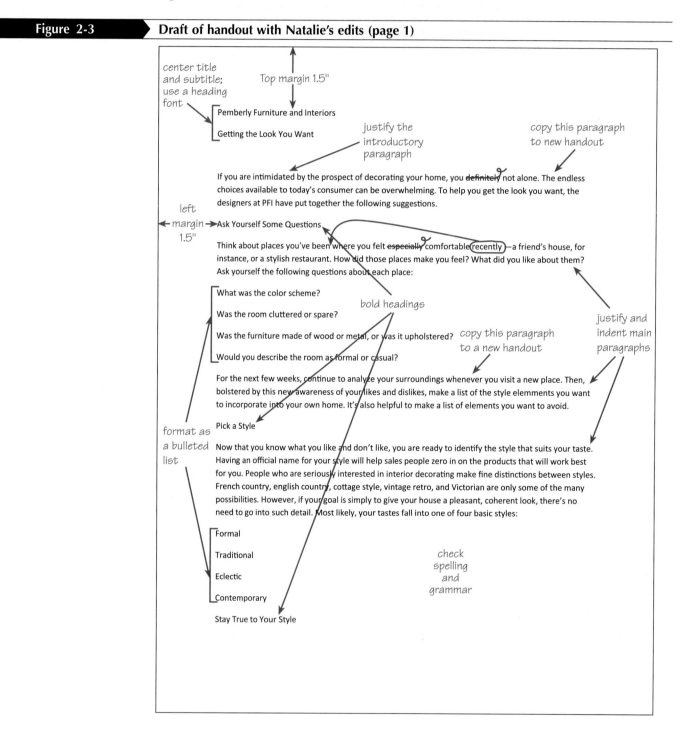

Draft of handout with Natalie's edits (page 2) ◀ Figure 2-3 (cont.)

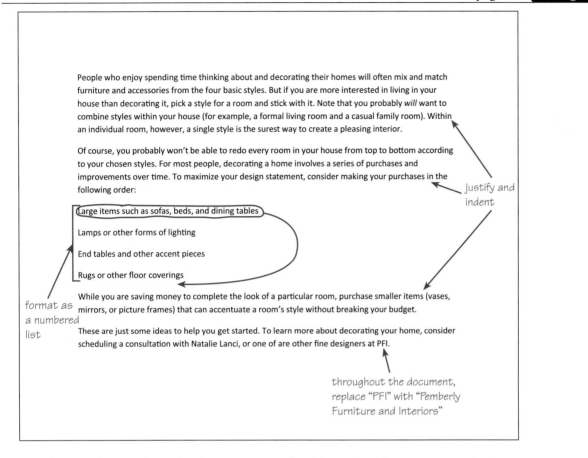

People who enjoy spending time thinking about and decorating their homes will often mix and match furniture and accessories from the four basic styles. But if you are more interested in living in your house than decorating it, pick a style for a room and stick with it. Note that you probably *will* want to combine styles within your house (for example, a formal living room and a casual family room). Within an individual room, however, a single style is the surest way to create a pleasing interior.

Of course, you probably won't be able to redo every room in your house from top to bottom according to your chosen styles. For most people, decorating a home involves a series of purchases and improvements over time. To maximize your design statement, consider making your purchases in the following order:

justify and indent

Large items such as sofas, beds, and dining tables

Lamps or other forms of lighting

End tables and other accent pieces

Rugs or other floor coverings

format as a numbered list

While you are saving money to complete the look of a particular room, purchase smaller items (vases, mirrors, or picture frames) that can accentuate a room's style without breaking your budget.

These are just some ideas to help you get started. To learn more about decorating your home, consider scheduling a consultation with Natalie Lanci, or one of are other fine designers at PFI.

throughout the document, replace "PFI" with "Pemberly Furniture and Interiors"

Before you begin editing the document, you should save it with a new name. Saving the document with a different filename creates a copy of the file and leaves the original file unchanged in case you want to work through the tutorial again.

To save the document with a new name:

▶ **1.** Click the **Office Button** 🔘, and then click **Save As**. The Save As dialog box opens with the current filename highlighted in the File name text box. You could type an entirely new filename, or you could edit the current one.

▶ **2.** Click to the right of the current filename to place the insertion point after the "n" in "Design."

▶ **3.** Press the **spacebar**, and then type **Handout** so that the filename is "Design Handout."

▶ **4.** Verify that the **Tutorial** folder is selected as the location for saving the file.

▶ **5.** Click the **Save** button. The document is saved with the new filename "Design Handout" in the Tutorial folder, and the original Design file closes, remaining unchanged.

Now you're ready to begin working with the document. First, you will check it for spelling and grammatical errors.

Using the Spelling and Grammar Checker

As you type a document, Word marks possible spelling errors with a red wavy underline. When you're working on a document that someone else typed, it's a good idea to start by using the **Spelling and Grammar Checker**, a feature that checks a document word by word for a variety of errors.

Reference Window | **Checking a Document for Spelling and Grammar Errors**

- Move the insertion point to the beginning of the document, click the Review tab on the Ribbon, and then, in the Proofing group, click the Spelling & Grammar button.
- In the Spelling and Grammar dialog box, review any items highlighted in color. Possible grammatical errors appear in green; possible spelling errors appear in red. Review the suggested corrections in the Suggestions list box.
- To accept a suggested correction, click on it in the Suggestions list box, click the Change button to make the correction, and then continue searching the document for errors.
- To skip the current instance of the highlighted text and continue searching the document for errors, click the Ignore Once button.
- Click the Ignore All button to skip all instances of the highlighted text and continue searching the document for errors. Click the Ignore Rule button to skip all instances of a highlighted grammatical error.
- To type your correction directly in the document, click outside the Spelling and Grammar dialog box, make the correction, and then click the Resume button in the Spelling and Grammar dialog box.
- To add an unrecognized word to the dictionary, click the Add to Dictionary button.
- When you see a dialog box informing you that the spelling and grammar check is complete, click the OK button.

You'll see how the Spelling and Grammar Checker works as you check the Design Handout document for mistakes.

To check the Design Handout document for spelling and grammatical errors:

1. Press the **Ctrl+Home** keys to verify that the insertion point is located at the beginning of the document, to the left of the "P" in "Pemberly Furniture and Interiors."

2. Click the **Review** tab on the Ribbon, and then, in the Proofing group, click the **Spelling & Grammar** button. The Spelling and Grammar: English (United States) dialog box opens with the word "Pemberly" displayed in red, indicating a possible spelling error. In the document, "Pemberly" is highlighted in blue. Typically, the Suggestions box would contain one or more possible corrections for you to choose from, but in this case, Word doesn't recognize the name of Natalie's company because it is not included in the main dictionary. This isn't really an error. See Figure 2-4.

Spelling and Grammar dialog box | Figure 2-4

Tip

The Check grammar check box is selected, indicating that grammar is being checked along with spelling. If you wanted to check only for spelling errors, you could deselect the Check grammar check box.

▶ **3.** Click the **Ignore All** button. This tells Word to ignore all instances of "Pemberly" throughout the document. Now the first sentence of the document appears in green in the dialog box and in a blue highlight in the document. The Suggestions box tells you that the highlighted text is a sentence fragment. The last part of the sentence should read "you definitely are not alone," but the word "are" is missing. You can fix this problem by clicking outside the Spelling and Grammar dialog box and typing the change directly in the document.

▶ **4.** Click the blue highlighted sentence outside the Spelling and Grammar dialog box. The blue highlight disappears, and the insertion point appears at the end of the sentence.

Trouble? If you can't see the entire highlighted sentence, move the mouse pointer over the title bar of the Spelling and Grammar dialog box, press and hold the left mouse button, drag the mouse pointer until the dialog box is out of the way, and then release the mouse button.

▶ **5.** Click to the left of the "n" in "not," type **are**, and then press the **spacebar**. Verify that the last part of the sentence now reads "you definitely are not alone." (You might notice that the word "definitely" makes the sentence awkward; you will delete this word in the next section.)

You've edited the document to correct the error. Now you need to return to the Spelling and Grammar dialog box to continue checking the document.

To continue checking the document:

▶ **1.** Click the **Resume** button in the Spelling and Grammar dialog box to continue checking the rest of the document. The misspelled word "elemments" is highlighted in the Spelling and Grammar dialog box and in the document. The correct spelling, "elements," appears in the Suggestions box.

▶ **2.** Verify that "elements" is highlighted in the Suggestions box, and then click the **Change** button. "Elements" is inserted into the document, and the word "english" is highlighted in the document. This should be "English," with an uppercase "E," instead.

▶ **3.** Verify that "English" is selected in the Suggestions box, and then click the **Change** button. The word "English" is inserted in the document. A message box opens indicating that the spelling and grammar check is complete.

▶ **4.** Click the **OK** button. The Spelling and Grammar dialog box closes. You return to the Design Handout document.

▶ **5.** Click the **Home** tab to display the options related to editing a document again. You'll need to use these options as you continue the tutorial.

Although the Spelling and Grammar Checker is a useful tool, there is no substitute for careful proofreading. Always take the time to read through your document to check for errors the Spelling and Grammar Checker might have missed. Keep in mind that the Spelling and Grammar checker cannot pinpoint phrases that are inaccurate. You'll have to find those yourself. To produce a professional document, you must read it carefully several times. It's a good idea to ask a coworker to read your documents, too.

To proofread the Design Handout document:

▶ **1.** Scroll to the beginning of the document and proofread the document. In the last sentence of the document, notice that the word "are" is used instead of the word "our." You will correct this error in the next section.

▶ **2.** Finish proofreading the Design Handout document, and then click the **Save** button 🖫 on the Quick Access Toolbar to save the changes you've made so far.

Your next job is to delete some text (as shown earlier in Figure 2-3).

Deleting Text

You already have experience using the Backspace and Delete keys to delete a few characters. To delete an entire word or multiple words, it's faster to select the text first. Then you can either replace it with something else by typing over it, or you can delete it by pressing the Delete key. Right now, you need to change the word "are" to "our."

To replace "are" with "our":

▶ **1.** Press the **Ctrl+End** keys. The insertion point moves to the end of the document.

▶ **2.** In the last line of the document, double-click the word **are** (in the phrase "are other fine designers...").

▶ **3.** Type **our**. The selected word is replaced with the correction. The phrase now correctly reads: "...our other fine designers...."

Next, Natalie wants you to delete the word "definitely" in the introductory paragraph at the beginning of the document and the word "especially" in the paragraph below the heading "Ask Yourself Some Questions." You can do this quickly by selecting multiple items and then pressing the Delete key.

To select and delete multiple items:

▶ **1.** Press the **Ctrl+Home** keys. The insertion point is now located at the beginning of the document.

2. In the introductory paragraph, which begins "If you are intimidated by...," double-click the word **definitely**. The word and the space following it are selected.

3. Press and hold the **Ctrl** key, double-click the word **especially** in the paragraph below the heading "Ask Yourself Some Questions," and then release the **Ctrl** key. At this point the words "definitely" and "especially" should be selected. See Figure 2-5.

Text to be deleted ◄ **Figure 2-5**

Trouble? If you don't get Step 3 right the first time, click anywhere in the document, and then repeat Steps 2 and 3.

4. Press the **Delete** key. The selected items are deleted, and the words around them move in to fill the space. See Figure 2-6.

Paragraphs after deleting text ◄ **Figure 2-6**

> **Trouble?** If you deleted the wrong text, click the Undo button on the Quick Access Toolbar to reverse your mistake, and then begin again with Step 2.
>
> ▶ **5.** Scroll down to display the last line of the document, drag the mouse pointer to select "Natalie Lanci," press the **Delete** key, press the **spacebar** if necessary, and then type your first and last name. This change will make it easier for you to find your document if you print it on a network printer used by other students.
>
> ▶ **6.** Save the document.

You have edited the document by replacing "are" with "our" and by removing the text that Natalie marked for deletion. Now you are ready to make the rest of the edits she suggested.

Moving Text in a Document

One of the most useful features of a word-processing program is the ability to move text. For example, Natalie wants to reorder the four points in the section "Stay True to Your Style" on page 2. You could reorder the list by deleting an item and then retyping it at a new location, but it's easier to select and then move the text. Word provides several ways to move text: drag and drop, cut and paste, and copy and paste.

Dragging and Dropping Text

To move text with **drag and drop**, you select the text you want to move, press and hold down the mouse button while you drag the selected text to a new location, and then release the mouse button.

Reference Window | **Dragging and Dropping Text**

- Select the text you want to move.
- Press and hold down the mouse button until the drag-and-drop pointer appears, and then drag the selected text to its new location.
- Use the dotted insertion point as a guide to determine exactly where the text should be inserted.
- Release the mouse button to "drop" the text at the insertion point.

Natalie wants you to change the order of the items in the list on page 2 of the document. You'll use the drag-and-drop method to reorder these items. Because you need to select text before you can move it, you'll get practice using the selection bar (the white space in the left margin) to highlight a line of text as you do these steps.

To move text using drag and drop:

▶ **1.** Scroll up slightly until you see the list of suggested purchases, which begins "Large items such as sofas, beds, and dining tables." Natalie wants you to move the first item to the bottom of the list.

▶ **2.** Move the pointer to the selection bar to the left of the line "Large items such as sofas, beds, and dining tables." The pointer changes to a right-facing arrow ⤢ .

▶ **3.** Click in the selection bar to the left of the line "Large items such as sofas, beds, and dining tables." The line is selected. Notice that the paragraph mark at the end of the line is also selected. See Figure 2-7.

Selected text to drag and drop ◀ **Figure 2-7**

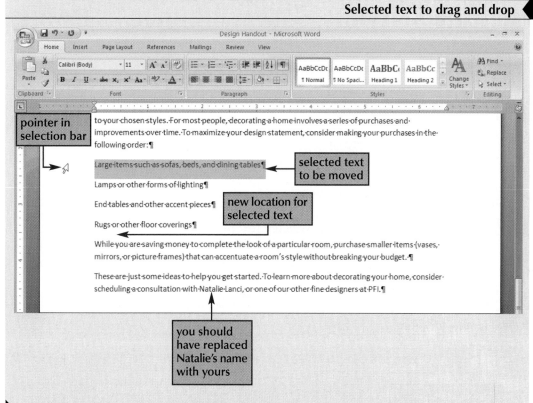

▶ **4.** Position the pointer over the selected text. The pointer changes from a right-facing arrow ⤢ to a left-facing arrow ⤡ .

▶ **5.** Press and hold down the mouse button until the drag-and-drop pointer ⤡ appears. Note that a dotted insertion point appears within the selected text. (You may have to move the mouse pointer slightly left or right to see the drag-and-drop pointer or the dotted insertion point.)

▶ **6.** Without releasing the mouse button, drag the selected text down until the dotted insertion point is positioned to the left of the first paragraph below the list (to the left of the "W" in "While you are saving..."). Make sure you use the dotted insertion point, rather than the mouse pointer, to guide the text to its new location. The dotted insertion point indicates exactly where the text will appear when you release the mouse button. See Figure 2-8.

Figure 2-8 **Moving text with drag-and-drop pointer**

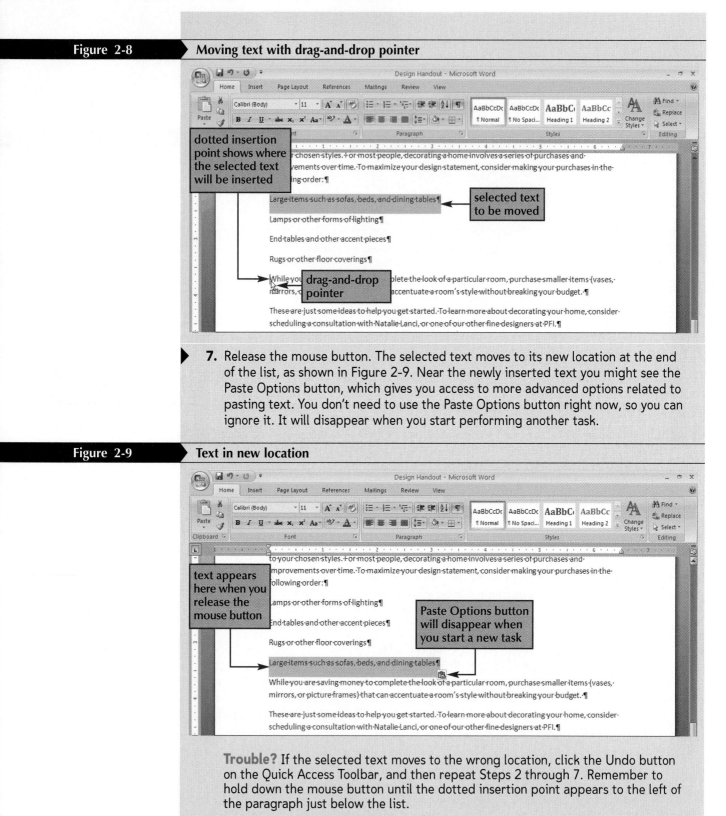

7. Release the mouse button. The selected text moves to its new location at the end of the list, as shown in Figure 2-9. Near the newly inserted text you might see the Paste Options button, which gives you access to more advanced options related to pasting text. You don't need to use the Paste Options button right now, so you can ignore it. It will disappear when you start performing another task.

Figure 2-9 **Text in new location**

Trouble? If the selected text moves to the wrong location, click the Undo button on the Quick Access Toolbar, and then repeat Steps 2 through 7. Remember to hold down the mouse button until the dotted insertion point appears to the left of the paragraph just below the list.

8. Deselect the highlighted text by clicking anywhere in the document, and then save the document.

Dragging and dropping works well if you're moving text a short distance in a document. For moving text longer distances, another method, called cut and paste, works better. You can also use cut and paste to move text short distances, if you find that you prefer it over drag and drop.

Cutting or Copying and Pasting Text

The key to cutting and pasting is the **Clipboard**, a temporary storage area on your computer that holds text or graphics until you need them. To **cut** means to remove something from a document and place it on the Clipboard. Once you've cut something, you can paste it somewhere else. To **paste** means to place a copy of whatever is on the Clipboard into the document; it gets pasted at the insertion point.

To **cut and paste**, you select the text you want to cut (or remove) from the document, click the Cut button, and then use the Paste button to paste (or insert) it into the document in a new location. If you don't want to remove the text from its original location, you can copy it (rather than cutting it), and then paste the copy in a new location. To **copy** means to copy text (or other material, such as pictures) to the Clipboard, leaving the material in its original location.

Note that when you paste an item from the Clipboard into a document, the item also remains on the Clipboard so you can paste it again somewhere else if you want.

Cutting (or Copying) and Pasting Text | Reference Window

- Select the text or graphics you want to cut or copy.
- To remove the text or graphics, click the Cut button in the Clipboard group on the Home tab, or to copy, click the Copy button in the Clipboard group on the Home tab.
- Move the insertion point to the target location in the document.
- Click the Paste button in the Clipboard group on the Home tab.

If you need to keep track of multiple pieces of cut or copied text, it's helpful to open the **Clipboard task pane**, a special part of the Word window that displays the contents of the Clipboard. You open the Clipboard task pane by clicking the Clipboard button on the Home tab. When the Clipboard task pane is not displayed, the Clipboard can hold only one item at a time. (Each newly copied item replaces the current contents of the Clipboard.) However, when the Clipboard task pane is displayed, the Clipboard can store up to 24 items. The last item cut or copied to the Clipboard is the first item listed in the Clipboard task pane.

As indicated in Figure 2-3, Natalie suggested moving the word "recently" (in the paragraph under the heading "Ask Yourself Some Questions") to a new location. You'll use cut and paste to move this word.

To move text using cut and paste:

1. Scroll up until you can see the paragraph below the heading "Ask Yourself Some Questions" on page 1.

2. Double-click the word **recently**. As you can see in Figure 2-10, you need to move this word to after the phrase "places you've been."

Figure 2-10 Text to move using cut and paste

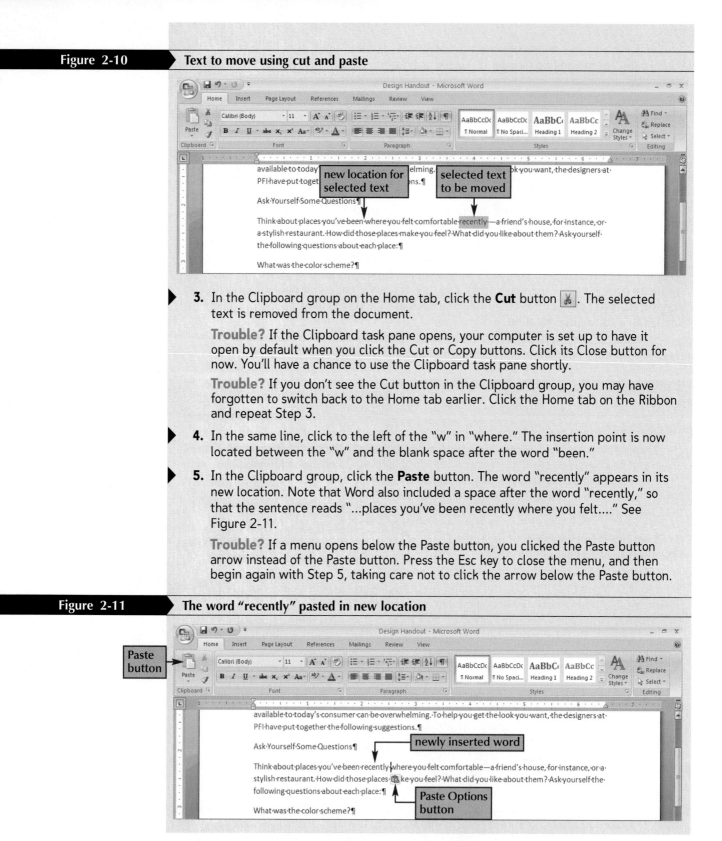

▶ **3.** In the Clipboard group on the Home tab, click the **Cut** button 🔏. The selected text is removed from the document.

Trouble? If the Clipboard task pane opens, your computer is set up to have it open by default when you click the Cut or Copy buttons. Click its Close button for now. You'll have a chance to use the Clipboard task pane shortly.

Trouble? If you don't see the Cut button in the Clipboard group, you may have forgotten to switch back to the Home tab earlier. Click the Home tab on the Ribbon and repeat Step 3.

▶ **4.** In the same line, click to the left of the "w" in "where." The insertion point is now located between the "w" and the blank space after the word "been."

▶ **5.** In the Clipboard group, click the **Paste** button. The word "recently" appears in its new location. Note that Word also included a space after the word "recently," so that the sentence reads "...places you've been recently where you felt...." See Figure 2-11.

Trouble? If a menu opens below the Paste button, you clicked the Paste button arrow instead of the Paste button. Press the Esc key to close the menu, and then begin again with Step 5, taking care not to click the arrow below the Paste button.

Figure 2-11 The word "recently" pasted in new location

Natalie mentions that she'll be using two paragraphs from the Design Handout document as the basis for a new handout entitled "Formal Designs." She asks you to copy that information and paste it in a new document. You can do this using copy and paste. In the process, you'll have a chance to use the Clipboard task pane.

To copy and paste text into a new document:

▶ **1.** In the Clipboard group, click the **Dialog Box Launcher**. The Clipboard task pane opens on the left side of the document window. It contains the word "recently," which you copied to the Clipboard in the last set of steps. The document zooms out so that you can still see the full width of the page, even though the Clipboard task pane is open. See Figure 2-12. To minimize the clutter on the Clipboard, you will delete its current contents in the next step.

Clipboard task pane ◀ **Figure 2-12**

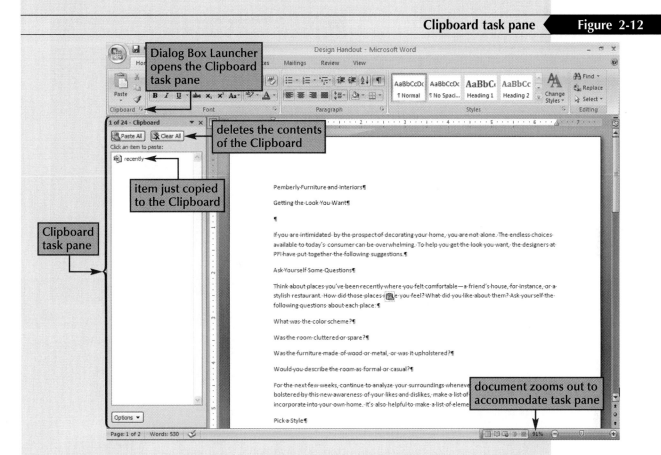

▶ **2.** Click the **Clear All** button near the top of the task pane. The current contents of the Clipboard are deleted, and you see the following message on the Clipboard task pane: "Clipboard empty. Copy or cut to collect items."

▶ **3.** Move the mouse pointer to the selection bar and double-click in the margin next to the paragraph that begins "If you are intimidated by the prospect...." The entire paragraph is selected.

▶ **4.** In the Clipboard group, click the **Copy** button 🖺. The first part of the paragraph appears in the Clipboard task pane, but a copy of all the text you selected—the whole paragraph—is now stored on the Clipboard.

▶ **5.** If necessary, scroll down until you can see the paragraph below the list of questions, which begins "For the next few weeks, continue...."

▶ **6.** Select the paragraph that begins "For the next few weeks, continue...."

▶ **7.** Click the **Copy** button. The first part of the paragraph appears in the Clipboard task pane, as shown in Figure 2-13.

Tip

To have the Clipboard task pane open each time you cut or copy an item, click Options at the bottom of the Clipboard task pane, and then select Show Office Clipboard Automatically.

Figure 2-13	Items in the Clipboard task pane

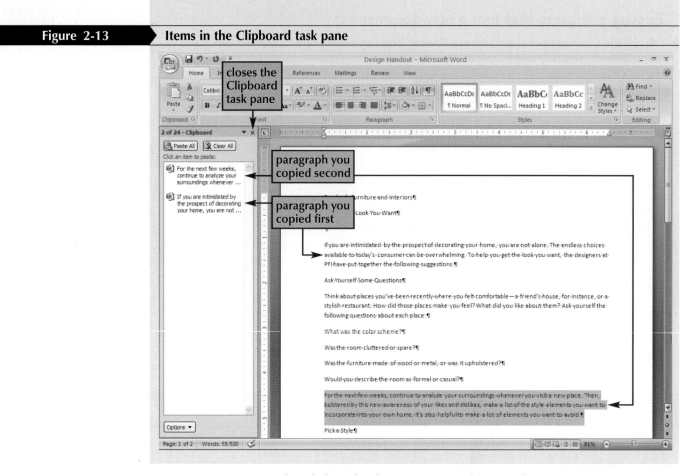

Now you can use the Clipboard task pane to insert the copied text into a new document. You'll start by opening a new, blank document.

To insert the copied text into the new document:

▶ 1. Click the **Office Button** (🔘), click **New**, verify that **Blank document** is selected, and then click the **Create** button. A new, blank document opens.

▶ 2. If the Clipboard task pane is not open, click the **Dialog Box Launcher** in the Clipboard group to open it.

▶ 3. In the Clipboard task pane, click the item that begins "**For the next few weeks**...." The text is inserted in the document.

▶ 4. Click the item that begins "**If you are intimidated by**...." The text is inserted as the second paragraph in the document.

▶ 5. Save the document as **Formal Designs** in the Tutorial.02\Tutorial folder.

▶ 6. Close the Formal Designs document. Natalie will be using this document later. You return to the Design Handout document, where the Clipboard task pane is still open. You are finished using the Clipboard task pane. In the next step you will clear the Clipboard so that you can start with an empty Clipboard when you begin work on the Review Assignments and Case Problems at the end of this tutorial.

▶ 7. Click the **Clear All** button on the Clipboard task pane. The copied items are removed from the Clipboard.

▶ 8. Click the **Close** button ⊠ on the Clipboard task pane. The Clipboard task pane closes.

▶ 9. Click anywhere in the document to deselect the highlighted paragraph, and then save the document.

Finding and Replacing Text

When you're working with a longer document, the quickest and easiest way to locate a particular character, word, or phrase is to use the **Find and Replace dialog box**. This dialog box contains three tabs:

- Find, for finding a word or phrase in a document (for example, you need to know where you referred to "textiles" in a document on interior design)
- Replace, for finding a word or phrase in a document and replacing it with something else (for example, you want to replace "formal design" with "formal style" throughout a document)
- Go To, for moving the cursor directly to a specific part of a document (for example, you want to go directly to page 29)

To open the Find and Replace dialog box, click the Find button or the Replace button (in the Editing group on the Home tab), depending on what you want to do. For example, to find a word or phrase, click the Find button, type the text you want to find in the Find what text box, and then click the Find Next button. The text you type in the Find what text box is known as the **search text**. After you click the Find Next button, Word finds and highlights the first instance of the search text. You continue clicking Find Next to find more occurrences of the search text in your document.

To replace text with something else, click the Replace button, and then type your search text in the Find what text box and the text you want to substitute in the Replace with text box. As with the Find feature, you click the Find Next button to find the next occurrence of the search text; Word stops and highlights each occurrence, allowing you to determine whether or not to substitute the replacement text. If you want to substitute the highlighted occurrence, click the Replace button. If you want to substitute every occurrence of the search text with the replacement text, without locating and reviewing each occurrence, you can click the Replace All button.

Finding and Replacing the Right Words | InSight

When using the Replace All button with single words, keep in mind that the search text might be found within other words. To prevent Word from making incorrect substitutions in such cases, it's a good idea to select the Find whole words only check box. (If you don't see this check box, click the More button to display additional options.) For example, suppose you want to replace the word "figure" with "illustration." Unless you select the Find whole words only check box, Word replaces "figure" in "configure" with "illustration" so the word becomes "conillustration."

- Click either the Find button or the Replace button on the Home tab.
- Click the More button to expand the dialog box to display additional options, including the Find whole words only option. If you see the Less button, the additional options are already displayed.
- In the Search list box, select Down if you want to search from the insertion point to the end of the document, select Up if you want to search from the insertion point to the beginning of the document, or select All to search the entire document.
- Type the characters you want to find in the Find what text box.
- If you are replacing text, type the replacement text in the Replace with text box.
- Click the Find whole words only check box to search for complete words.
- Click the Match case check box to insert the replacement text with the same case (upper or lower) as in the Replace with text box. For example, if the Replace with text box contained the words "Pemberly Interiors," this would ensure that Word inserted the text with a capital (uppercase) "P" and a capital (uppercase) "I."
- Click the Find Next button.
- Click the Replace button to substitute the found text with the replacement text and find the next occurrence.
- Click the Replace All button to substitute all occurrences of the found text with the replacement text, without reviewing each occurence.

Throughout the document, Natalie wants to replace the initials "PFI" with the full company name, "Pemberly Furniture and Interiors." You'll use the Replace feature to make this change quickly and easily.

To replace "PFI" with "Pemberly Furniture and Interiors":

▶ **1.** Press the **Ctrl+Home** keys to move the insertion point to the beginning of the document.

▶ **2.** In the Editing group on the Home tab, click the **Replace** button. The Find and Replace dialog box opens, with the Replace tab displayed.

▶ **3.** If you see a **More** button in the lower-left corner of the dialog box, click it to display the additional search options. (If you see a Less button, the additional options are already displayed.) Verify that **All** is selected in the Search list box, so Word will search the entire document.

▶ **4.** Click the **Find what** text box if necessary, type **PFI**, press the **Tab** key, and then, in the Replace with text box, type **Pemberly Furniture and Interiors**.

   Trouble? If you already see the text "PFI" and "Pemberly Furniture and Interiors" in your Find and Replace dialog box, someone has recently performed these steps on your computer without closing Word afterward. Skip Step 4 and continue with Step 5.

▶ **5.** Click the **Match case** check box to insert a check. This ensures that Word will search only for "PFI" and not "pfi" in the document.

▶ **6.** Click the **Find whole words only** check box to insert a check. Your Find and Replace dialog box should look like Figure 2-14.

Find and Replace dialog box ◄ Figure 2-14

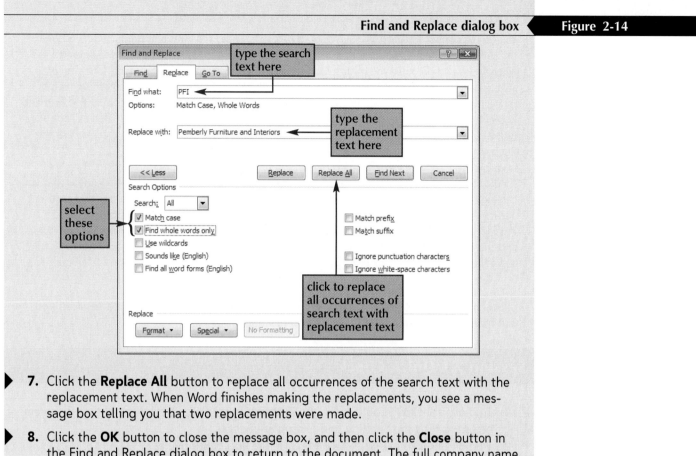

7. Click the **Replace All** button to replace all occurrences of the search text with the replacement text. When Word finishes making the replacements, you see a message box telling you that two replacements were made.

8. Click the **OK** button to close the message box, and then click the **Close** button in the Find and Replace dialog box to return to the document. The full company name has been inserted near the beginning of the document, as shown in Figure 2-15. If you scroll down to the end of the document, you'll see that it was also inserted in the last sentence.

Document with "Pemberly Furniture and Interiors" inserted ◄ Figure 2-15

9. Save the document.

You can search for formatting, such as bold or italics, using the Find and Replace dialog box in the same way that you can find text. For example, you might want to check a document to see where you used bold. Or you might need to find where you used a certain font, font size, or style. This is especially useful in long documents where scrolling to look for something would take a long time. To search for formatting, click the Format button at the bottom of the Find and Replace dialog box, click the category of formatting that you want to look for (such as Font, Paragraph, Style, and so on), and then select the formatting you want to find. You can also use the Replace tab to replace formatting in the same way you use it to replace text. To replace formatting, click the Replace tab, and then repeat the previous steps to specify the formatting that should replace the other formatting. Whether you are replacing formatting or not, note that you can look for formatting that occurs only on specific text, or you can look for formatting that occurs anywhere in a document. If you're looking for formatting on certain text (such as all instances of "Contemporary Furniture" that are bold), enter the text in the Find what text box and then specify the formatting you're looking for. To find formatting on any text in a document, leave the Find what text box empty and then specify the formatting.

You have completed the content changes Natalie requested. In the next session, you will make changes that affect the document's appearance.

Review | **Session 2.1 Quick Check**

1. True or False: You should move the insertion point to the beginning of the document before starting the Spelling and Grammar checker.
2. True or False: You need to select text before you can move it.
3. Explain how to drag and drop text.
4. Explain how to cut and paste text.
5. Suppose you want to find a word in a document. How do you open the Find and Replace dialog box?
6. How can you ensure that Word will insert "ZIP code" instead of "zip code" when you use the Find and Replace dialog box?

Session 2.2

Changing Margins

When you **format** a document, you make changes that affect the way the document looks. You'll start formatting Natalie's handout by adjusting the document's margins. By default, the margins for a Word document are one inch on the top, bottom, and sides.

When adjusting a document's margins, you'll find that the rulers are essential. They show you the current margin settings, as well as the amount that individual paragraphs are indented from the margin. On the horizontal ruler, the right edge of the left margin serves as the zero point, with the numbers to the right measuring the distance to the right edge of the page, and the numbers on the left measuring the distance to the left edge of the page. This allows you to see the exact width of the left margin at a glance. See Figure 2-16. The measurements on the vertical ruler work similarly, with the bottom edge of the top margin serving as the zero point from which all other vertical distances are measured.

Using the horizontal ruler to view margins | **Figure 2-16**

As you'll see in the upcoming steps, you can change the page margins in the Page Setup dialog box. You can also quickly adjust a document's margins in Print Layout view by clicking an option in the Margins menu. You'll have a chance to practice these techniques in the Case Problems at the end of this tutorial.

Changing Margins for a Document | Reference Window

- Make sure no text is selected, and then, in the Page Setup group on the Page Layout tab, click the Dialog Box Launcher. If necessary, click the Margins tab to display the margin settings.
- Use the arrows to change the settings in the Top, Bottom, Left, or Right text boxes, or type a new margin value in each text box.
- Make sure the Apply to list box displays Whole document.
- Click the OK button.
- To choose from groups of predefined margin settings, click the Margins button in the Page Setup group on the Page Layout tab. In the Margins menu, click the group of margin settings that is appropriate for your document.

You need to change the top and left margins of the Design Handout document to 1.5 inches, per Natalie's note in Figure 2-3. The left margin needs to be wider than the right to allow space for holes so that the document can be inserted in a three-ring binder. Also, the top margin needs to be wider than the bottom margin so the document can be printed on the company letterhead. In the next set of steps, you'll change the margins using the Page Setup dialog box.

To change the margins in the Design Handout document:

▶ **1.** Click anywhere in the document to make sure no text is selected.

▶ **2.** Click the **Page Layout** tab on the Ribbon, and then, in the Page Setup group, click the **Margins** button. The Margins menu appears, displaying some common margin settings. The Normal option contains the default margin settings. You can always click Normal to return a document to the default margin settings. The item at the top of the menu, Last Custom Setting, reflects the last margin settings selected in the Page Setup dialog box. See Figure 2-17.

Figure 2-17 | **Margins menu**

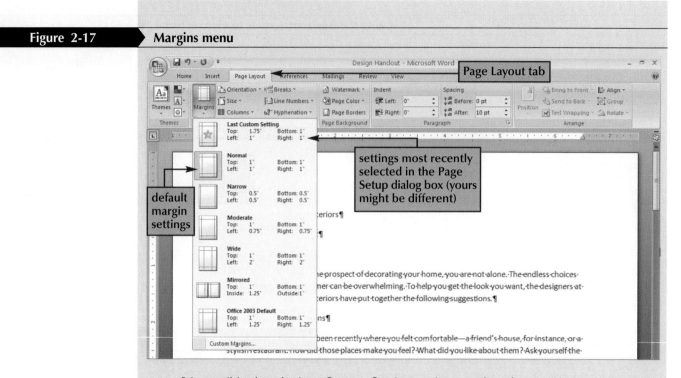

It's possible that the Last Custom Setting option matches the margin settings you want to use in the Design Handout document, but if so, ignore it. Instead, you'll open the Page Setup dialog box in the next step, so you can practice using it. You can open the Page Setup dialog box via the Custom Margins option at the bottom of the Margins menu, or you can use the Dialog Box Launcher in the Page Setup group on the Page Layout tab. You'll try the Custom Margins option now.

▶ **3.** At the bottom of the Margins menu, click **Custom Margins**. The Page Setup dialog box opens.

▶ **4.** Click the **Margins** tab, if it is not already selected, to display the margin settings. The Top margin setting is selected. See Figure 2-18. As you complete the following steps, keep an eye on the Preview in the bottom-left part of the dialog box, which changes to reflect changes you make to the margins.

Page Setup dialog box   Figure 2-18

5. Type **1.5** to change the Top margin setting. (You do not have to type the inches symbol.)

6. Press the **Tab** key twice to select the Left text box and highlight the current margin setting. The text area in the Preview box moves down to reflect the larger top margin.

7. Verify that the insertion point is in the Left text box, type **1.5**, and then press the **Tab** key. The left margin in the Preview box increases.

8. In the Apply to list box, make sure **Whole document** is selected, and then click the **OK** button to return to your document. Notice that the ruler has changed to reflect the new margin settings and the resulting reduced page area. The document text is now 6 inches wide. See Figure 2-19.

Figure 2-19 | Rulers after setting top and left margins to 1.5 inches

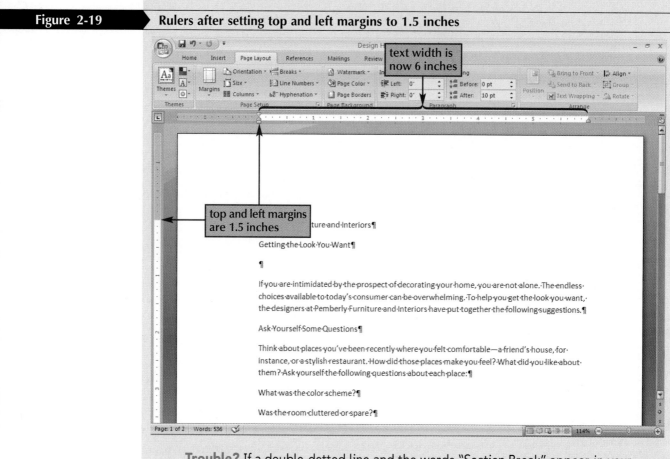

Trouble? If a double-dotted line and the words "Section Break" appear in your document, Whole document wasn't selected in the Apply to list box. If this occurs, click the Undo button ⤺ on the Quick Access Toolbar and repeat Steps 1 through 8, making sure you select the Whole document option in the Apply to list box.

▶ **9.** Save the document and then click the **Home** tab.

InSight | **Using Margins to Insert Space**

Recall that in Tutorial 1 you inserted a series of blank paragraphs at the beginning of a document in order to allow room for the company letterhead. Now that you know how to change margins, you should use this method to insert extra space in a document rather than inserting blank paragraphs. Adjusting margins allows you to be more precise, because you can specify an exact amount. Also, if you know you will usually need to use a particular margin setting for your documents, you can click the Default button on the Margins tab of the Page Setup dialog box to make your settings the default for all new documents.

In the next section, you will make some changes that will affect the way certain paragraphs are positioned between the left and right margins.

Aligning Text

The term **alignment** refers to the way a paragraph lines up horizontally between the margins. By default, text is aligned along the left margin and is **ragged**, or uneven, along the right margin. This is called **left alignment**. With **right alignment**, the text is aligned along the right margin and is ragged along the left margin. With **center alignment**, text is centered between the left and right margins and is ragged along both the left and right margins. With **justified alignment**, full lines of text are spaced between both the left and the right margins, and the text is not ragged. Text in newspaper columns is often justified. See Figure 2-20.

Varieties of text alignment | **Figure 2-20**

left alignment
If you are intimidated by the prospect of decorating your home, you are not alone. The endless choices available to today's consumer can be overwhelming. To help you get the look you want, the designers at Pemberly Furniture and Interiors have put together the following suggestions.

right alignment
If you are intimidated by the prospect of decorating your home, you are not alone. The endless choices available to today's consumer can be overwhelming. To help you get the look you want, the designers at Pemberly Furniture and Interiors have put together the following suggestions.

center alignment
If you are intimidated by the prospect of decorating your home, you are not alone. The endless choices available to today's consumer can be overwhelming.

justified alignment
If you are intimidated by the prospect of decorating your home, you are not alone. The endless choices available to today's consumer can be overwhelming. To help you get the look you want, the designers at Pemberly Furniture and Interiors have put together the following suggestions.

The Paragraph group on the Home tab includes a button for each of the four major types of alignment. The Mini toolbar, which appears when you select text in a document, includes just the Center button, which is commonly used to center titles in a document.

To align a single paragraph, click anywhere in that paragraph and then click the appropriate alignment button. To align multiple paragraphs, select the paragraphs first, and then click an alignment button.

Figure 2-3 indicates that the title and subtitle of the Design Handout should be centered and that the main paragraphs should be justified. First, you'll center the title and subtitle using the Center button on the Mini toolbar.

To center-align the title:

▶ **1.** Click and drag in the selection bar to select the title ("Pemberly Furniture and Interiors") and the subtitle ("Getting the Look You Want"). A faint image of the Mini toolbar appears near the selected text. To fully display the Mini toolbar, you need to move the mouse pointer over it.

▶ **2.** Move the mouse pointer near the Mini toolbar. The Mini toolbar is now fully visible and remains visible until you move the mouse pointer away from it. It contains one alignment button, the Center button. The Align Text Left button on the Home tab is highlighted in orange, indicating that the selected text is currently left-aligned. See Figure 2-21.

Figure 2-21	Mini toolbar visible over selected text

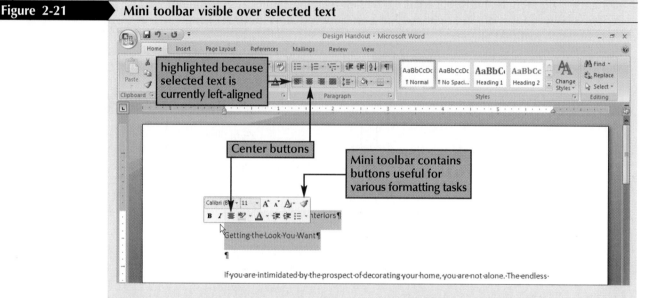

▶ **3.** On the Mini toolbar, click the **Center** button. The text is centered between the left and right margins. Both Center buttons are now highlighted in orange, indicating that the selected text is centered. The Mini toolbar remains visible until you move the mouse pointer away from it.

Trouble? If the Mini toolbar disappears before you click the Center button, click anywhere in the document to deselect the text, and then repeat Steps 1 through 3.

Next, you'll justify the text in the first two main paragraphs.

To justify the first two main paragraphs:

▶ **1.** Click anywhere in the paragraph that begins "If you are intimidated by...." If the Mini toolbar was still visible, it disappears and the insertion point is now located in the paragraph you want to align. The Align Text Left button in the Paragraph group is highlighted in orange, indicating that the paragraph containing the insertion point is left-aligned.

▶ **2.** In the Paragraph group, click the **Justify** button. The paragraph text spreads out so that it lines up evenly along the left and right margins.

▶ **3.** Scroll down if necessary and click in the paragraph that begins "Think about places you've been recently.... "

▶ **4.** Click the **Justify** button in the Paragraph group again. The text is evenly spaced between the left and right margins. See Figure 2-22.

Justified paragraphs | Figure 2-22

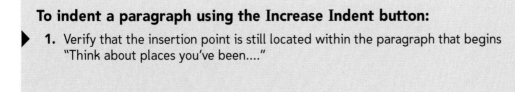

You'll justify the other paragraphs later. But first, you turn your attention to indenting a paragraph.

Indenting a Paragraph

When you **indent** a paragraph, you move the entire paragraph to the right. You can use the indent buttons on the Home tab to increase or decrease paragraph indenting in increments of 0.5 inches. The **indent markers** on the horizontal ruler allow you to see at a glance a paragraph's current indent settings. See Figure 2-23.

Indent markers on horizontal ruler | Figure 2-23

By dragging the indent markers individually, you can create specialized indents, such as a **hanging indent** (where all lines except the first line of the paragraph are indented from the left margin) or a **right indent** (where all lines of the paragraph are indented from the right margin). You'll have a chance to try some of these specialized indents in the Case Problems at the end of this tutorial. In this document, though, you only need to indent the main paragraphs 0.5 inches. When you do a simple indent like this, the three indent markers, shown stacked on top of one another in Figure 2-23, move as a unit along with the paragraphs you are indenting.

To indent a paragraph using the Increase Indent button:

▶ **1.** Verify that the insertion point is still located within the paragraph that begins "Think about places you've been...."

    2. In the Paragraph group, click the **Increase Indent** button 📑 twice. (Be careful not to click the Decrease Indent button by mistake.) The entire paragraph and the stacked indent markers in the horizontal ruler move right 0.5 inches each time you click the Increase Indent button. The paragraph is indented 1 inch, which is 0.5 inches more than Natalie wants.

    3. Click the **Decrease Indent** button 📑 in the Paragraph group to move the paragraph left 0.5 inches. The paragraph is now indented 0.5 inches from the left margin. Don't be concerned about the list of questions. You will indent this list later, when you format it as a bulleted list. See Figure 2-24.

Figure 2-24 ▶ **Indented paragraph**

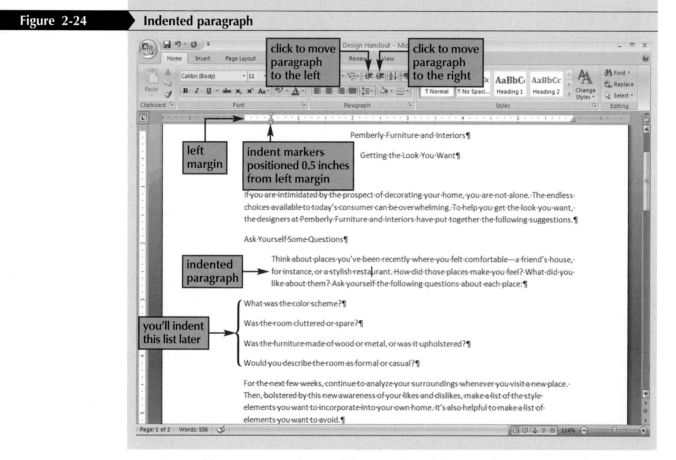

You could continue to indent and then justify each paragraph. However, it's faster to use the Format Painter button. With the Format Painter, you can easily copy both the indentation and alignment changes to the remaining paragraphs in the document.

Using the Format Painter

The **Format Painter** makes it easy to copy all the formatting features of one paragraph to other paragraphs (or from one heading to other headings, or from one word to other words). You can use this button to copy formatting to just one item or to multiple items.

Using the Format Painter

- Select the text whose formatting you want to copy. If you are trying to copy the formatting of an entire paragraph, you can just click anywhere in the paragraph.
- To copy formatting to one item, click the Format Painter button in the Clipboard group on the Home tab, and then select the text you want to format, or click anywhere in the paragraph you want to format.
- To copy formatting to multiple items, double-click the Format Painter button in the Clipboard group on the Home tab, and then select, one by one, each text item you want to format, or click anywhere in each paragraph you want to format. When you are finished, click the Format Painter button again to deselect it.

You'll use the Format Painter now to copy the formatting of the second paragraph to the other main paragraphs. The first step is to move the insertion point to the paragraph whose formatting you want to copy.

To copy paragraph formatting with the Format Painter:

▶ **1.** Verify that the insertion point is located in the paragraph that begins "Think about places you've been...."

▶ **2.** In the Clipboard group, double-click the **Format Painter** button 🖋. When you double-click the Format Painter button, it stays selected until you click it again; you can paste the copied formatting as many times as you wish. Also, notice that when you move the pointer over text, the pointer changes to 🖌I to indicate that the format of the paragraph containing the insertion point can be "painted" (or copied) onto another paragraph.

▶ **3.** Scroll down, and then click anywhere in the paragraph that begins "For the next few weeks...." The format of this paragraph changes to match the format of the indented and justified paragraph above it. See Figure 2-25. Two paragraphs are now indented and justified. The Format Painter pointer is still visible, indicating that you can continue formatting paragraphs with it.

Formatting copied with Format Painter ◀ Figure 2-25

Now you need to continue copying the indented and justified formatting to the main paragraphs of text. You do not want to copy this formatting to the document headings or to the several lists. (You'll format these elements later in this tutorial.)

▶ **4.** Scroll down and click in the paragraph below the "Pick a Style" subheading, which begins "Now that you know what you like...." Also, click the paragraphs that begin "People who enjoy spending time..." and "Of course you probably won't be able...." Finally, click the paragraph that begins "While you are saving money...." Do not click the document title or subtitle, the lists, or the last paragraph of text.

Trouble? If you click a paragraph and the formatting doesn't change to match the indented and justified paragraphs, you single-clicked the Format Painter button rather than double-clicked it. Move the insertion point to a paragraph that has the desired format, double-click the Format Painter button, and then repeat Step 4.

Trouble? If you accidentally click a heading or one line of a list, click the Undo button on the Quick Access Toolbar to return the line to its original formatting. Then select a paragraph that has the desired format, double-click the Format Painter button, and repeat Step 4 to finish copying the format to the desired paragraphs.

▶ **5.** After you are finished formatting paragraphs with the Format Painter pointer, click the **Format Painter** button 🖌 to turn off the feature.

▶ **6.** Save the document.

You've saved considerable time using the Format Painter to format all the main paragraphs in your document with the correct indentation and alignment. Your next job is to make the lists easier to read by adding bullets and numbers.

Adding Bullets and Numbers

You can emphasize a list of items by adding a heavy dot, or **bullet**, before each item in the list. Bulleted lists are usually much easier to read and follow than lists that do not have bullets. For a list of items that have a particular order (such as steps in a procedure), you can use numbers instead of bullets. Natalie's printout requests that you add bullets to the list of questions on page 1 to make them stand out. She also wants you to add bullets to the list of four basic styles on page 1.

To apply bullets to a list of questions:

▶ **1.** Scroll up until you see the list of questions on page 1, which begins "What was the color scheme?"

▶ **2.** Select the four questions in the list.

▶ **3.** In the Paragraph group, click the **Bullets** button ▤. Black circles called bullets appear before each item in the list. Also, the list is indented and the paragraph spacing between the items is reduced. After reviewing the default, circular bullet style in the document, Natalie decides she would prefer square bullets.

Trouble? If no bullets are applied and a menu opens instead, you clicked the Bullets button arrow instead of the Bullets button. Press the Esc key to close the menu, and then repeat Step 3, taking care to click the Bullets button.

▶ **4.** In the Paragraph group, click the **Bullets button arrow** ▤▾ (make sure to click the arrow, not just the button). A gallery of bullet styles opens.

At the top of the gallery of bullet styles is the Recently Used Bullets section; these are the bullet styles that have been used since you started Word. You'll probably see just the round black bullets, which were applied by default when you clicked the Bullets button. However, if you had used several different bullet styles, you would see them here. Below the Recently Used Bullets section is the **Bullet Library**, which offers a variety of bullet styles. For the Design Handout, you want to use a black square, which is an option in the Bullet Library. See Figure 2-26.

Bullets gallery ◄ Figure 2-26

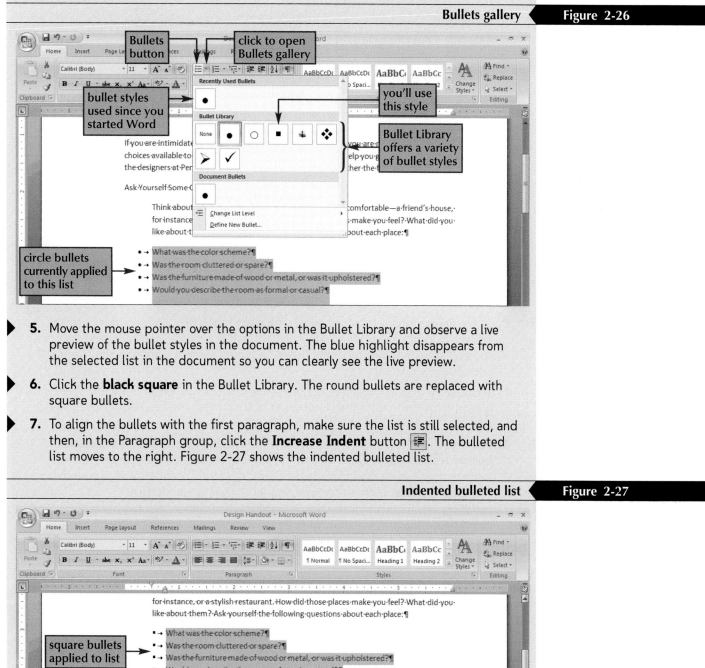

5. Move the mouse pointer over the options in the Bullet Library and observe a live preview of the bullet styles in the document. The blue highlight disappears from the selected list in the document so you can clearly see the live preview.

6. Click the **black square** in the Bullet Library. The round bullets are replaced with square bullets.

7. To align the bullets with the first paragraph, make sure the list is still selected, and then, in the Paragraph group, click the **Increase Indent** button 📇. The bulleted list moves to the right. Figure 2-27 shows the indented bulleted list.

Indented bulleted list ◄ Figure 2-27

Next, you need to format the list of decorating styles on page 1 with square bullets. When you first start Word, the Bullets button applies the round bullets you saw earlier. But after you select a new bullet style, the Bullets button applies that last bullet style you used. So, to add square bullets to the decorating styles list, you just have to select the list and click the Bullets button.

To add bullets to the list of decorating styles:

▶ **1.** Scroll down and select the list of four basic decorating styles (**Formal**, **Traditional**, **Eclectic**, **Contemporary**) at the bottom of page 1.

▶ **2.** In the Paragraph group, click the **Bullets** button ▤, and then click the **Increase Indent** button ▤. The list is now formatted with square black bullets. The list is also indented, similar to the list of questions shown earlier in Figure 2-27.

Your next step is to format the list of suggested purchases on page 2. Natalie wants you to format this information as a numbered list because it specifies purchases in a sequential order. Adding numbers to a list of items is a quick task thanks to the Numbering button, which numbers selected paragraphs with consecutive numbers. If you insert a new paragraph, delete a paragraph, or reorder the paragraphs, Word adjusts the numbers to make sure they remain consecutive.

To apply numbers to the list of suggested purchases:

▶ **1.** Scroll down and select the list that begins with **Lamps or other forms of lighting** and ends with **Large items such as sofas, beds, and dining tables**.

▶ **2.** In the Paragraph group, click the **Numbering** button ▤. Consecutive numbers appear in front of each item in the list, with a period after each number. As you'll see in the next step, you can choose from more options by clicking the Numbering button arrow instead.

   Trouble? If you see a gallery of numbering options, you clicked the Numbering button arrow instead of the Numbering button. Press the Esc key to close the gallery, and then click the Numbering button.

▶ **3.** Make sure the list is still selected in the document, and then click the **Numbering button arrow** ▤ ▾. A gallery of numbering formats opens. Recently used numbering formats appear at the top of the list. Below the recently used formats you see the **Numbering Library**, which contains a variety of numbering formats. The style currently applied to the numbered list is highlighted in orange. You can move the mouse pointer over the options in the Numbering Library to see a live preview of the other formats in the document. See Figure 2-28.

Numbering Gallery ◄ Figure 2-28

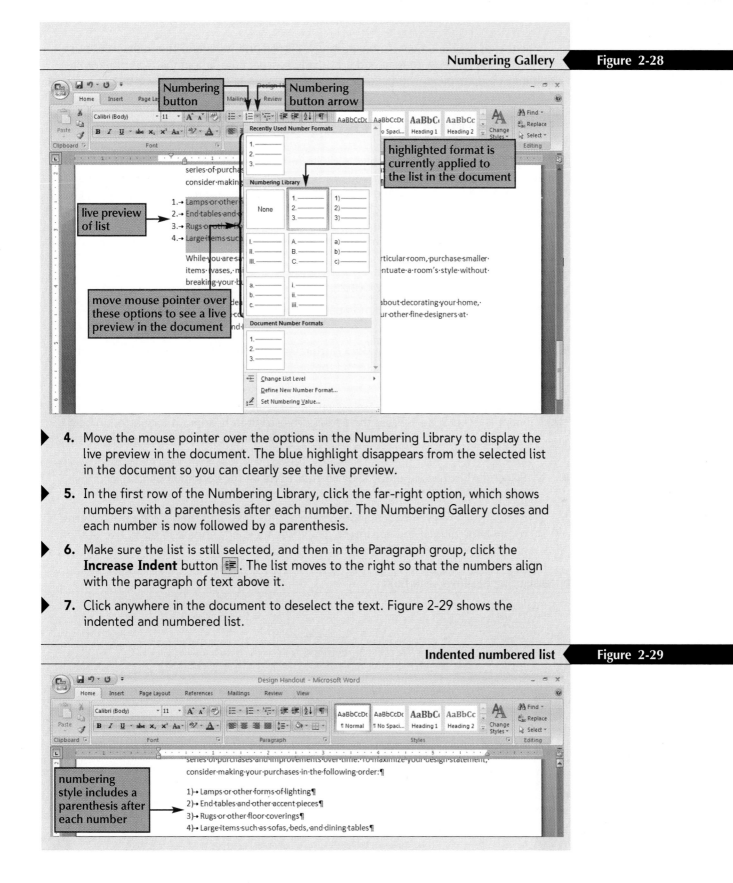

4. Move the mouse pointer over the options in the Numbering Library to display the live preview in the document. The blue highlight disappears from the selected list in the document so you can clearly see the live preview.

5. In the first row of the Numbering Library, click the far-right option, which shows numbers with a parenthesis after each number. The Numbering Gallery closes and each number is now followed by a parenthesis.

6. Make sure the list is still selected, and then in the Paragraph group, click the **Increase Indent** button ⎘. The list moves to the right so that the numbers align with the paragraph of text above it.

7. Click anywhere in the document to deselect the text. Figure 2-29 shows the indented and numbered list.

Indented numbered list ◄ Figure 2-29

The text of the document is now properly aligned and indented. The bullets and numbers make the lists easy to read and give readers visual clues about the type of information they contain. Next, you need to adjust the formatting of individual words.

Emphasizing Text Using Bold and Italic

You can emphasize text by formatting it with bold, underline, or italic. These styles help make specific words or phrases stand out. You add bold, underline, or italics by using the corresponding buttons in the Font group on the Home tab. These buttons are **toggle buttons**, which means you can click them once to format the selected text, and click again to remove the formatting from the selected text.

Natalie wants to draw attention to the headings by formatting them in bold.

To format the headings in bold:

1. On page 1, click in the selection bar to select the heading **Ask Yourself Some Questions**.

2. In the Font group, click the **Bold** button B. The heading is formatted in bold. In the next step, you'll learn a useful method for repeating the task you just performed.

3. Scroll down and click in the selection bar to select the next heading in the document ("Pick a Style"). Press the **F4** key. The selected heading is formatted in bold. The F4 key repeats your most recent action. It is especially helpful when formatting parts of a document.

4. Select the last heading, **Stay True to Your Style** (at the bottom of page 1), and then press the **F4** key.

5. Click anywhere in the document to deselect the text, and then scroll up to return to the beginning of the document. The three headings appear in bold. Two of them are shown in Figure 2-30.

Figure 2-30 — **Formatting headings with bold**

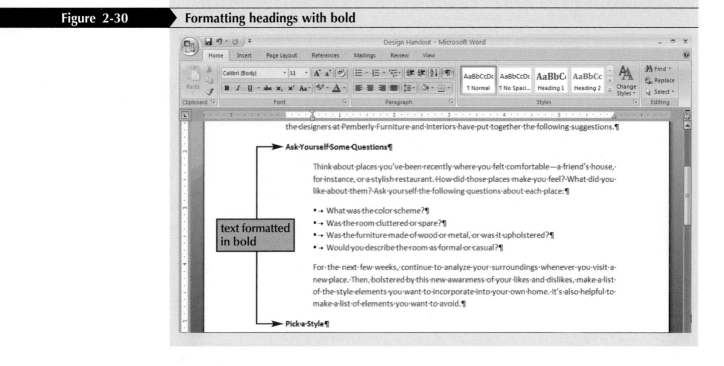

Now that it is formatted in bold, it's easy to see that the last heading, "Stay True to Your Style," is stranded at the bottom of page 1. The handout would look better if the heading was at the top of page 2, just above the first paragraph of the "Stay True to Your Style" section. To fix this problem, you need to tell Word to keep one paragraph (the heading paragraph) on the same page as the next paragraph.

To keep one paragraph with another:

▶ **1.** Scroll down and click anywhere in the heading **Stay True to Your Style**.

▶ **2.** In the Paragraph group, click the **Dialog Box Launcher**, and then, in the Paragraph dialog box, click the **Line and Page Breaks** tab.

▶ **3.** Click the **Keep with next** check box to insert a check mark, and then click the **OK** button. The Paragraph dialog box closes, and the "Stay True to Your Style" heading moves to the top of page 2.

The Underline and Italic buttons on the Home tab work in the same way as the Bold button. You'll try formatting the title and subtitle in italics now, to see how they look.

To format the title and subtitle in italics:

▶ **1.** On page 1, select the title **Pemberly Furniture and Interiors** and the subtitle **Getting the Look You Want**.

▶ **2.** In the Font group, click the **Italic** button *I* . The title and subtitle are italicized, meaning they lean slightly to the right. The Italic button is selected, indicating that the selected text is italicized. See Figure 2-31.

Formatting headings with italics ◀ **Figure 2-31**

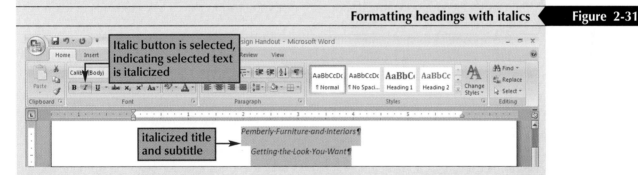

▶ **3.** After reviewing the change, Natalie decides she doesn't care for the italics and asks you to remove them.

▶ **4.** Click the **Italic** button *I* . The italic formatting toggles off. The selected text looks the way it did before you italicized it.

▶ **5.** Save the document, leaving the title and subtitle selected.

Helpful Keyboard Shortcuts

For common tasks, such as applying bold and italics, it's often faster to use a **keyboard shortcut** (a combination of keys pressed at the same time) instead of clicking buttons with the mouse. For each of the keyboard shortcuts listed below, press and hold the Ctrl key, press the indicated number or letter key, and then release both keys.

- Bold selected text: Ctrl+B
- Italicize selected text: Ctrl+I

- Underline selected text: Ctrl+U
- Single-space lines within paragraph that currently contains the insertion point: Ctrl+1
- Double-space lines within paragraph that currently contains the insertion point: Ctrl+2
- Select entire document: Ctrl+A
- Cut selected text: Ctrl+X
- Copy selected text to Clipboard: Ctrl+C
- Paste most recently copied item at location of insertion point: Ctrl+V
- Undo your most recent action: Ctrl+Z

You can also save time by using **KeyTips**, sometimes called access keys, to select buttons and commands. To use KeyTips, press the Alt key and notice the letters that are displayed over each tab. Press the letter for the tab that contains the feature you want. For example, "P" is the KeyTip for the Page Layout tab; pressing it displays the Page Layout tab, with KeyTips showing for each feature on that tab. Press the KeyTip for the feature you want (for example, "B" for the Breaks button), and then notice the KeyTips that appear in the menu or gallery that opens. Press the KeyTip for the option you want. The change you select is applied to your document, and the KeyTips are hidden. You can press the Alt key to display them again for your next task. To hide KeyTips without using them, press the Esc key.

Working with Themes and Fonts

In addition to drawing attention to text with bold, italics, or underlining, you can change the shape and size of the individual letters by changing the font and font size. (As you learned in Tutorial 1, the term "font" refers to the shape of the characters in a document, and "font size" refers to the size of the characters.) You'll learn how to change the font in the Design Handout document soon, but first you need to take a few moments to learn about a related topic, document themes.

The document **theme** controls the variety of fonts, colors, and other visual effects available to you as you format a document. Twenty different themes are included in Word, with each offering a coordinated assortment of fonts, colors, and visual effects. By default, the Office theme is selected in each new Word document, including the Design Handout document you are working on now. You'll learn more about themes as you gain experience with Word. For now, you need to focus only on the relationship between themes and fonts.

One secret to creating a harmonious-looking document is to use no more than two fonts. For this reason, each theme includes only two fonts: one for headings and one for body text (that is, anything that is not a heading). In the Office theme, the heading font is Cambria, and the body font is Calibri. These two fonts were designed specifically for easy reading onscreen as well as on the printed page. A long list of other fonts is available. You can experiment with them and use them in your documents, but take care not to use too many fonts. This will create a document with a cluttered, disjointed appearance.

Applying a New Font and Font Size

To apply a font, select the text you want to format, then in the Font group on the Home tab, click the Font arrow, and click the font you want. The heading and body font for a document's theme are listed first, at the top of the font list.

To select a font size, make sure the text you want to format is selected, then in the Font group, click the Font Size arrow, and click the font size you want. Both the Font and Font Size lists allow you to see a live preview of selections by moving the mouse pointer over a font name or font size.

Natalie typed the entire Design Handout document in the Calibri font, which is intended primarily for body text, and the font size for the entire document is 11-point. She wants you to format the title and the subtitle in Cambria, which is the heading font for the Office theme. She also wants you to increase the size of the title and subtitle to 14-point.

To apply the Cambria heading font to the Design Handout document:

▶ **1.** On page 1, verify that the title **Pemberly Furniture and Interiors** and the subtitle **Getting the Look You Want** are selected.

▶ **2.** In the Font group, click the **Font** arrow. A list of available fonts appears. The heading and body font for the Office theme (Cambria and Calibri) appear at the top of the list. The intended use of these two fonts (Headings or Body) is specified after each font name. Calibri (Body) is highlighted in orange, indicating that this font is currently applied to the selected text. (Calibri also appears in the Font box, above the list, for the same reason.) Below the heading and body fonts is a list of fonts that have been used recently on your computer, followed by a complete alphabetical list of all available fonts. (You need to scroll the list to see all the fonts.) Each name in the list is formatted with the relevant font. For example, "Cambria" appears in the Cambria font, and "Calibri" appears in the Calibri font. See Figure 2-32.

Font list ◀ **Figure 2-32**

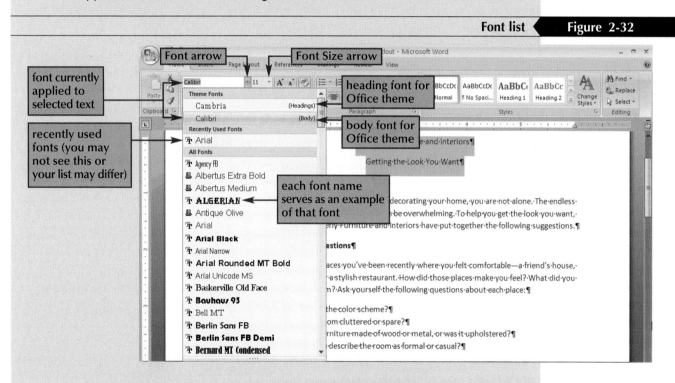

▶ **3.** Without clicking, move the mouse pointer over a dramatic-looking font in the font list, such as Algerian or Arial Black, and then drag the pointer over another font. The selected text in the document shows a live preview of the font, changing again to a new font when you drag the mouse pointer to a different font name.

▶ **4.** At the top of the list, click **Cambria (Headings)**. Take care to select Cambria (Headings) at the top of the list. Do not click Cambria where it appears farther down, in the alphabetical list of fonts. (The reason for this will become clear in the next section, when you learn more about document themes.) The selected title and subtitle are now formatted in Cambria, and the font list closes. "Cambria (Headings)" appears in the Font box, indicating the font currently applied to the selected text. Next, you need to increase the font size of the selected text from 11 point to 14 point.

Trouble? If you see "Cambria" in the font box rather than "Cambria (Headings)," you selected Cambria where it appears in the alphabetical list of fonts rather than at the top of the list. Begin again with Step 2, taking care to select Cambria (Headings) at the top of the list.

Tip

The font and font size settings in the Font group reflect the settings of the text that is currently selected, or, if no text is selected, of the text currently containing the insertion point.

▶ **5.** Verify that the title and subtitle are still selected, and then in the Font group click the **Font Size** arrow (shown earlier in Figure 2-32). A list of font sizes appears, with the currently selected font size (11) displayed in the Font Size box. Like the Font box, the Font Size box allows you to preview options before selecting one.

▶ **6.** Drag the mouse pointer over a few font sizes, and notice how the size of the selected text changes accordingly.

▶ **7.** Click **14**. The Font Size list closes and the selected text increases from 11-point to 14-point Cambria. Click within the title to deselect the text.

You've finished formatting the document's title and subtitle in the Cambria font, the preferred heading font for the Office theme. You could also apply the Cambria font to the headings within the document (such as the heading "Ask Yourself Some Questions"). However, Natalie thinks the bold you applied earlier emphasizes them enough, so you'll leave the headings as they are.

The only remaining font change has to do with the company name. Wherever it appears in the body of the document, Natalie wants to format it in the Arial font, so that it matches the sign outside the company's storefront. Arial is not one of the suggested fonts for the Office theme, and using it breaks the general rule of two fonts per document, but this is a small change that won't affect the overall look of the document.

To format the company name in the Arial font:

▶ **1.** At the end of the introductory paragraph, select **Pemberly Furniture and Interiors**.

▶ **2.** In the Font group click the **Font** arrow, and then click **Arial** in either in the Recently used Fonts section of the list or in the All Fonts section. The font for the company name changes from Calibri to Arial. Arial appears in the Font box, indicating that the selected text is formatted in this font.

Trouble? If you don't see Arial in your font list, choose another font in the All Fonts section that is easy to distinguish from Calibri or Cambria but still looks suitable for a business document.

▶ **3.** Scroll down to the last paragraph of the document, select **Pemberly Furniture and Interiors**, and format it in the Arial font. See Figure 2-33.

Figure 2-33 | Company name formatted in Arial

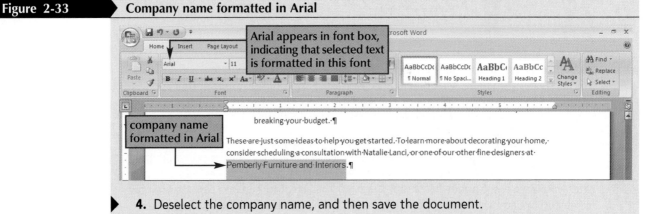

▶ **4.** Deselect the company name, and then save the document.

You are finished changing the document fonts. In the next section, you'll select a new theme for the document and observe how this affects your font choices.

Changing the Document's Theme

Each document theme is designed to convey a specific look and feel. For example, the Office theme is designed to be appropriate for standard business documents. By contrast, some of the other themes are designed to give documents a more informal look, such as sleek for a new product announcement or earthy for a flyer on environmental news.

The advantage of sticking with a theme's suggested heading and body fonts (the two fonts at the top of the font list) is that if you switch to a different theme, the fonts in the document automatically change to the body and heading fonts for that theme. If you select any fonts on the font list other than the two heading and body fonts at the top of the list, they will remain unchanged in the document as you switch from one theme to another.

Natalie is considering using a different theme for future handouts. She asks you to apply the Metro theme to the Design Handout document to see how it looks.

To change the document's theme:

▶ **1.** Make sure that you saved the document using the current name (Design Handout) at the end of the last section. If you aren't sure, save the document again.

▶ **2.** Save the document as **Design Handout Metro** in the Tutorial folder.

▶ **3.** Press the **Ctrl+Home** keys to move the insertion point up to the headings at the beginning of the document. With the title and subtitle visible, you will more easily be able to see what happens when you change the document's theme.

▶ **4.** Click the **Page Layout** tab, and then click the **Themes** button. The Themes gallery opens. You might have to wait a moment until the various themes appear in the gallery. See Figure 2-34.

Themes gallery | Figure 2-34

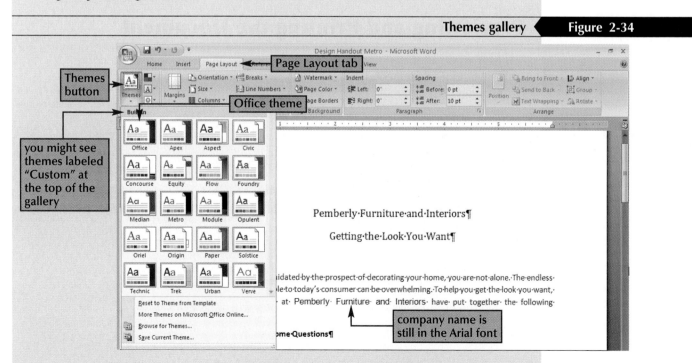

5. Without clicking, hold the mouse over the various themes in the gallery, and observe the live preview of each theme in the document. The heading and body fonts change to reflect the fonts associated with the various themes.

6. Click **Metro**. Except for the two instances of the company name (which you formatted earlier in Arial), the text in the Design Handout Metro document changes to the body and heading fonts of the Metro theme. To see exactly what the Metro theme fonts are, you can point to the Theme Fonts button in the Themes group.

7. Point to the **Theme Fonts** button ⒜⁻ in the Themes group. A ScreenTip appears, listing the currently selected theme (Metro), the heading font (Consolas), and the body font (Corbel).

   Trouble? If a menu appears, you clicked the Theme Fonts button instead of pointing to it. Press the Esc key, and then repeat Step 7.

8. Save the document and then close it. You can give the Design Handout Metro file to Natalie later, so she can decide whether or not to use the Metro theme for future handouts. Because you saved the Design Handout document before changing the theme, you can reopen it now and continue with the tutorial.

9. Reopen the Design Handout document, which is formatted with the Office theme.

Tip

To quickly open a document you were recently working on in Word, click the Office Button and then click the document you want in the Recent Documents list.

InSight | **Changing Fonts by Changing Themes**

The two fonts at the top of the font list are not actually specific fonts; they are instructions that tell Word to use the heading and body fonts for the currently selected theme. By contrast, the other fonts in the Font list (such as Arial or Calibri where they appear in the alphabetical list of fonts) are more straightforward. When you apply one of these fonts to text in a document, it doesn't change when you change the document theme. The same is true for other kinds of formatting, such as bold, italics, or font size changes. These types of formatting remain unchanged no matter what theme you choose.

Previewing and Printing the Document

You have made all the editing and formatting changes that Natalie requested for the Design Handout document. It's helpful to preview a document after formatting it. The Print Preview window makes it easy to spot things you need to change before printing, such as text that is not aligned correctly.

To preview and print the document:

1. Click the **Office Button** ⊙, point to **Print**, and then click **Print Preview**. The document is displayed in Print Preview.

2. In the Zoom section, click the **Two Pages** button. You see both pages of the document side by side. Review the document's formatting.

   Trouble? If you notice any alignment or indentation errors, click the Close Print Preview button, correct the errors in Print Layout view, save your changes, and then return to the Print Preview window.

3. On the Print Preview tab in the Print group, click the **Print** button, check the print settings, and then click the **OK** button. After a pause, the document prints.

> **4.** Click the **Close Print Preview** button. You return to Print Layout view.
>
> **5.** Save the document if necessary and then close it.

You now have a printed copy of the final Design Handout document, as shown in Figure 2-35.

Final version of Design Handout document ◀ **Figure 2-35**

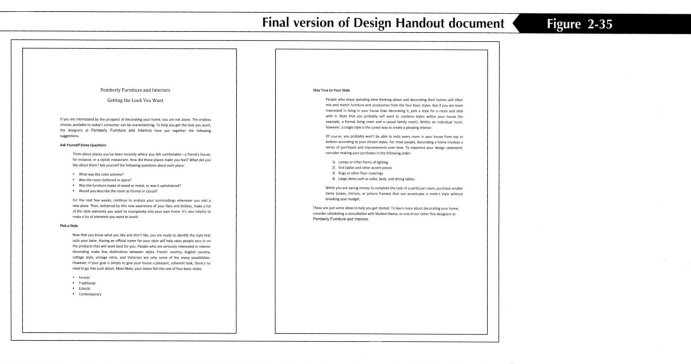

Session 2.2 Quick Check | Review

1. The term _____ refers to the way a paragraph lines up horizontally between the margins.
2. Explain how to indent a paragraph 1 inch or more from the left margin.
3. Explain how to copy formatting to multiple paragraphs.
4. What is the Numbering Library?
5. Explain the effect a theme has on the overall look of a document.
6. Explain how to change a paragraph's font.
7. Explain the relationship between the two items at the top of the Font list and the document's theme.

Tutorial Summary | Review

In this tutorial, you learned how to use the Spelling and Grammar checker, select parts of a document, delete text, and move text within a document. You also learned how to find and replace text. Next, you focused on formatting a document, including changing margins, aligning text, indenting paragraphs, using the Format Painter, and emphasizing text with bold and italics. Finally, you learned how to change the font and font size for selected text and you explored the relationship between fonts and themes.

Key Terms

alignment
bullet
Bullet Library
center alignment
Clipboard
Clipboard task pane
copy
cut
cut and paste
drag and drop
Find and Replace
    dialog box

format
Format Painter
hanging indent
indent
indent markers
justified alignment
keyboard shortcut
Key Tips
left alignment
Numbering Library
paste

ragged
right alignment
right indent
search text
Spelling and Grammar
    checker
theme
toggle buttons

| Practice | **Review Assignments** |

Apply the skills you learned in the tutorial using the same case scenario.

Data Files needed for the Review Assignments: Getting.docx, Staff.docx

Natalie asks you to work on a document that explains how to get started working with the designers at Pemberly Furniture and Interiors. The document starts by introducing the entire Pemberly design staff and then lists the steps involved in a major home renovation. Natalie also asks you to create a document listing the names of the firm's interior designers and interior decorators.

1. Open the file **Getting** located in the Tutorial.02\Review folder included with your Data Files, and then check your screen to make sure your settings match those in the tutorial.
2. Save the document as **Getting Started** in the same folder.
3. Use the Spelling and Grammar checker to correct any errors in the document. Assume that all names in the document and the term "Feng Shui" are spelled correctly.
4. Proofread the document carefully to check for any additional errors. Look for and correct errors in the last two paragraphs of the document that were not reported when you used the Spelling and Grammar checker.
5. Change the left and top margins to 1.5 inches using the Page Setup dialog box. Make sure to apply the change to the whole document.
6. In the list on the second page of the document, select the paragraph that begins "Interview potential construction..." and move it so that it follows the paragraph that reads "Review the final design plan."
7. Format the heading and subheading in the suggested heading font for the Office theme. Change the font size to 16 point.
8. Make all edits and formatting changes shown in Figure 2-36, and then save your work.

Figure 2-36

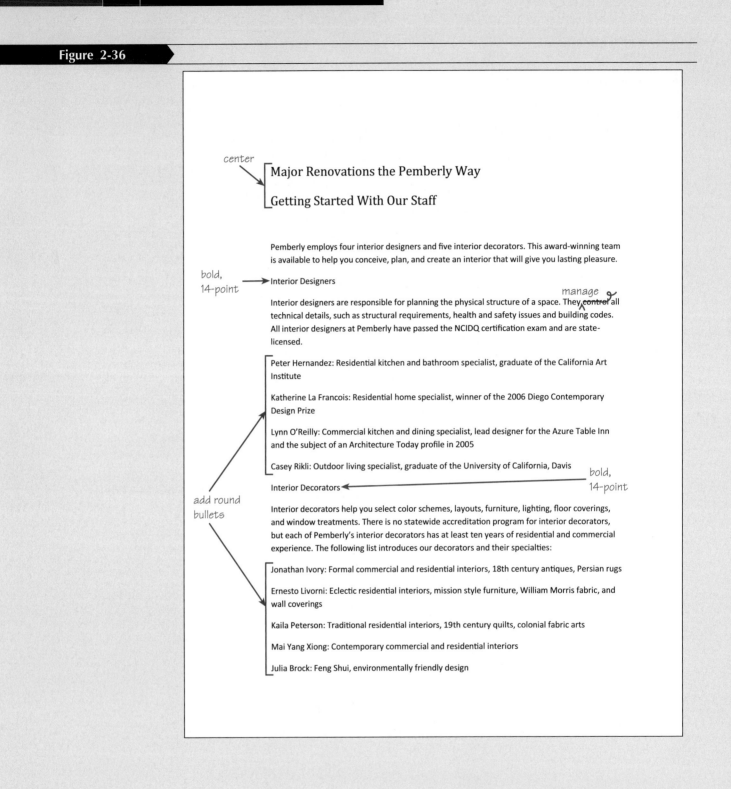

center

Major Renovations the Pemberly Way

Getting Started With Our Staff

Pemberly employs four interior designers and five interior decorators. This award-winning team is available to help you conceive, plan, and create an interior that will give you lasting pleasure.

bold, 14-point

Interior Designers

manage

Interior designers are responsible for planning the physical structure of a space. They control all technical details, such as structural requirements, health and safety issues and building codes. All interior designers at Pemberly have passed the NCIDQ certification exam and are state-licensed.

Peter Hernandez: Residential kitchen and bathroom specialist, graduate of the California Art Institute

Katherine La Francois: Residential home specialist, winner of the 2006 Diego Contemporary Design Prize

Lynn O'Reilly: Commercial kitchen and dining specialist, lead designer for the Azure Table Inn and the subject of an Architecture Today profile in 2005

Casey Rikli: Outdoor living specialist, graduate of the University of California, Davis

bold, 14-point

Interior Decorators

add round bullets

Interior decorators help you select color schemes, layouts, furniture, lighting, floor coverings, and window treatments. There is no statewide accreditation program for interior decorators, but each of Pemberly's interior decorators has at least ten years of residential and commercial experience. The following list introduces our decorators and their specialties:

Jonathan Ivory: Formal commercial and residential interiors, 18th century antiques, Persian rugs

Ernesto Livorni: Eclectic residential interiors, mission style furniture, William Morris fabric, and wall coverings

Kaila Peterson: Traditional residential interiors, 19th century quilts, colonial fabric arts

Mai Yang Xiong: Contemporary commercial and residential interiors

Julia Brock: Feng Shui, environmentally friendly design

Figure 2-36 (cont.)

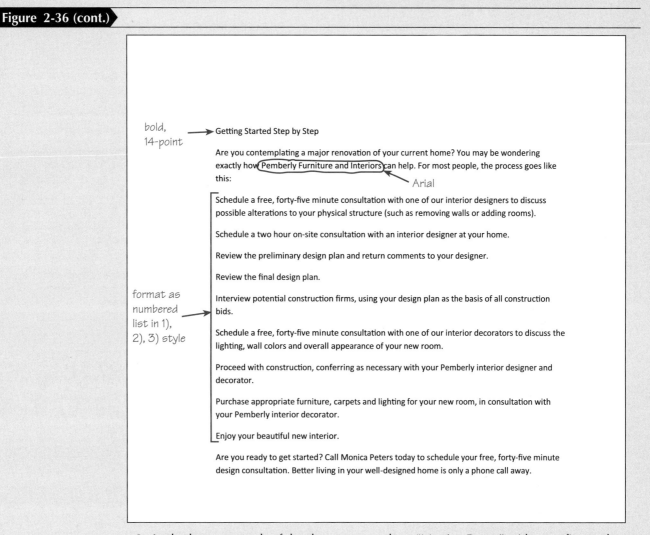

bold,
14-point

format as
numbered
list in 1),
2), 3) style

Arial

9. In the last paragraph of the document, replace "Monica Peters" with your first and last name.

10. Below the heading "Interior Designers," justify the paragraph that begins "Interior designers are responsible for...." Click the Increase Indent button once. Note that Word indents the justified paragraph slightly to match the bulleted list below it. Click the Increase Indent button again to indent the paragraph a full 0.5 inch. Similarly, justify and indent the paragraph below the heading "Interior Decorators" and the paragraph below the heading "Getting Started Step by Step." Finally, justify and indent the last paragraph in the document, and then indent the two bulleted lists and the numbered list to match the other indented paragraphs. When you are finished, the text and lists below the three boldface headings should all be indented by 0.5 inch. Save the document.

11. If necessary, move the heading "Getting Started Step by Step" to the top of page 2.

12. Display the Clipboard task pane. Copy the list of interior designers and their specialties (starting with Peter Hernandez and ending with Casey Rikli) to the Clipboard. Also copy the list of interior decorators and their specialties (beginning with Jonathan Ivory and ending with Julia Brock) to the Clipboard.

13. Open the file **Staff** located in the Tutorial.02\Review folder included with your Data Files, and save the document as **Pemberly Staff** in the same folder. In the subtitle, insert your first and last name after the word "by."

14. Display the Clipboard task pane. Below the heading "Interior Designers," paste the list of interior designers, which begins "Peter Hernandez." Below the heading "Interior Decorators," paste the list of interior decorators, which begins "Jonathan Ivory." In each case, start by moving the insertion point to the blank paragraph below the heading. Notice that text inserted from the Clipboard retains its original formatting.

15. Clear the contents of the Clipboard task pane, and then print the document.

16. Save the Pemberly Staff document and close it. Close the Clipboard task pane.

17. Save the Getting Started document, deselect any selected text, preview the document, and print it.

18. Save the Getting Started document as **Verve Sample** in the same folder.

19. Select the Verve theme, and then review the newly formatted document and its list of fonts. Check the company name in the paragraph below the heading "Getting Started Step by Step" and make sure it is still formatted in Arial.

20. Save the Verve Sample document, preview it, print it, and close it. Close any other open documents. Submit the finished documents to your instructor, either in printed or electronic form, as requested.

Apply	**Case Problem 1**

Apply the skills you learned to create a one-page flyer.

Data File needed for this Case Problem: New.docx

Peach Tree School of the Arts   Students at Peach Tree School of the Arts, in Savannah, Georgia, can choose from a wide range of after-school classes in fine arts, music, and theater. Amanda Reinhard, the school director, has created a flyer informing parents of some additional offerings. It's your job to format the flyer to make it professional looking and easy to read.

1. Open the file **New** located in the Tutorial.02\Case1 folder included with your Data Files, and save the file as **New Classes** in the same folder.

2. Correct any spelling or grammar errors. Ignore the sentence fragments highlighted by the grammar checker. These fragments will make sense once they are formatted as part of a bulleted list.

3. Proofread for other errors, such as words that are spelled correctly but used incorrectly. Use the Replace command to replace "P.M." with "p.m." throughout the document.

4. Replace "Marcus Cody" with your name.

5. Change the top, left, right, and bottom margins to 1.5 inches, and then save your work.

6. Format everything in the document except the title and subtitle in 12-point Times New Roman font. Format the title and subtitle in Arial, 16 point, bold.

7. Format the list of new classes (which begins "Advanced Drawing") as a bulleted list, using the square bullet style.

8. Move the third bulleted item (which begins "Jazz Dance...") up to make it the first bulleted item in the list.

9. Format the four-step check list near the end of the document as a numbered list, using the default numbering style.

10. Save your work, preview the document, switch back to Print Layout view to make any changes you think necessary, print the document, and then close it. Submit the finished document to your instructor, either in printed or electronic form, as requested.

Apply | **Case Problem 2**

Use your skills to format the summary document shown in Figure 2-37.

Data File needed for this Case Problem: Moth.docx

Hamilton Polytechnic Institute   Finn Hansen is an associate researcher in the Department of Entomology at Hamilton Polytechnic Institute. He is working on a nationwide program that aims to slow the spread of a devastating forest pest, the gypsy moth. He has created a one-page document that will be used as part of a campaign to inform the public about current efforts to manage gypsy moths in North America. Format the document by completing the following steps.

1. Open the file **Moth** located in the Tutorial.02\Case2 folder included with your Data Files, and then check your screen to make sure your settings match those in the tutorial.
2. Save the file as **Gypsy Moth** in the same folder.
3. Format the document as shown in Figure 2-37.

Figure 2-37

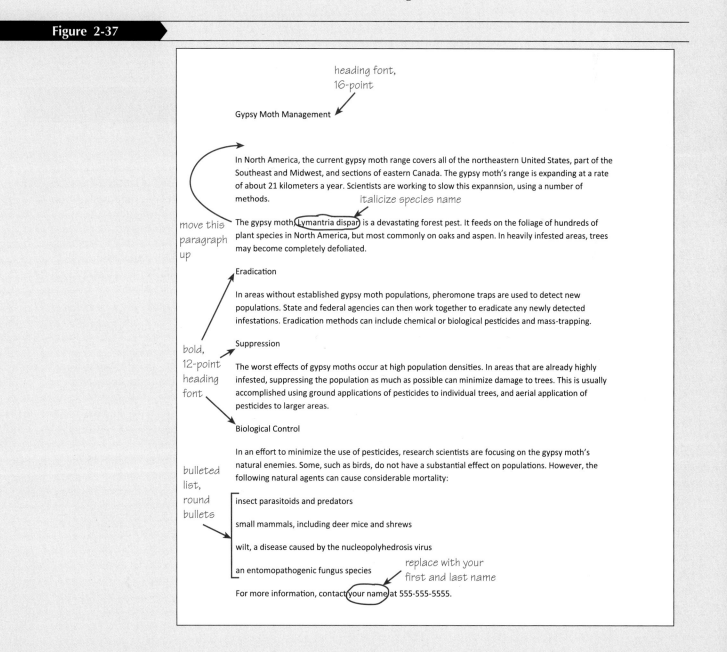

⊕ EXPLORE

4. Use the ruler to indent a paragraph, as follows:
    a. Make sure the horizontal ruler is displayed and the document is in Print Layout view.
    b. Click anywhere in the paragraph below the heading "Eradication."
    c. Position the pointer on the small gray rectangle on the ruler at the left margin (the rectangle is below the two triangles). A ScreenTip with the words "Left Indent" appears.
    d. Press and hold down the mouse button. A vertical dotted line appears in the document window, indicating the current left margin. Drag the Left Indent marker right to the 0.5-inch mark on the ruler, and then release the mouse button.

5. Use the Format Painter to copy the indent to the paragraph below the heading "Suppression" and the heading "Biological Control."

6. Indent the bulleted list so it aligns below the preceding paragraph.

7. Use the Spelling and Grammar checker to make corrections as needed, proofread for additional errors, save, and preview the document.

8. Print the document, and then close it. Submit the finished document to your instructor, either in printed or electronic form, as requested.

Challenge | Case Problem 3

Expand your formatting skills to create a resume for an aspiring sales representative.

Data File needed for this Case Problem: Resume.docx

Educational Publishing Elena Pelliterri has over a decade of experience in education. She worked as a writing teacher and then as a college supervisor of student teachers. Now she would like to pursue a career as a sales representative for a company that publishes textbooks and other educational materials. She has asked you to edit and format her resume. Complete the resume by completing the following steps.

1. Open the file **Resume** located in the Tutorial.02\Case3 folder included with your Data Files, and then check your screen to make sure your settings match those in the tutorial.

2. Save the file as **Elena Resume** in the same folder.

3. Search for the text "your name", and replace it with your first and last name.

4. Replace all occurrences of "Aroyo" with "Arroyo."

5. Use the Spelling and Grammar checker to correct any errors in the document. Note that this document contains lines that the Spelling and Grammar checker might consider sentence fragments but that are acceptable in a resume.

6. Delete the word "traveling" from the sentence below the "OBJECTIVE" heading.

7. Change the document theme to Metro.

8. Format the resume as described in Figure 2-38. Use the Format Painter to copy formatting as necessary.

Figure 2-38

Resume Element	Format
Name "Elena Pelliterri"	16-point, heading font, bold, with underline
Address, phone number, and e-mail address	14-point, heading font, bold
Uppercase headings (OBJECTIVE, EXPERIENCE, etc.)	11-point, heading font, bold
Two subheadings below EXPERIENCE, which begin "Rio Mesa College..." and "Middleton Public Schools..."	11-point, heading font, bold, italic
Lists of teaching experience, educational history, and so on, below the resume headings and subheadings	Bulleted list with square bullets

9. Reorder the two items under the "COMPUTER SKILLS" heading so that the second item becomes the first.

EXPLORE 10. Open a new, blank document, type some text, and experiment with the Change Case button in the Font group on the Home tab. Close the document without saving it, and then change the name "Elena Pelliterri" at the top of the resume to all uppercase.

11. Save, preview, and print the document.

EXPLORE 12. Experiment with two special paragraph alignment options: first line and hanging.

   a. Save the document as **Alignment Samples**. Make sure the horizontal ruler is displayed and the document is in Print Layout view.

   b. Select the two bulleted items under the subheading "Middleton Public Schools." Click the Bullets button to remove the bulleted list format.

   c. With the paragraphs still selected, locate the alignment markers on the left side of the horizontal ruler. Position the pointer over the bottom, triangle-shaped alignment marker. A ScreenTip with the words "Hanging Indent" appears. (If you see a different ScreenTip, such as "Left Indent," you don't have the pointer positioned properly.)

   d. Press and hold down the mouse button. A vertical dotted line appears in the document window, indicating the current left margin. Drag the Hanging Indent marker right to the 1-inch mark on the ruler, and then release the mouse button.

   e. Select the two bulleted items under the heading "Educational History" and remove the bulleted list formatting. Position the mouse pointer over the top, triangle-shaped alignment marker until you see the ScreenTip "First Line Indent." Drag the First Line Indent marker right to the 1-inch mark on the ruler, and then release the mouse button.

13. Save, preview, and print the document.

14. Close the document. Close any other open documents. Submit the finished documents to your instructor, either in printed or electronic form, as requested.

Challenge | **Case Problem 4**

Explore new ways to format an order form for a baking supply company.

Data File needed for this Case Problem: Flour.docx

McElmeel Baking Supply Melissa Martinez is the sales manager for McElmeel Baking Supply, a wholesale distributor of gourmet baking ingredients based in Ames, Iowa. The company is currently offering a special on flour. Melissa has started work on an order form that explains the special offer. She plans to include the form with each invoice sent out next month. It's your job to format the order form to make it easy to use.

1. Open the file **Flour** located in Tutorial.02\Case4 folder included with your Data Files, and save the file as **Flour Form** in the same folder.

⊕ EXPLORE

2. When you type Web addresses or e-mail addresses in a document, Word formats them as links. When you click a Web address formatted as a link, Windows opens a Web browser (such as Microsoft Internet Explorer) and, if your computer is connected to the Internet, displays that Web page. Likewise, Word recognizes text that looks like an e-mail address, and formats such text as links as well. If you click an e-mail address formatted as a link, Windows opens a program in which you can type an e-mail message. The address you clicked is included, by default, as the recipient of the e-mail. You'll see how this works as you add a Web address and e-mail address to the order form. At the top of the document, click at the end of the company name, add a new line, and then type the address for the company's Web site: **www.McElmeelBaking.course.com**. (The company is fictitious and does not really have a Web site.) When you are finished, press the Enter key. Word formats the address in blue with an underline, marking it as a link. Move the mouse pointer over the link and read the ScreenTip.

⊕ EXPLORE

3. In the line below the Web address, type **McElmeel_Baking@course.com** and then press the Enter key. Word formats the e-mail address as a link. Press and hold the Ctrl key and then click the e-mail link. Your default e-mail program opens, displaying a window where you could type an e-mail message to McElmeel Baking Supply. (If your computer is not set up for email, close any error messages or wizard dialog boxes that open.) Close the e-mail window without saving any changes. The e-mail link is now formatted in a color other than blue, indicating that the link has been clicked.

⊕ EXPLORE

4. Right-click the Web site address, and then click Remove Hyperlink in the shortcut menu. Do the same for the e-mail address. The links are now formatted as ordinary text.

5. Delete the phrase "regular clients," and replace it with "loyal customers."

6. Use the Margins menu to change the top and bottom margins to 1 inch and the left and right margins to 2 inches.

7. Format the entire document in the Arial font.

8. At the top of the document, center and single space the company name, Web address, and e-mail address. Remove extra paragraph spacing from all three paragraphs.

9. Change the font size for the company name at the top of the document to 16 points.

10. Near the middle of the document, bold and single space the company address. Remove extra paragraph spacing from all three paragraphs.

11. Format the blank ruled lines at the bottom of the order form as a numbered list.

12. Insert your name in the form to the right of "Name:".

⊕ EXPLORE

13. Save your work and preview the document. Click the One Page button on the Print Preview tab to view the entire document on the screen at one time. Print the document and then close the Print Preview window.

⊕EXPLORE

14. The Words box in the bottom, left-hand corner of the document window shows you the number of words in a document. To see more useful statistics, you can use the Word Count dialog box. Click the Words box in the lower-left corner of the document window to open the Word Count dialog box. Note the number of characters (not including spaces), paragraphs, and lines in the document, and then write these statistics in the upper-right corner of the printout. Close the Word Count dialog box.

15. Save and close the document. Submit the finished document to your instructor, either in printed or electronic form, as requested.

Research | Internet Assignments

Go to the Web to find information you can use to create documents.

The purpose of the Internet Assignments is to challenge you to find information on the Internet that you can use to work effectively with this software. The actual assignments are updated and maintained on the Course Technology Web site. Log on to the Internet and use your Web browser to go to the Student Online Companion for New Perspectives Office 2007 at **www.course.com/np/office2007**. Then navigate to the Internet Assignments for this tutorial.

Assess | SAM Assessment and Training

If you have a SAM user profile, you may have access to hands-on instruction, practice, and assessment of the skills covered in this tutorial. Log in to your SAM account (**http://sam2007.course.com**) to launch any assigned training activities or exams that relate to the skills covered in this tutorial.

Review | Quick Check Answers

Session 2.1

1. True
2. True
3. Select the text you want to move. Press and hold down the mouse button until the drag-and-drop pointer appears, and then drag the selected text to its new location. Use the dotted insertion point as a guide to determine exactly where the text will be inserted. Release the mouse button to drop the text at the insertion point.
4. Select the text you want to cut, and then click the Cut button in the Clipboard group on the Home tab. Move the insertion point to the target location in the document, and then click the Paste button in the Clipboard group on the Home tab.
5. Click the Find button in the Editing group on the Home tab.
6. Select the Match case check box.

Session 2.2

1. alignment
2. Click the Increase Indent button in the Paragraph group on the Home tab.
3. Move the insertion point to the paragraph whose formatting you want to copy, double-click the Format Painter button, and then click each paragraph you want to format. When you are finished, click the Format Painter button again to deselect it.
4. A gallery of numbered list styles. To display it (along with other numbered list options), click the Numbering button arrow in the Paragraph group on the Home tab.
5. A theme controls the variety of fonts, colors, and other visual effects available to you as you format a document. Each theme is designed to provide a coordinated, harmonious-looking document.
6. Select the text you want to change. Click the Font arrow in the Font group to display the list of fonts. Move the mouse pointer over the list of font names and observe a preview of the fonts in the selected text. Click the font you want to use.
7. They are the heading and body fonts for the document's theme. They are really instructions that tell Word to use the heading and body fonts for the currently selected theme.

Ending Data Files

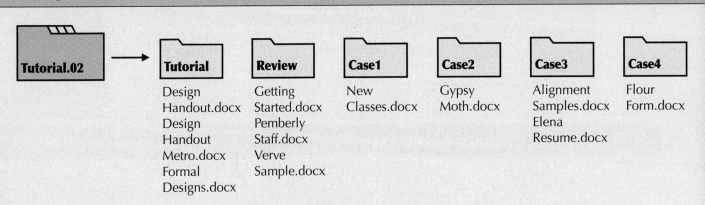

Tutorial.02 →

Tutorial
Design Handout.docx
Design Handout Metro.docx
Formal Designs.docx

Review
Getting Started.docx
Pemberly Staff.docx
Verve Sample.docx

Case1
New Classes.docx

Case2
Gypsy Moth.docx

Case3
Alignment Samples.docx
Elena Resume.docx

Case4
Flour Form.docx

Objectives

Session 3.1
- Format headings with Quick Styles
- Insert a manual page break
- Create and edit a table
- Sort rows in a table
- Modify a table's structure
- Format a table

Session 3.2
- Set tab stops
- Create footnotes and endnotes
- Divide a document into sections
- Create a SmartArt graphic
- Create headers and footers
- Insert a cover page

Creating a Multiple-Page Report

Writing a Recommendation

Case | Parkside Housing Coalition

Robin Kinsella is the director of Parkside Housing Coalition, a nonprofit organization that provides low-cost rental housing in Evanston, Illinois, at more than 50 properties it owns and manages in the Evanston area. Robin has been investigating a plan to reduce utility bills for Parkside residents through a process known as an energy audit. Robin has written a multiple-page report for the board of directors at Parkside Housing Coalition summarizing basic information about energy audits. It's your job to finish formatting the report. She also needs some help adding a table to the end of the report.

In this tutorial, you will format headings with Quick Styles and insert a manual page break. Then you will insert a table, select all or part of a table, sort a table's rows, insert and delete rows or columns, change column widths, and format a table to improve its appearance. You will also set tab stops, create footnotes and endnotes, and insert a section break. Finally, you will create a SmartArt graphic, add headers and footers, and insert a cover page.

Starting Data Files

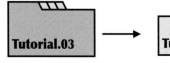 **Tutorial.03** →

 Tutorial
Audit.docx

 Review
Class.docx

 Case1
Textiles.docx

 Case2
WiFi.docx

 Case3
Clients.docx
Expenses.docx

 Case4
(none)

Session 3.1

Planning the Document

Robin saved her draft of the report as a Word document named Audit. In its current form, the report is two pages long. By the time you are finished, it will be five pages long, containing a title page, a table, and an illustration, each on a separate page. Figure 3-1 illustrates the revisions you'll be making to the report.

Figure 3-1	Revisions planned for Audit document

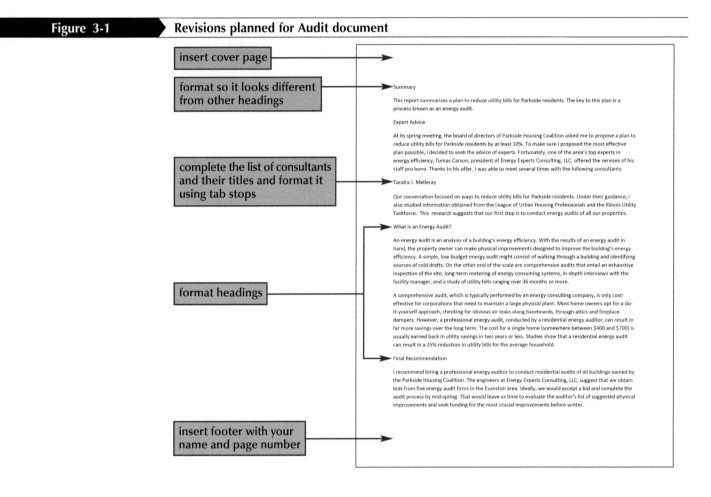

Revisions planned for Audit document (page 2) ◀ **Figure 3-1 (cont.)**

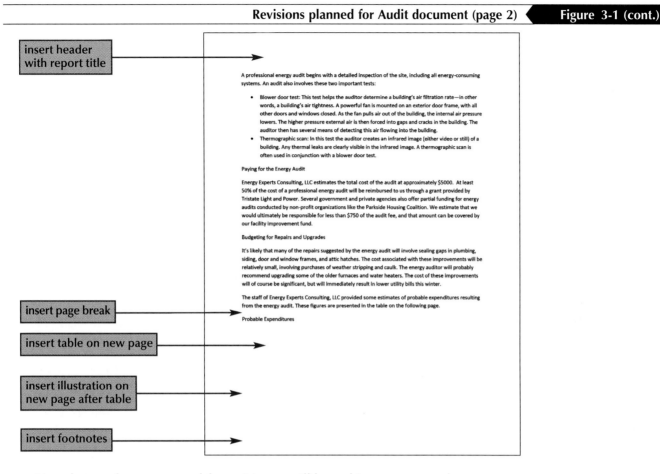

Now that you have a sense of the revisions you'll be making, you are ready to get started.

To open the document:

▶ **1.** Start Word, and then open the file **Audit** located in the Tutorial.03\Tutorial folder included with your Data Files.

▶ **2.** To avoid altering the original file, save the document as **Audit Report** in the same folder.

▶ **3.** Check your settings to make sure your screen matches the figures in this tutorial. In particular, be sure to display the nonprinting characters, switch to Print Layout view if necessary, display the rulers, and set the zoom so you can see the entire width of the page.

Formatting Headings with Quick Styles

Your first job is to format the headings to make them easier to distinguish from the body text. You already know how to draw attention to text by adding bold, italic, or underline formatting. You also know how to use a heading font. To give a document a really polished look, you can use **Quick Styles**, which allow you to apply an entire set of formatting choices with one click. A Quick Style typically applies many formatting options at once, such as, bold, a specific font, a specific indent setting, and a new color for the text (that is, a new **font color**).

Some Quick Styles apply **paragraph-level formatting**—that is, they are set up to format an entire paragraph (for example, adding space before and after a heading paragraph). Other Quick Styles apply **character-level formatting**—that is, they are set up to format only a few characters or words (for example, formatting a book title in italics).

The Quick Styles gallery on the Home tab gives you access to the document's Quick Styles (or just "styles," as they are sometimes called). One row of the gallery is always visible on the Home tab. When you first open a document, the visible row contains the four most commonly used Quick Styles (Normal, No Spacing, Heading 1, and Heading 2). These are all paragraph-level Quick Styles, so to use one, you place the insertion point anywhere in the paragraph you want to format, and then click one of the four visible styles. To use any other Quick Style, click the More button in the Styles group to display the entire Quick Styles gallery, and then click the Quick Style you want.

The Quick Styles that are available in a given document are controlled by the document's theme. Each theme uses the same names for its Quick Styles (starting with Normal, No Spacing, Heading 1, and Heading 2), but the formatting applied by a given Quick Style depends on the document's theme. For example, in the Office theme (the default theme for new documents), the Heading 1 style applies the Cambria font in blue. But in the Equity theme, the Heading 1 style applies the Franklin Gothic Book font in dark red.

Robin decided that the Office theme (the default) works fine for the Energy Audit document, so you'll be working with the Quick Styles that come with that theme. She would like you to apply the Intense Quote style to the Summary heading and the Heading 1 style to the other headings. As its name suggests, the Intense Quote style is useful for drawing attention to quotations from a document; however, because it indents text, it's also useful for certain types of headings. It applies paragraph-level formatting, so you need to start by moving the insertion point to the paragraph you want to format.

To format the "Summary" heading with the Intense Quote style:

▶ **1.** Click in the paragraph containing the heading **Summary** at the beginning of the document (if necessary), and then on the Home tab, locate the More button in the Styles group, as shown in Figure 3-2.

| Figure 3-2 | **Locating the More button** |

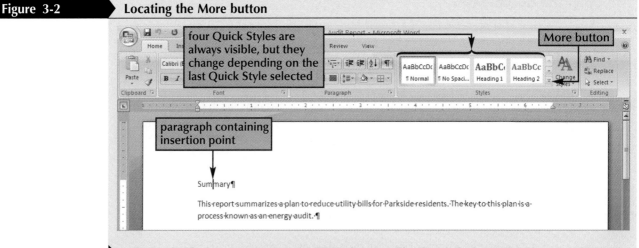

▶ **2.** In the Styles group, click the **More** button. The Quick Styles gallery opens, displaying a total of 16 possible Quick Styles.

▶ **3.** Move the mouse pointer over the styles in the Quick Styles Gallery. When you point to a style, a ScreenTip displays the style's full name, and the text in your document that contains the insertion point is formatted with a preview of that style.

4. Point to (but don't click) the **Intense Quote** style. A preview of the style appears in the document, as shown in Figure 3-3. The Intense Quote style indents text 0.5 inch, inserts a blue line below the text, changes the font color to blue, and adds bold and italic to the text. It does not change the font, which remains 11-point Calibri.

Quick Styles Gallery | **Figure 3-3**

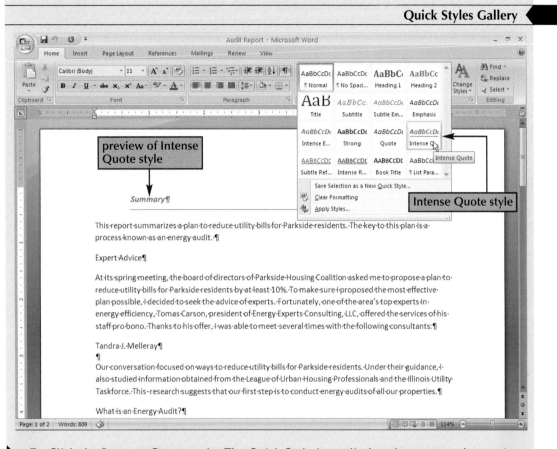

5. Click the **Intense Quote** style. The Quick Style is applied to the paragraph containing the heading "Summary." The row of buttons visible on the Ribbon is now the row containing the Intense Quote style. Next, you need to indent the summary itself so it matches the heading.

6. Click anywhere in the paragraph that begins "The report summarizes..." and then in the Paragraph group, click the **Increase Indent** button twice. (Make sure to click it twice.) The summary paragraph indents to match the "Summary" heading.

Trouble? If the summary paragraph is not indented as far as the "Summary" heading, you probably clicked the Increase Indent button just once. Try clicking it again.

Next, Robin would like you to format the remaining headings in the document with the Heading 1 style. She would also like the table heading at the end of the document to be formatted with the Heading 2 style.

To format the remaining headings with the Heading 1 style:

1. Click the heading **Expert Advice**. The Heading 1 style is no longer visible in the Styles group because when you used the Intense Quote style in the last set of steps, the default row was replaced with the row containing the button you just used. This means that you need to open the Quick Styles gallery again.

2. In the Styles group, click the **More** button, and then click the **Heading 1** style in the Quick Styles gallery. The heading is formatted in blue, 14-point Cambria, with bold. The Heading 1 style also inserts some extra space above the heading. The gallery row containing the Heading 1 style is now visible in the Styles group.

3. If necessary, scroll down, click the heading **What is an Energy Audit?**, and then press the **F4** key to apply the Heading 1 Quick Style. (Recall that the F4 key repeats your most recent action.) Continue to format these headings with the Heading 1 style: **Final Recommendation**, **Paying for the Energy Audit**, and **Budgeting for Repairs and Upgrades**.

4. At the end of the document, click the heading **Probable Expenditures** (the caption for the table that you will create later in this tutorial), and format it with the **Heading 2** Quick Style.

5. Save your work. Figure 3-4 shows two headings formatted with the Heading 1 Quick Style and one with the Heading 2 Quick Style.

Figure 3-4 | **Formatted headings**

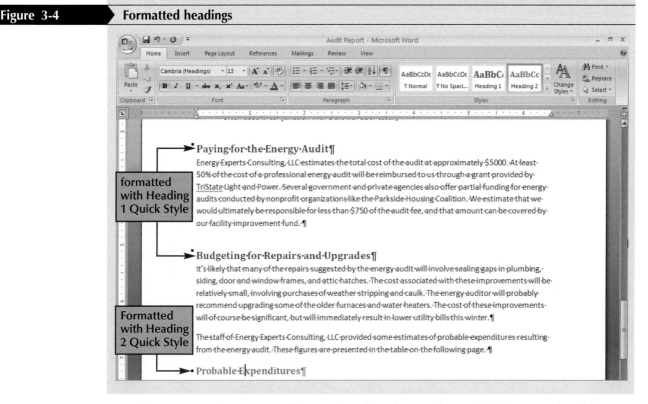

Next, you need to start working on the table of expenditures. Robin wants the table to appear on its own page (to allow plenty of room for the board of directors to make notes on it), so first you need to insert a page break.

Inserting a Manual Page Break

There are two kinds of page breaks in Word—automatic page breaks and manual page breaks. You've already seen how Word inserts automatic page breaks, by starting a new page every time the current page fills up. A **manual page break** is one you insert at a specific location; it doesn't matter if the previous page is full or not. You insert a manual page break by clicking the Page Break button on the Insert tab or by holding down the Ctrl key and pressing the Enter key. Note that the Page Break button and the Ctrl+Enter keys insert a new page *after* the insertion point. To insert a new page *before* the insertion point, use the Blank Page button (also on the Insert tab).

You need to insert a manual page break just before the table caption. This will ensure that the caption and the table are on their own page.

To insert a manual page break:

▶ **1.** If necessary, scroll down to the bottom of page 2 until you can see the table caption "Probable Expenditures," and then click to the left of the "P" in "Probable."

▶ **2.** Click the **Insert** tab, and then, in the Pages group, click the **Page Break** button. The caption "Probable Expenditures" moves to the top of the new page 3. A dotted line with the words "Page Break" is inserted on page 2, where you positioned the insertion point in Step 1.

   Trouble? If you don't see the dotted line with the words "Page Break," check to make sure your document is displayed in Print Layout view and that nonprinting characters are displayed.

You are now ready to insert the table on the new page 3, just below the table caption.

Organizing Information in Tables

A **table** is information arranged in horizontal rows and vertical columns. It's common to organize text or numerical data in a table, but you can also insert graphics, charts, and other kinds of art into tables. You can format text in various ways in different parts of a table, turning some text so it stretches vertically from top to bottom, while centering other text between the left and right margins. You can even insert one table inside another. All of these options make tables extremely useful for setting up complicated documents. You'll have a chance to explore some of the more advanced table features in the Case Problems at the end of this tutorial. Right now, you'll focus on creating the simple table Robin needs for her report. In the process, you'll gain a good understanding of how to work with tables in Word.

When you first insert a table into a document, it appears as a simple grid structure, with black **gridlines** defining the rows and columns. The area where a row and column intersect is called a **cell**. Depending on your needs, you can create a blank table and then insert information into it (as you'll do next), or you can convert existing text into a table (as you'll do in the Case Problems at the end of this tutorial).

Inserting a Blank Table

Figure 3-5 shows a sketch of what Robin wants the table to look like. The top row of the table, called the **header row**, identifies the type of information in each column. Some tables also include a **header column**, which is a column on the left that identifies the type of information in each row.

Table sketch | Figure 3-5

Item	Materials Cost
Weather stripping	$350
High-efficiency water heaters	$8,500
High-efficiency furnaces	$10,000
Insulation	$700

In the following steps, you will insert a blank table by using the Table button on the Insert tab. The Table button allows you to drag the mouse pointer across a blank grid to select the numbers of rows and columns you want to include in your table. A live preview of the table structure appears in the document as you drag the mouse pointer. The table is inserted in the document when you click the mouse button. Keep in mind that the table you insert has the same paragraph and line spacing settings as the paragraph that currently contains the insertion point.

To insert a blank table:

▶ **1.** Press the **Ctrl+End** keys to move the insertion point to the end of the document (to the blank paragraph below the heading "Probable Expenditures").

▶ **2.** Make sure the Insert tab is displayed and then, in the Tables group, click the **Table** button. A table grid opens, with a menu at the bottom.

▶ **3.** Position the pointer in the upper-left cell of the grid, and then drag the pointer down and across the grid until you highlight **two columns** and **five rows**. (The outline of a cell turns orange when it is highlighted.) As you drag the pointer across the grid, Word indicates the size of the table (columns by rows) at the top of the grid. A live preview of the table structure appears in the document. See Figure 3-6.

   Trouble? If the rows of the live preview table are spaced more widely than shown in Figure 3-6, the insertion point is located in a heading, rather than at the end of the document. Press the Esc key to close the Table grid, and begin again with Step 1, taking care to press the Ctrl+End keys as instructed.

Figure 3-6 ▶ **Inserting a blank table**

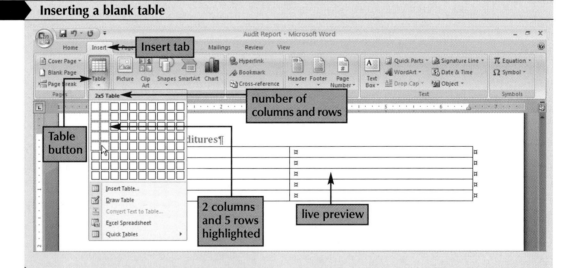

▶ **4.** When the table size is 2 × 5 (as in Figure 3-6), click the mouse button. An empty table, two columns by five rows, appears below the table caption, with the insertion point in the upper-left cell. The two columns are of equal width. Each cell contains an end-of-cell mark, and each row contains an end-of-row mark, which are important for selecting parts of a table. Two new tabs appear on the Ribbon; the label "Table Tools" identifies them as Table contextual tabs. They are visible only when the table is selected or the insertion point is located inside the table.

   Trouble? If you inserted a table with the wrong number of rows or columns, click the Undo button to remove the table, and then repeat Steps 1 through 4.

5. Move the mouse pointer over the empty table. The Table Move handle appears in the table's upper-left corner, and the Table Resize handle appears in the lower-right corner. See Figure 3-7. You don't need to use either of these handles now, but you should understand their function. To select the entire table quickly, you can click the Table Move handle. Then you can move the entire table by dragging the Table Move handle. To change the size of the entire table, you can drag the Table Resize handle.

Trouble? If you don't see the end-of-cell and end-of-row marks, you need to display nonprinting characters. Click the Show/Hide ¶ button on the Home tab.

Blank table inserted in document **Figure 3-7**

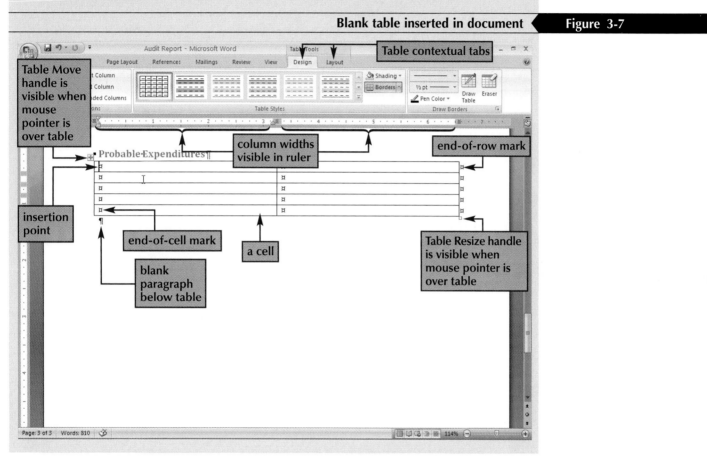

The blank table is ready for you to begin entering information. You'll do that next.

Entering Data in a Table

You can enter data in a table by moving the insertion point to a cell and typing. If the data takes up more than one line in the cell, Word automatically wraps the text to the next line and increases the height of that cell (and all the cells in that row). To move the insertion point to another cell in the table, you can click in that cell, use the arrow keys, or use the Tab key.

To enter data into the table:

1. Verify that the insertion point is located in the upper-left cell.

2. Type **Item**. As you type, the end-of-cell mark moves right to accommodate the text.

> **3.** Press the **Tab** key to move to the next cell to the right.
>
> **Trouble?** If Word created a new paragraph in the first cell rather than moving the insertion point to the second cell, you pressed the Enter key instead of the Tab key. Press the Backspace key to remove the paragraph mark, and then press the Tab key to move to the second cell in the first row.
>
> **4.** Type **Materials Cost**, and then press the **Tab** key to move to the first cell in the second row. Notice that when you press the Tab key in the right column, the insertion point moves to the first column in the next row.

You have finished entering the header row—the row that identifies the information in each column. Now you can enter the information about the various expenditures.

> **To continue entering information in the table:**
>
> **1.** Type **weather stripping**, and then press the **Tab** key to move to the second cell in the second row. Notice that the "w" in "weather stripping" is capitalized, even though you typed it in lowercase. By default, AutoCorrect capitalizes the first letter in a cell entry.
>
> **2.** Type **$350**, and then press the **Tab** key to move the insertion point to the first cell in the third row.
>
> **3.** Type the following information to complete the table, pressing the Tab key to move from cell to cell. When you are finished, your table should look like the one in Figure 3-8.
>
> | | |
> |---|---|
> | **High-efficiency water heaters** | **$8,500** |
> | **High-efficiency furnaces** | **$10,000** |
> | **Insulation** | **$700** |

Figure 3-8   Table with all data entered

• Probable·Expenditures¶		
Item¤	Materials·Cost¤	¤
Weather·stripping¤	$350¤	¤
High-efficiency·water·heaters¤	$8,500¤	¤
High-efficiency·furnaces¤	$10,000¤	¤
Insulation¤	$700¤	¤

> **Trouble?** If a new row (row 6) appears at the bottom of your table, you pressed the Tab key when the insertion point was in the last cell in the table. Click the Undo button on the Quick Access Toolbar to remove row 6 from the table.

The table you've just created presents information about expenditures in an easy-to-read structure. Your next job is to format the header row in bold so it stands out from the rest of the table. To do that, you need to know how to select a table row.

Selecting Part of a Table

As you have learned, you can select the entire table by clicking the Table Move handle (just above the upper-left corner of the table). You can also click the Select button on the Table Tools Layout tab and then click Select Table.

To select part of a table, you can drag the mouse pointer, just as you would to select regular text in a document—but that's not a good idea, because you can easily miss the end-of-cell mark in a cell or the end-of-row mark at the end of a row. This can produce unpredictable results when you are performing certain formatting or editing tasks. The most foolproof way to select part of a table is to use the Select button on the Table Tools Layout tab. A third method, which is often the most convenient, is to select a row by clicking in the left margin next to the row. Similarly, to select a column, you can click just above the column. After you've selected an entire row or column, you can drag the mouse to select more rows or columns.

You'll get some practice selecting a row in the following steps, as you format the header row in bold. Formatting the header row in bold is helpful for two reasons: (1) it makes it easier to distinguish between the header row and the rest of the data in the table; and (2) when you are using certain table commands, it allows Word to recognize the header row as a special part of the table. Later in this tutorial, you'll apply more elaborate formatting to the table.

To select and format the header row:

▶ 1. Move the mouse pointer to the left of the table next to the first row (which contains the word "Item"). The pointer changes to a right-facing arrow ⤢.

▶ 2. Click the left mouse button. The entire header row, including the end-of-cell mark in each cell and the end-of-row mark, is selected. See Figure 3-9. To format this row in bold, you could switch to the Home tab and click the Bold button or use the Mini toolbar, but it's faster to use a keyboard shortcut.

Header row selected ◀ Figure 3-9

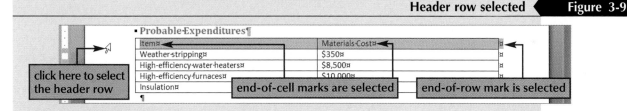

▶ 3. Press the **Ctrl+B** keys. The headers are formatted in bold.

▶ 4. Click anywhere in the table to deselect the header row, and then save your work.

You've created a very basic table. Now you can sort the information in the table and improve its appearance.

Sorting Rows in a Table

The term **sort** refers to the process of rearranging information in alphabetical, numerical, or chronological order. You can sort a series of paragraphs, such as a list or the rows of a table.

When you sort a table, you arrange the rows based on the contents of one of the columns. For example, you could sort the table you just created based on the contents of the Item column—either in ascending alphabetical order (from A to Z) or in descending alphabetical order (from Z to A). Alternately, you could sort the table based on the contents of the Materials Cost column—either in ascending numerical order (lowest to highest) or in descending numerical order (highest to lowest).

To sort a table, select the table, then, on the Table Tools Layout tab, click the Sort button. This opens the Sort dialog box, which provides a number of options that allow you to fine-tune the sorting process. You'll have to change fewer settings in the Sort dialog box if you first take the time to format the headers in bold, as you just did. That way Word recognizes the bold text as headers and excludes them from the sorting process, leaving them unsorted at the top of the table.

Reference Window | **Sorting the Rows of a Table**

- Format the column headers in bold, and then select the entire table.
- In the Data group on the Table Tools Layout tab, click the Sort button.
- In the Sort dialog box, click the Sort by arrow, and then select the header for the column you want to sort by. For example, if you want to organize the rows in the table according to the contents of the Last Name column, click "Last Name."
- In the Type list box located to the right of the Sort by list box, select the type of information stored in the column you want to sort by. You can choose to sort text, dates, or numbers.
- To sort in alphabetical, chronological, or numeric order, click the Ascending option button. To sort in reverse order, click the Descending option button.
- If you also want to sort by a second column, click the Then by arrow and click a column header. This is useful if, for example, you want to organize the table rows by last name, and then, within each last name, by first name. You can also specify the type of information in the Then by column, and whether you want to sort in ascending or descending order.
- Make sure the Header row option button is selected. This tells Word that the table you want to sort includes a header row that should not be sorted along with the other rows.
- Click the OK button.

Robin would like you to sort the table in ascending alphabetical order, based on the contents of the Item column.

To sort the information in the table:

▶ **1.** Make sure the insertion point is somewhere in the table, and then click the **Table Tools Layout** tab.

▶ **2.** In the Table group, click the **Select** button, and then click **Select Table**. The entire table is selected.

▶ **3.** In the Data group, click the **Sort** button. The Sort dialog box opens, as shown in Figure 3-10. By default, the far-left column heading ("Item") is already selected in the Sort by list box. This tells Word to sort the rows of the table according to the contents of the Item column, which is what you want. Word recognizes the information in the Item column as text, so "Text" is selected by default in the Type list box. (If the column contained dates or numbers, you would see Date or Number in the Type list box instead.) The Ascending option button next to the Sort by list box is selected by default, indicating that Word will sort the contents of the Item column from *A* to *Z*. The Header row option button is selected in the lower-left corner of the dialog box. This indicates that the table contains a header row that should not be sorted along with the rest of the rows. The default settings in the Sort dialog box are all correct, so you can go ahead and complete the sort process.

Sort dialog box ◀ Figure 3-10

▶ **4.** Click the **OK** button. The Sort dialog box closes.

▶ **5.** Click anywhere in the table to deselect it. Rows 2 through 5 are now arranged alphabetically according to the text in the Item column, with the "Weather stripping" row now at the bottom. When you sort a table, all the items in a row move together as one entity. In this table, that means the materials cost doesn't become separated from its item during the sort process. Also note that the header row remains in its original position at the top of the table. See Figure 3-11.

Trouble? If the sort was unsuccessful, click the Undo button on the Quick Access Toolbar, and then repeat Steps 1 through 5.

Table after being sorted ◀ Figure 3-11

The table looks good, but after reviewing it, Robin decides that she should include an estimate of the labor cost for each item. She asks you to insert a "Labor Cost" column.

Inserting Rows and Columns in a Table

You will often need to modify a table structure by adding or deleting rows and columns. With the buttons in the Rows & Columns group on the Table Tools Layout tab, this is a straightforward task. You'll see how these buttons work in the following steps, as you insert a new column between the Item column and the Materials Cost column. To insert a column, you begin by selecting a column to the left or right of the location where you want to insert a column.

To insert a column in the table:

1. Click any cell in the Item column, click the **Select** button in the Table group, and then click **Select Column**. The Item column is selected.

Tip

Word inserts the same number of new columns as are selected. For example, if you had selected two columns in Step 1, Word would have inserted two new columns in the table.

2. In the Rows & Columns group, click the **Insert Right** button. A new, blank column is inserted to the right of the Item column. The three columns in the table are narrower than the original two columns; the overall width of the table does not change.

3. Click in the top cell of the new column, and enter the following header and data. Use the ↓ key to move the insertion point down through the column.

Labor Cost

$3,000 to $4,500

$2,000 to $3,000

$1,000

$1,500

When you are finished, your table should look like the one in Figure 3-12. Because you selected the entire header row when you formatted the original headers in bold, the newly inserted header, "Labor Cost," is also formatted in bold.

Figure 3-12 ▶ New Labor Cost column

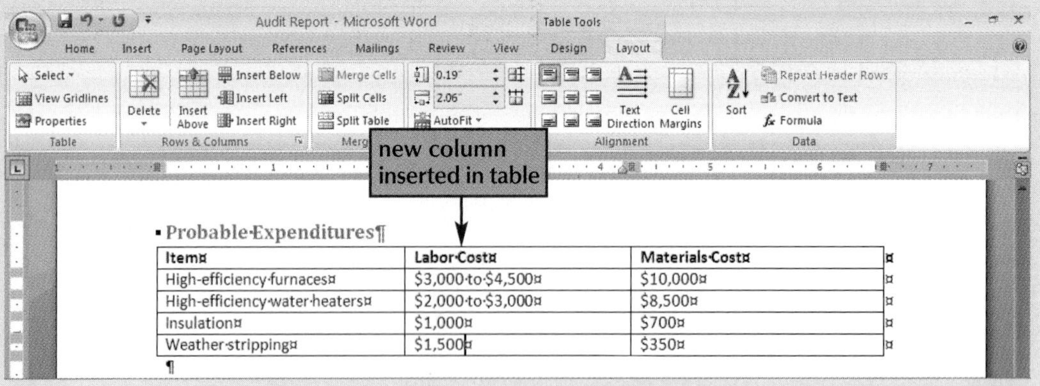

Inserting a row is similar to inserting a column. First, you select a row below the location where you want to insert a row, and then, in the Rows & Columns group, click the Insert Above button. Alternatively, you could select a row above where you want to insert a row, and then click the Insert Below button.

You're almost finished adjusting the structure of the table. But first Robin would like to delete the Insulation row because she's just learned that the costs listed for weather stripping actually cover both weather stripping and insulation.

Deleting Rows and Columns

When you consider deleting a row, you need to be clear about whether you want to delete the *contents* of the row, or the contents and the *structure* of the row. You can delete the *contents* of a row by selecting the row and pressing the Delete key. The same is true for deleting the contents of an individual cell, a column, or the entire table. To delete the *structure* of a row, column, or the entire table—including its contents—you select the row (or column or the entire table) and then use the Delete button in the Rows & Columns group. To delete multiple rows or columns, start by selecting all the rows or columns you want to delete.

Before you delete the Insulation row, you need to edit the bottom row.

To delete the Insulation row:

▶ **1.** In the cell containing the text "Weather stripping," click to the right of the "g," press the **spacebar**, and then type **and insulation**. The cell now reads "Weather stripping and insulation." Next, you can delete the Insulation row, which is no longer necessary.

▶ **2.** Select the Insulation row by clicking to the left of the row in the left margin.

▶ **3.** In the Rows & Columns group, click the **Delete** button. The Delete menu opens, displaying options for deleting cells, columns, rows, or the entire table. See Figure 3-13.

Deleting a row | **Figure 3-13**

▶ **4.** Click **Delete Rows**. The Insulation row is removed from the table.

▶ **5.** Save your work.

The table now contains all the information Robin wants to include. Your next job is to adjust the widths of the three columns to make the table attractive and easy to read.

Changing Column Widths

Columns that are too wide for the material they contain can make a table hard to read. You can quickly change a column's width by dragging the column's right border to a new position. Or, if you prefer, you can double-click a column border to make the column width adjust automatically to accommodate the widest entry in the column.

You'll adjust the columns in Robin's table by double-clicking the right column borders. You need to start by making sure that no part of the table is selected. Otherwise, when you double-click the border, only the width of the selected part of the table will change.

To change the width of the columns in the table:

▶ **1.** Verify that no part of the table is selected, and then position the mouse pointer over the right border of the Labor Cost column until the pointer changes to ◀┃▶ . See Figure 3-14.

Figure 3-14 **Changing the column width**

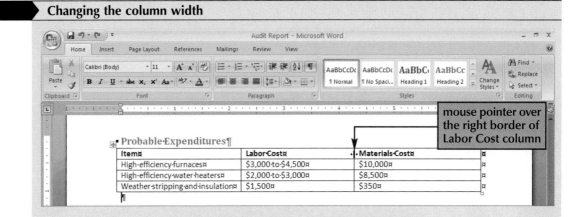

▶ **2.** Double-click the left mouse button. The right column border moves left so that the column is just wide enough to accommodate the widest entry in the column.

▶ **3.** Double-click the right border of the Materials Cost column. The Materials Cost column becomes narrower, leaving just enough room for the widest entry in the column (the column header "Materials Cost").

▶ **4.** Repeat this procedure to adjust the width of the Item column. All three columns in the table are now just wide enough to accommodate their widest entries.

Tip

To change the height of a row, position the mouse pointer over the bottom row border and drag the border up or down.

The table is almost finished. Your final job is to add some color and modify the cell borders. As you'll see in the next section, Word's predefined table styles make quick work of these tasks.

Formatting Tables with Styles

Word includes a variety of built-in table styles that you can use to add shading, color, borders, and other design elements with a single click. You can choose a style that includes different formatting for the header row than for the rest of the table. Or you can choose a style that instead applies different formatting to the **first column**, or header column (that is, the far-left column, which sometimes contains headers that identify the type of information in each row). Some styles format the rows in alternating colors, called banded rows, while others format the columns in alternating colors, called banded columns.

At first, the variety of styles available for formatting your tables may seem overwhelming, but once you become familiar with the basic variations (header row formatting, first row formatting, banded rows, banded columns, etc.), you'll grow comfortable with choosing a style that suits your needs. Six table styles are always visible in the Table Styles group on the Table Tools Design tab. To see the complete collection, click the More button in the Table Styles group. After you apply a table style, you can modify it by selecting or deselecting the check boxes in the Table Style Options group on the Table Tools Design tab.

| Formatting a Table with a Built-In Table Style | | Reference Window |

- Click in the table you want to format, and then click the Table Tools Design tab.
- In the Table Styles group, click the More button to display the Table Styles gallery.
- Position the mouse pointer over a style in the Table Styles gallery to see a live preview of the style in the document.
- In the Table Styles gallery, click the style you want.
- To apply or remove style elements (such as special formatting for the header row, banded rows, or banded columns), select or deselect check boxes as necessary in the Table Style Options group.

Robin wants to use a table style that emphasizes the header row with special formatting, that does not include column borders, and that uses color to separate the rows.

To apply a table style to the Probable Expenditures table:

▶ **1.** Click anywhere in the table, and then click the **Table Tools Design** tab. Within the six visible styles, the plain black and white grid style is highlighted, indicating that it is the current style of the table in the document. See Figure 3-15.

Table styles visible on the Table Tools Design tab ◀ Figure 3-15

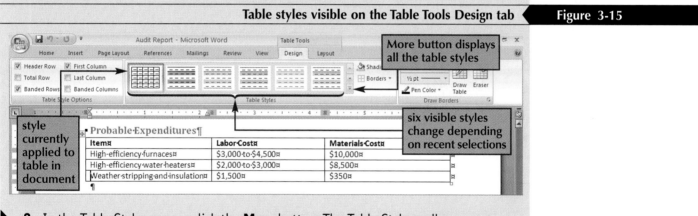

▶ **2.** In the Table Styles group, click the **More** button. The Table Styles gallery opens. Now the plain black and white grid style appears at the top of the gallery, under the heading "Plain Tables." The more elaborate Table Styles appear below, in the "Built-In" section of the gallery.

▶ **3.** Use the gallery's vertical scroll bar to view the complete collection of table styles. When you are finished looking, scroll up until you can see the Built-In heading again.

▶ **4.** Move the mouse pointer over the style located in the fourth row down, second column from the left. See Figure 3-16. A ScreenTip displays the style's official name, "Medium Shading 1 – Accent 1." The style consists of a dark blue heading row, with alternating rows of light blue and white below and no borders between the columns. A live preview of the style is visible in the document, although the size of the Table Styles gallery makes this hard to see.

Figure 3-16   Table Styles gallery

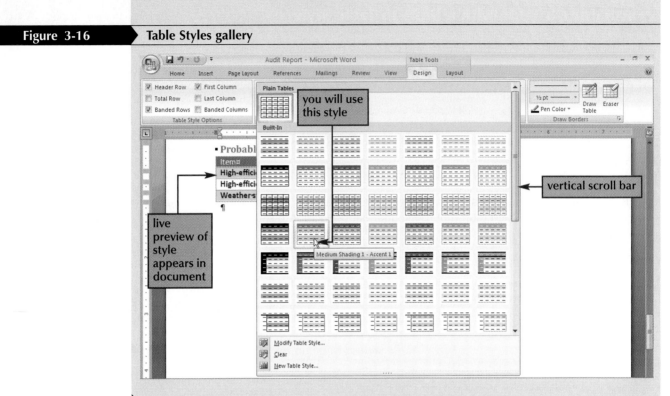

▶ **5.** Click the **Medium Shading 1 – Accent 1** style. The Table Styles gallery closes. The table's header row is formatted with dark blue shading and white text. The rows below are shaded light blue and white.

The only problem with the newly formatted table is that the text in the first column is formatted in bold. In tables where the first column contains headers, bold would be appropriate, but this isn't the case with Robin's table. You'll fix this by deselecting the First Column check box in the Table Style Options group.

To remove the bold formatting from the first column:

▶ **1.** In the Table Style Options group, click the **First Column** check box to remove the check. The bold formatting is removed from the entries in the Item column. Note that the Header Row check box is selected. This indicates that the table's header row is emphasized with special formatting (dark blue shading with white text). The Banded Rows check box is also selected because the table is formatted with banded rows of blue and white. See Figure 3-17.

Figure 3-17   Deselecting the First Column check box

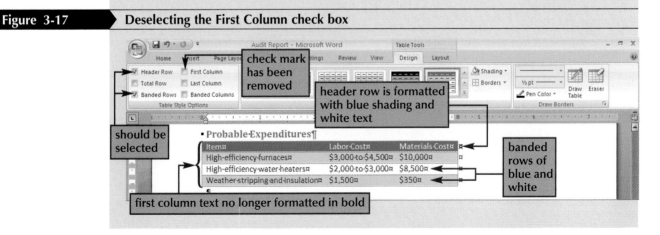

Using Table Styles vs. Manually Formatting a Table | InSight

You can create a table by formatting it "manually" with the buttons on the Table Tools Design tab. For example, you can change the thickness and color of the table borders using the options in the Draw Borders group, and you can add shading using the Shading button in the Table Styles group. However, applying formatting by clicking individual buttons is time consuming. Also, it's easy to make mistakes. For example, you might omit a necessary column border or apply color inconsistently. Instead of formatting a table manually, it's better to start with the built-in table style that most closely resembles the formatting you want. Then you can fine tune the formatting. And remember, if you don't like the selection of table styles available in your document, change the document's theme and look again at the available table styles. Each theme includes a complete set of table styles.

The completed table looks crisp and professional. In the next session, you'll turn your attention to completing the rest of the report.

Session 3.1 Quick Check | Review

1. Explain how to format a heading with a Quick Style.
2. True or False: To insert a manual page break, you can press the Ctrl+End key combination.
3. Explain how to insert a table in a document.
4. What key can you press to move the insertion point from one cell to another in a table?
5. What's the most foolproof way to select part of a table?
6. Explain how to sort a table.
7. True or False: To insert a column, you begin by selecting a column to the left or right of the location where you want to insert a column.

Session 3.2

Setting Tab Stops

A **tab stop** (often called just a **tab**) is a location on the horizontal ruler where the insertion point moves when you press the Tab key. Tab stops are useful for aligning small amounts of data in columns. There are default tab stops every one-half inch on the horizontal ruler, indicated by the small gray tick marks along the bottom edge of the ruler. When you press the Tab key, the insertion point moves to the next tab stop to the right. It's helpful to have the Show/Hide ¶ button selected when you work with tab stops, because then you can see the nonprinting tab character (→) that is inserted when you press the Tab key. A tab is just like any other character you type; you can delete it by pressing the Backspace key or the Delete key.

Text next to tab stops can be aligned in a variety of ways. The five major styles are Left, Center, Right, Decimal, and Bar, as shown in Figure 3-18. The Left style is selected by default and is probably the tab style you'll use most often.

Figure 3-18 **Tab stop alignment styles**

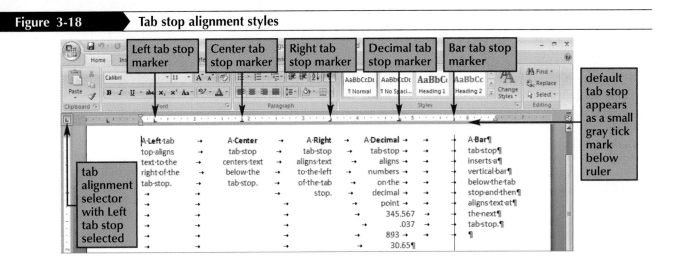

You can set tab stops a few different ways. The simplest is to first select an alignment style from the tab alignment selector, located at the left end of the horizontal ruler, and then click the horizontal ruler where you want the tab stop. When you insert a tab stop in this way, all of the default tab stops to its left are removed. This means you have to press the Tab key only once to move the insertion point to your new tab stop.

Reference Window | **Setting and Clearing Tab Stops**

- To set a tab stop, click the tab alignment selector on the far left of the horizontal ruler until the appropriate tab stop alignment style appears, and then click the horizontal ruler where you want to position the tab stop. Press the Tab key to move the insertion point to the new tab stop.
- To align text that already contains a nonprinting tab character, select the text and then insert a tab stop on the horizontal ruler.
- To remove a tab stop, locate it on the ruler, click it, and drag it off the ruler (into the document window).
- To clear all tab stops in the document or in a selected paragraph, click the Dialog Box Launcher in the Paragraph group, click the Indents and Spacing tab, click the Tabs button, and then click the Clear All button. Click the OK button to close the Tabs dialog box.

In the report, you need to type the list of consultants and their titles. As you type, you'll discover whether Word's default tab stops are appropriate for this document or whether you need to add a new tab stop.

To enter the list of consultants using tabs:

1. If you took a break after the previous session, make sure Word is running and that the Audit Report document is open. Check that the ruler and nonprinting characters are displayed and that the document is displayed in Print Layout view.

2. Scroll as necessary to display the Expert Advice section, and then click to the right of the "y" in "Tandra J. Melleray."

3. Press the **Tab** key. A tab character appears, and the insertion point moves to the first tab stop after the "y" in "Melleray." This tab stop is one of the default tabs and is located at the 1.5-inch mark on the horizontal ruler. See Figure 3-19.

Tab character ◀ **Figure 3-19**

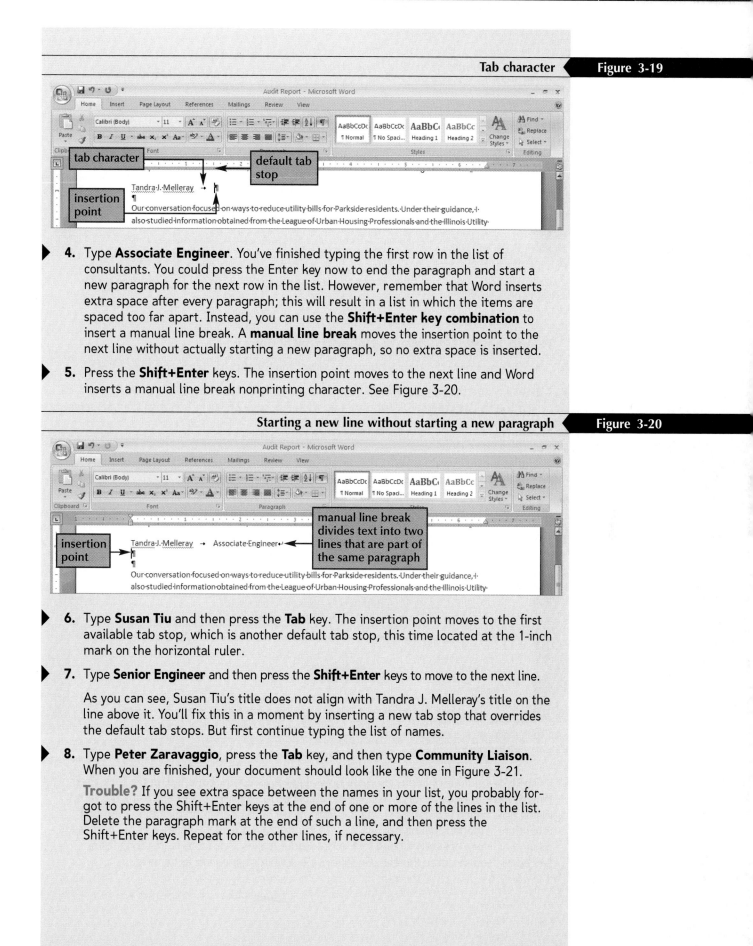

4. Type **Associate Engineer**. You've finished typing the first row in the list of consultants. You could press the Enter key now to end the paragraph and start a new paragraph for the next row in the list. However, remember that Word inserts extra space after every paragraph; this will result in a list in which the items are spaced too far apart. Instead, you can use the **Shift+Enter key combination** to insert a manual line break. A **manual line break** moves the insertion point to the next line without actually starting a new paragraph, so no extra space is inserted.

5. Press the **Shift+Enter** keys. The insertion point moves to the next line and Word inserts a manual line break nonprinting character. See Figure 3-20.

Starting a new line without starting a new paragraph ◀ **Figure 3-20**

6. Type **Susan Tiu** and then press the **Tab** key. The insertion point moves to the first available tab stop, which is another default tab stop, this time located at the 1-inch mark on the horizontal ruler.

7. Type **Senior Engineer** and then press the **Shift+Enter** keys to move to the next line.

As you can see, Susan Tiu's title does not align with Tandra J. Melleray's title on the line above it. You'll fix this in a moment by inserting a new tab stop that overrides the default tab stops. But first continue typing the list of names.

8. Type **Peter Zaravaggio**, press the **Tab** key, and then type **Community Liaison**. When you are finished, your document should look like the one in Figure 3-21.

Trouble? If you see extra space between the names in your list, you probably forgot to press the Shift+Enter keys at the end of one or more of the lines in the list. Delete the paragraph mark at the end of such a line, and then press the Shift+Enter keys. Repeat for the other lines, if necessary.

Figure 3-21 ▶ **List of consultants**

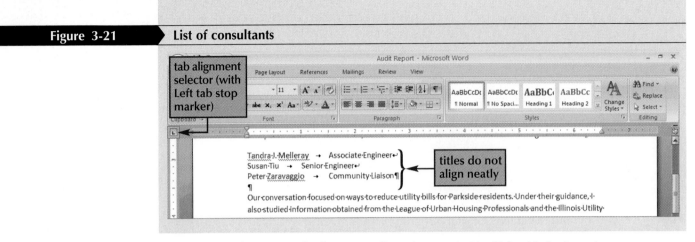

The list of names and titles is not aligned properly. You'll fix this by inserting a new tab stop.

To add a new tab stop to the horizontal ruler:

▶ **1.** Click and drag the mouse pointer to select the list of consultants and their titles.

▶ **2.** Make sure the current tab stop alignment style is Left tab ⬛, as shown in Figure 3-21. If the Left tab marker is not displayed as in Figure 3-21, click the tab alignment selector one or more times until ⬛ appears.

▶ **3.** Click the tick mark on the ruler that is at 2.5 inches. Word inserts a Left tab stop at that location and removes the default tab stops to its left. The column of titles shifts to the new tab stop.

▶ **4.** Click anywhere in the list of names and titles. See Figure 3-22.

Figure 3-22 ▶ **Titles aligned at the new tab stop**

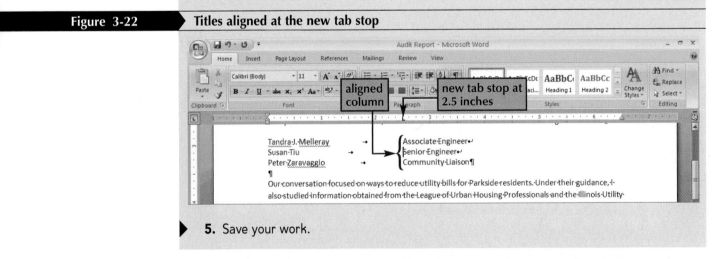

▶ **5.** Save your work.

The two columns of information are now aligned, as Robin requested. In the Case Problems at the end of this tutorial, you'll have a chance to work with tab stops using the Tabs dialog box, which you can open via the Tabs button in the Paragraph dialog box. Among other things, the Tabs dialog box allows you to insert a **dot leader**, which is a row of dots (or other characters) between tabbed text. A dot leader makes it easier to read a long list of tabbed material because the eye can follow the dots from one item to the next.

Choosing Between Tabs and Tables | InSight

What's the best way to align text in columns? It depends. Tabs work well for small amounts of information, such as two columns with three rows, but they become cumbersome when you need to organize a lot of data. For larger amounts of information, tables are better. Unlike with tabbed columns of data, it's easy to add data to tables by inserting columns. Also, you can format tables more elaborately than you can format tabbed columns.

Whatever you do, don't try to align columns of data by adding extra spaces with the spacebar. Although the text might seem precisely aligned on the screen, it might not be aligned when you print the document. Furthermore, if you edit the text, the spaces you inserted to align your columns will be affected by your edits; they get moved just like regular text, ruining your alignment. One of the main advantages of tab stops and tables is that when you edit data, the alignment remains intact.

Your next job is to add two footnotes to the document that provide further information about topics discussed in Robin's report.

Creating Footnotes and Endnotes

A **footnote** is an explanatory comment or reference that appears at the bottom of a page. When you create a footnote, Word inserts a small, superscript number (called a **reference marker**) in the text. The term "superscript" means that the number is raised slightly above the line of text. Word then inserts the same number in the page's bottom margin and positions the insertion point next to it so you can type the text of the footnote. **Endnotes** are similar, except that the text of an endnote appears at the end of a document. Also, by default, the reference marker for an endnote is a lowercase Roman numeral.

Word automatically manages the reference markers for you, keeping them sequential from the beginning of the document to the end, no matter how many times you add, delete, or move footnotes or endnotes. For example, if you move a paragraph containing footnote 4 so that it falls before the paragraph containing footnote 1, Word renumbers all the footnotes in the document to keep them sequential.

Working with Footnotes and Endnotes | Reference Window

- To create a footnote, click where you want to insert a footnote, click the References tab, in the Footnotes group click the Insert Footnote button, and then type the text of the footnote in the bottom margin.
- To create an endnote, click where you want to insert an endnote, click the References tab, in the Footnotes group click the Insert Endnote button, and then type the text of the endnote at the end of the document.
- When you are finished typing the text of a footnote or endnote, click in the body of the document to continue working on it.
- To delete a footnote or endnote, delete its reference marker (the small, superscript number) in the text.
- To edit the text of a footnote or endnote, click in the bottom margin or at the end of the document and edit the note.

Robin asks you to insert a footnote at the end of the paragraph just above the heading "Final Recommendation." The last sentence of this paragraph refers to studies on the effectiveness of residential energy audits. Robin wants a footnote that explains where more information about those studies can be found.

To add a footnote to the report:

▶ **1.** Near the bottom of page 1, locate the paragraph just above the heading "Final Recommendation."

▶ **2.** Click to the right of the period after "household" at the end of the paragraph. The insertion point is now located at the end of the paragraph, where you want the footnote.

▶ **3.** Click the **References** tab, and then in the Footnotes group, click the **Insert Footnote** button. A superscript "1" is inserted to the right of the period after "household." Word also inserts the number "1" in the bottom margin below a separator line. The insertion point is now located next to the number in the bottom margin, ready for you to type the text of the footnote. See Figure 3-23.

| Figure 3-23 | Inserting a footnote |

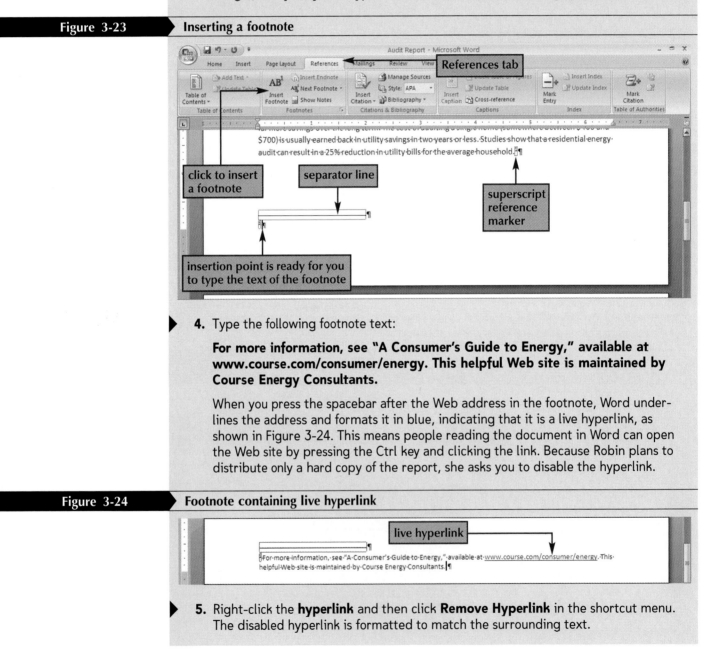

▶ **4.** Type the following footnote text:

For more information, see "A Consumer's Guide to Energy," available at www.course.com/consumer/energy. This helpful Web site is maintained by Course Energy Consultants.

When you press the spacebar after the Web address in the footnote, Word underlines the address and formats it in blue, indicating that it is a live hyperlink, as shown in Figure 3-24. This means people reading the document in Word can open the Web site by pressing the Ctrl key and clicking the link. Because Robin plans to distribute only a hard copy of the report, she asks you to disable the hyperlink.

| Figure 3-24 | Footnote containing live hyperlink |

▶ **5.** Right-click the **hyperlink** and then click **Remove Hyperlink** in the shortcut menu. The disabled hyperlink is formatted to match the surrounding text.

The first footnote is complete. Robin would like you to insert a second footnote explaining more about the cost of a typical residential home energy audit. You start by clicking the location in the main document where you want to insert the footnote's reference marker.

To insert a second footnote:

▶ **1.** In the same paragraph (the paragraph above the heading "Final Recommenda-tion"), locate the second to last sentence, which begins "The cost of auditing a single home..." and then click at the end of the sentence. The insertion point should be positioned to the right of the period after "less."

▶ **2.** In the Footnotes group, click the **Insert Footnote** button. Because this footnote is placed earlier in the document than the one you just created, Word inserts a super-script "1" for this footnote, and the other footnote is now numbered "2." See Figure 3-25.

Inserting a second footnote ◀ **Figure 3-25**

> far more savings over the long term. The cost of auditing a single home (somewhere between $400 and $700) is usually earned back in utility savings in two years or less. Studies show that a residential energy audit can result in a 25% reduction in utility bills for the average household.
>
> new footnote is number 1
>
> old footnote changed to 2
>
> For more information, see "A Consumer's Guide to Energy," available at www.course.com/consumer/energy. This helpful Web site is maintained by Course Energy Consultants.

▶ **3.** Type the following footnote text:

   While cost varies by auditor, the price of an audit is usually based on a home's square footage.

▶ **4.** Zoom out so you can see the entire page, with the footnotes at the bottom. Note that to make room for the two footnotes, the "Final Recommendation" heading and the paragraph that follows it were moved to the next page. One of the advantages of using Word's heading styles (such as the Heading 1 Quick Style you applied earlier) is that they tell Word to keep the heading and the paragraph that follows it together.

▶ **5.** Zoom back in so you can read the document, and then save your work.

The footnotes will provide helpful information for the board of directors. Next, Robin wants to include a sample of the type of handout she plans to post on community bulle-tin boards at Parkside, encouraging residents to take part in the energy audit process. Before you can create the handout, you need to divide the document into sections.

Formatting a Document in Sections

Robin wants to format the handout in **landscape orientation**—that is, with the page turned so it is wider than it is tall. The rest of the report is currently formatted in **portrait orientation** (with the page taller than it is wide), which is the default orientation for all Word documents and is appropriate for a report. To format part of a document in an orientation different from the rest of the document, you need to divide the document into sections.

A **section** is a part of a document that can have its own page orientation, margins, headers, footers, and so on. Each section, in other words, is like a document within a document. To divide a document into sections, you insert a **section break**, which appears as a dotted line with the words "Section Break." When you insert a section break, you can choose to have the section start a new page (a Next Page section break) or have the section start at the location of the insertion point, without changing the page flow (a Continuous section break). You insert section breaks with the Breaks button on the Page Layout tab.

To insert a section break below the table:

▶ 1. Press the **Ctrl+End** keys to move the insertion point to the end of the document (to the blank paragraph below the table).

▶ 2. Click the **Page Layout** tab, and then, in the Page Setup group, click the **Breaks** button. The Breaks menu opens, as shown in Figure 3-26. The Page Breaks part of the menu includes options for controlling how the text flows from page to page. The first option, Page, inserts a page break (just like the Page Break button on the Insert tab that you used earlier). The Section Breaks part of the menu includes four types of section breaks. The two you'll use most often are Next Page, which starts a section on a new page, and Continuous, which starts a new section at the location of the insertion point, without starting a new page.

Figure 3-26 ▶ Breaks menu

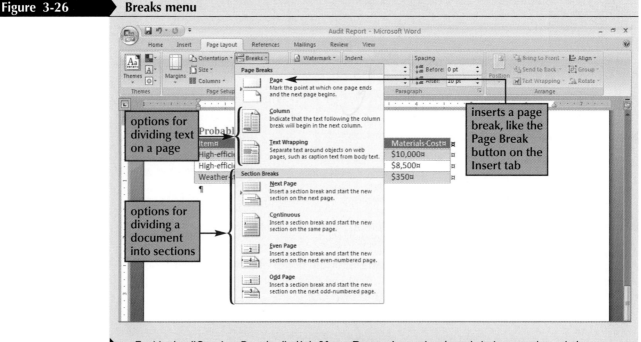

▶ 3. Under "Section Breaks," click **Next Page**. A section break is inserted, and the insertion point moves to the top of the newly inserted page.

▶ **4.** Scroll up until you can see the double-dotted line and the words "Section Break (Next Page)" below the table. This line indicates that a new section begins on the next page.

Trouble? If you see a single dotted line and the words "Page Break," you inserted a page break rather than a Next Page section break. Click the Undo button on the Quick Access Toolbar, and then repeat Steps 1 through 4.

▶ **5.** Save your work.

Tip

To delete a section break, click the line representing the break, and then press the Delete key.

You've created a new page that is a separate section from the rest of the report. The sections are numbered consecutively, so that the first part of the document is section 1 and the new page is section 2. Now you can format section 2 in landscape orientation without affecting the rest of the document.

To format section 2 in landscape orientation:

▶ **1.** Scroll down if necessary and verify that the insertion point is positioned at the top of the new page 4.

▶ **2.** Change the zoom setting to 50% (this will allow you to see clearly the page orientation change in the next steps), and then scroll down, if necessary, so you can see the page containing the table and the new page 4, which is blank.

▶ **3.** In the Page Setup group, click the **Orientation** button. The Orientation menu opens.

▶ **4.** Click **Landscape**. Section 2, which consists solely of page 4, changes to landscape orientation, as shown in Figure 3-27. Section 1, which consists of pages 1–3, remains in portrait orientation.

Page 4 formatted in landscape orientation ◀ **Figure 3-27**

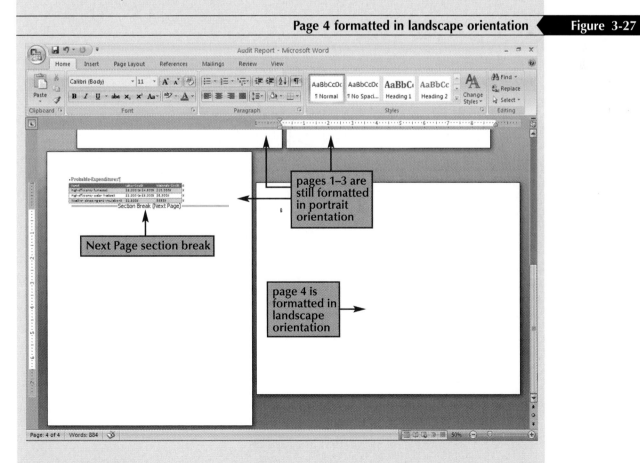

> **5.** Zoom back in so you can read the document text, and then save your work.

Page 4 is now formatted in landscape orientation, ready for you to create Robin's handout, which will consist of an illustration, or **graphic**, that explains the stages and ultimate goal of the energy audit process. With Word's SmartArt feature, you can quickly create great looking illustrations for a wide variety of purposes.

Creating SmartArt

The **SmartArt** feature allows you to create diagrams and charts to illustrate concepts that would otherwise require several paragraphs of explanation. To begin creating a SmartArt graphic, you switch to the Insert tab and then, in the Illustrations group, click the SmartArt button. This opens the Choose a SmartArt Graphic dialog box, where you can select from seven categories of graphics, including graphics designed to illustrate relationships, processes, and hierarchies. Within each category, you can then choose from numerous designs. Once inserted into your document, a SmartArt graphic contains placeholder text that you replace with something appropriate for your needs. When a SmartArt graphic is selected, the SmartArt tools appear on the Ribbon, with two tabs of editing options. In the following steps, you will begin creating a SmartArt graphic that summarizes the energy audit process.

To create a SmartArt graphic:

> **1.** Verify that the insertion point is located at the top of page 4, which is blank.

> **2.** Click the **Insert** tab, and then, in the Illustrations group, click the **SmartArt** button. The Choose a SmartArt Graphic dialog box opens. This dialog box consists of three panels. The left panel lists the categories of SmartArt Graphics; the middle panel displays the graphics associated with the category selected in the left panel; and the right panel displays a larger image of the graphic that is currently selected in the middle panel, along with an explanation of the graphic's purpose. Currently, All is selected in the left panel. This means you could use the scroll bar in the middle panel to see all of the possible SmartArt graphics.

> **3.** Explore the Choose a SmartArt Graphic dialog box by selecting categories in the left panel and viewing the graphics displayed in the middle panel.

> **4.** In the left panel, click **Relationship**, and then, in the middle panel, click the **Equation** graphic (in the far-left column, fifth row from the top), which shows three circles in an equation. In the right panel, you see an explanation of the Equation graphic, as shown in Figure 3-28.

Tip

To see a detailed view of a graphic, click that graphic in the middle panel and view the details that appear in the right panel.

Selecting a SmartArt graphic ◄ **Figure 3-28**

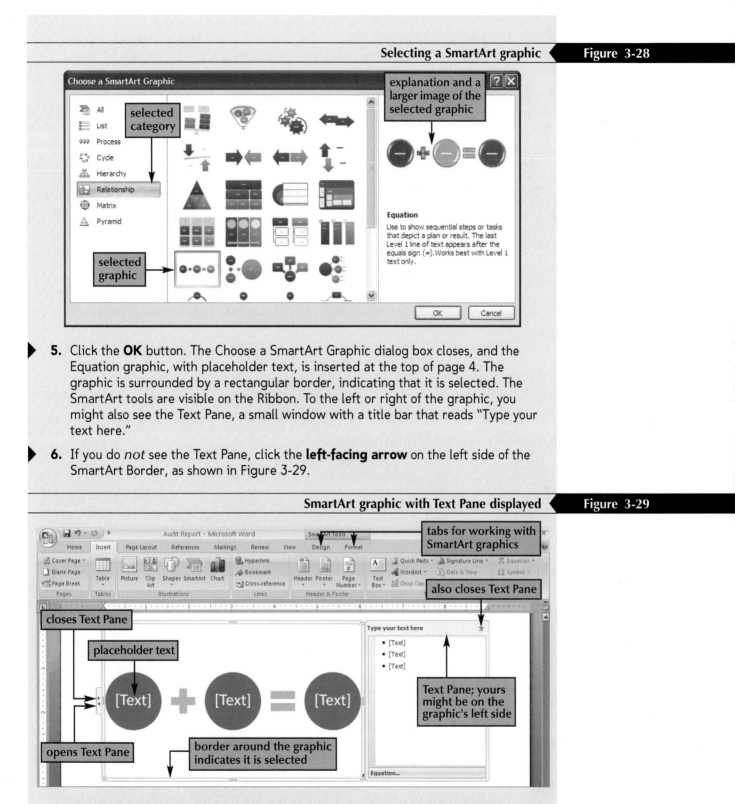

5. Click the **OK** button. The Choose a SmartArt Graphic dialog box closes, and the Equation graphic, with placeholder text, is inserted at the top of page 4. The graphic is surrounded by a rectangular border, indicating that it is selected. The SmartArt tools are visible on the Ribbon. To the left or right of the graphic, you might also see the Text Pane, a small window with a title bar that reads "Type your text here."

6. If you do *not* see the Text Pane, click the **left-facing arrow** on the left side of the SmartArt Border, as shown in Figure 3-29.

SmartArt graphic with Text Pane displayed ◄ **Figure 3-29**

The Text Pane is useful for complicated graphics containing many parts. However, the Equation graphic is simple enough that you can type the text directly in the circles, so you will close the Text Pane in the next step.

Trouble? If you inserted a graphic other than the equation graphic, click the Undo button on the Quick Access Toolbar and start again with Step 1.

Trouble? If you see other elements in your SmartArt graphic, such as a square border around one of the blue circles, or if you see the insertion point blinking inside the Text Pane, don't be concerned. Just continue with the steps.

▶ **7.** Click the **Close** button ⓧ in the upper-right corner of the Text Pane (shown in Figure 3-29). You will type the text directly into the circles.

Now you are ready to begin typing text in the graphic.

To add text to the SmartArt graphic:

▶ **1.** In the blue circle on the left, click the placeholder text (which reads "[Text]"). The placeholder text disappears and the insertion point blinks inside the left circle. (The insertion point might be hard to see on the dark blue background.) The left circle is surrounded by a box consisting of a dotted line, with small white circles on the corners and a small white square in the middle of each side. This box indicates that the blue circle is selected, ready for you to replace the placeholder text with your text. The circles and squares along the border of the box are called **handles**; you can drag them to change the shape of the item inside the box. You'll learn more about dragging handles to change the shape of a graphic in Tutorial 4. For now, you can ignore them. See Figure 3-30.

Trouble? If the circle is selected, but the placeholder text is still visible, you clicked the circle, but not the placeholder text within the circle. Repeat Step 1, but take care to click the placeholder text.

Figure 3-30 ▶ **Entering text in the SmartArt graphic**

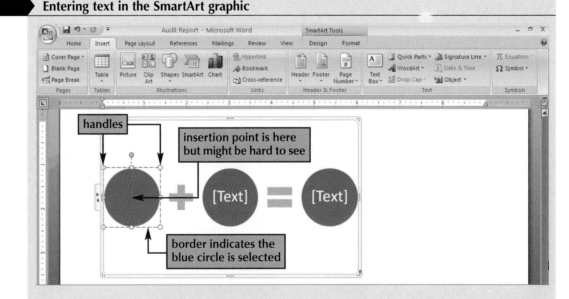

▶ **2.** Type **Energy Audit**. The font size gets smaller as you type, shrinking to accommodate each new letter without increasing the size of the circle.

▶ **3.** Click the placeholder text in the middle circle, type **Repairs and Upgrades**, click the **right circle** to select it, and type **Lower Utility Bills**. The right circle remains selected.

Trouble? If you make a typing mistake, click the circle containing the error and edit the text as you would ordinary text, using the Backspace or Delete keys as necessary.

▶ **4.** Click in the white area inside the SmartArt border to deselect the right circle. The equation now reads "Energy Audit + Repairs and Upgrades = Lower Utility Bills."

The graphic is almost finished. Your last task is to increase its size so it fills the page. To resize the entire SmartArt graphic, you drag the outer border.

To adjust the size of the SmartArt graphic:

▶ **1.** Zoom out so you can see the entire page.

▶ **2.** Position the mouse pointer over the lower-right corner of the SmartArt border. The pointer changes to a diagonal, double-sided arrow ⤡. As you can see on the ruler, the SmartArt border is currently about six inches wide. See Figure 3-31.

Mouse pointer on SmartArt border ◀ **Figure 3-31**

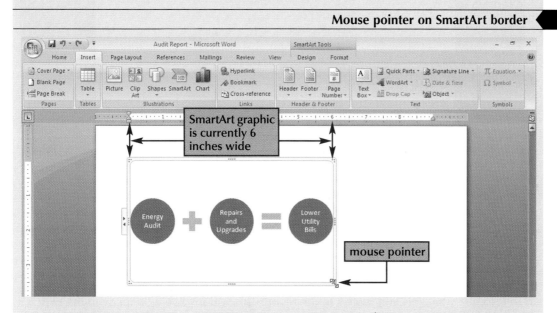

Trouble? If the pointer changes to a four-sided arrow ✥, you haven't positioned the pointer correctly over the lower-right corner. Reposition the pointer until it changes to a diagonal, double-sided arrow, as shown in Figure 3-31.

▶ **3.** Drag the pointer down and to the right. As you drag, the pointer changes to a crosshair ╋. A rectangular outline moves with the pointer, showing how the dimensions of the SmartArt border will appear when you release the mouse button. The size of the graphic won't actually change until you release the mouse button.

Trouble? If the graphic changes size, you released the mouse button too early. Undo the change, and begin again with Step 2.

▶ **4.** Position the pointer in the lower-right corner of the page, so the outline is approximately 9 inches wide and 6.5 inches high, but do *not* release the mouse button yet. Compare your screen to Figure 3-32 to make sure you have the pointer in the correct location.

Figure 3-32 | **Dragging the SmartArt border**

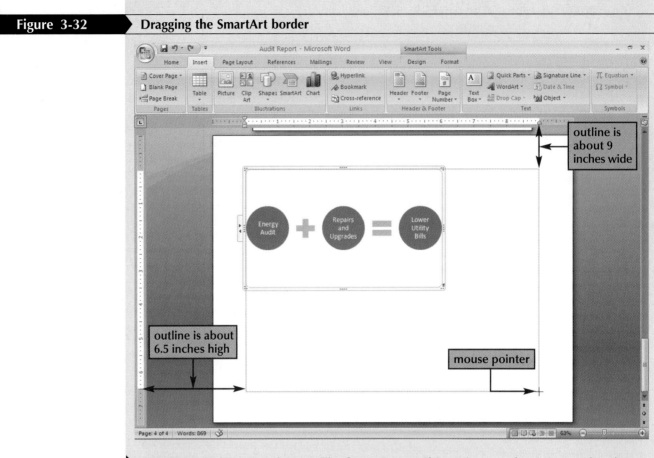

▶ **5.** Release the mouse button. The SmartArt graphic resizes, so that it is now 9 inches wide and 6.5 inches high, taking up most of the page.

▶ **6.** Click outside the SmartArt border to view the graphic centered on the page.

The SmartArt graphic is eye-catching and succinctly explains the goal of the energy audit. Robin will add a heading and some text introducing the graphic later. Your next job is to insert headers and footers in the report. This will involve working with the two sections separately.

Adding Headers and Footers

Text that is printed at the top of every page is called a **header**. For example, the information printed at the top of this textbook page is a header. A **footer** is text that is printed at the bottom of every page.

There are two ways to begin inserting a header or footer: (1) you can double-click in the header area (in a page's top margin) or in the footer area (in a page's bottom margin); or (2) you can click the Header button or the Footer button on the Insert tab. Either way, the document switches to **Header and Footer view**, with special tools related to working with headers and footers displayed on the Ribbon. In Header and Footer view, the document text is dimmed, indicating that it cannot be edited while you are in this view.

Some headers and footers also include **document controls**, which are similar to the kinds of controls (text boxes, list boxes, etc.) that you might encounter in a dialog box. Most of the document controls you'll see in headers and footers are text boxes, where you can enter important information such as the document title or the name of the document's author. Any information that you enter in a document control is displayed in the header or footer as ordinary text, but it is also stored in the Word file so that Word can easily reuse it in other parts of the document. For example, later in this tutorial you will create a cover page for the report. Word's predefined cover pages include document controls similar to those found in headers and footers. So if you use a document control to enter the document title in the header, that same document title will show up in the cover page; there's no need to retype it. You'll see how this works shortly.

Two Ways to Insert a Header or Footer | InSight

Double-clicking in the top or bottom margin is the simplest way to begin inserting a header or footer. After Word switches to Header and Footer view, you type the text of the header or footer. Three default tab stops allow you to left-align, center, or right-align the text in the header or footer. Many documents require page numbers; you can use the Page Number button on the Insert tab to insert the page number, which Word updates as you add and delete pages from your document.

For a more elaborate header or footer, use the Header and Footer buttons on the Insert tab. These buttons open menus that you can use to select from a number of predefined headers and footers, some of which include page numbers and graphic elements such as horizontal lines or shaded boxes.

You'll create a footer for the whole document (pages 1 through 4) that includes the page number and your name. You'll also create a header for section 1 (pages 1 through 3) that includes the document title and the date. When creating a header or footer for an entire document, you can work in the header or footer area for any page in the document. In the following steps, you'll start on page 1, so you can see how the footer fits below the footnotes at the bottom of the page.

To create a footer for the entire document:

▶ **1.** Zoom back in so you can read the text, and then scroll up until you can see the bottom of page 1.

▶ **2.** Double-click in the bottom margin of page 1, below the footnotes. The document switches to Header and Footer view. On the Ribbon, the Design tab appears below the label "Header & Footer Tools." The insertion point is positioned on the left side of the footer area, ready for you to begin typing. The label "Footer - Section 1" tells you that the insertion point is located in the footer for section 1. The document text (including the footnotes) is gray, indicating that you cannot edit it in Header and Footer view. The header area for section 1 is also visible on top of page 2. The default footer tab stops are visible on the ruler. See Figure 3-33.

Figure 3-33 ▸ **Creating a footer**

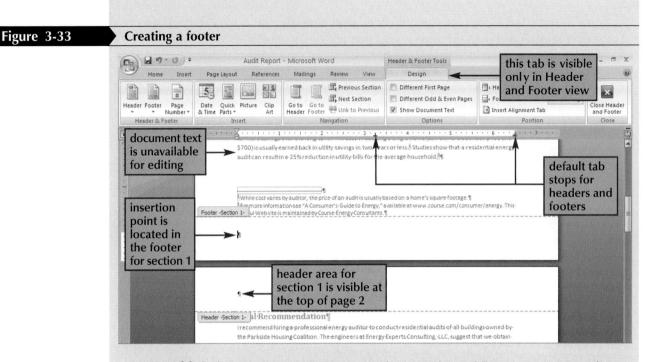

> **Trouble?** If the document does not switch to Header and Footer view, you probably did not double-click in the right place in Step 2. Try again.

▸ **3.** Type your first and last name, and then press the **Enter** key. The insertion point moves to the second line in the footer, on the left margin. This is where you will insert the page number.

▸ **4.** In the Header & Footer group, click the **Page Number** button. The Page Number menu opens. This menu allows you to insert a page number at the top, bottom, or side of the page. Because the insertion point is already located where you want to insert the page number, you need to use the Current Position option.

▸ **5.** Point to **Current Position**. A gallery of page number styles opens. The Plain Number style at the top simply inserts a page number, whereas other styles include the word "Page" or design elements such as special shapes or colors. Robin wants to use the Accent Bar 2 style. See Figure 3-34.

Inserting the page number in the footer   **Figure 3-34**

use this option when the insertion point is located where you want to insert the page number

you will use this page number style

6. Scroll down the page number gallery to get a sense of the types of page number styles available, then scroll back up and click the **Accent Bar 2** style (the third from the top). The word "Page," a vertical bar, and the page number are inserted in the document. Next, you'll check to make sure that the footer you just created for section 1 also appears in section 2.

7. Scroll down to the end of the document until you can see the footer at the bottom of page 4. Scroll left or right, if necessary, so you can see the entire footer. The label at the top of the footer area on page 4, "Footer – Section 2," tells you that you are looking at the footer for section 2. You see the same text (your name, plus the page number) in this footer as in section 1.

You have successfully created a footer for the entire document. Now you can turn your attention to creating a header for section 1. Robin does not want to include a header in section 2 because it would distract attention from the SmartArt graphic. So your first task is to separate the header for section 1 from the header for section 2.

To separate the headers for section 1 and section 2:

1. Click anywhere in the section 2 footer area, at the bottom of page 4. The insertion point moves to the section 2 footer.

2. In the Navigation group, click the **Go to Header** button. The insertion point moves to the section 2 header at the top of page 4. Notice that in the Navigation group, the Link to Previous button is selected. This tells you that the section 2 header is linked to the header in the previous section (that is, the section 1 header). In other words, anything you add to the section 1 header will also be added to the section 2 header—but Robin wants the header to appear only in section 1. To make the section 2 header a separate entity, you need to break that link.

3. In the Navigation group, click the **Link to Previous** button to deselect it. Deselecting this button ensures that the header you create in section 1 will not appear in section 2. See Figure 3-35.

Figure 3-35	Breaking the link between the section 1 and section 2 headers

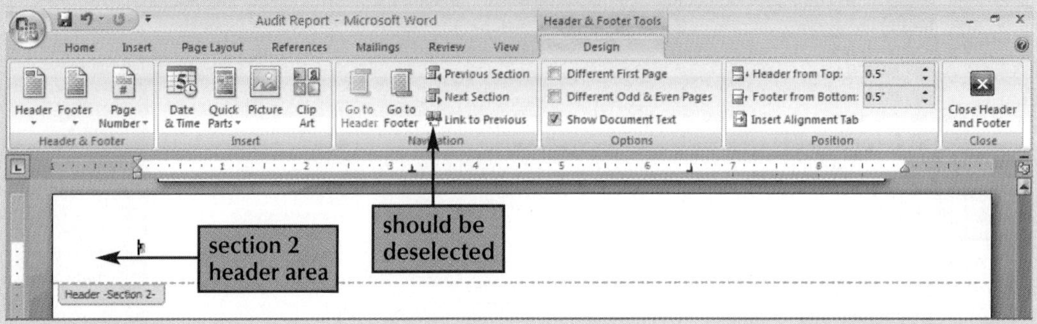

Tip

When you create a header for a section, it doesn't matter what page you're working on, as long as the insertion point is located in a header in that section.

Next, you need to move the insertion point to the section 1 header.

4. In the Navigation group, click the **Previous Section** button. The insertion point moves up to the nearest section 1 header, which is at the top of page 3. The label "Header – Section 1" identifies this as a section 1 header.

5. In the Header & Footer group, click the **Header** button. A gallery of header styles opens. See Figure 3-36.

Figure 3-36	Header gallery

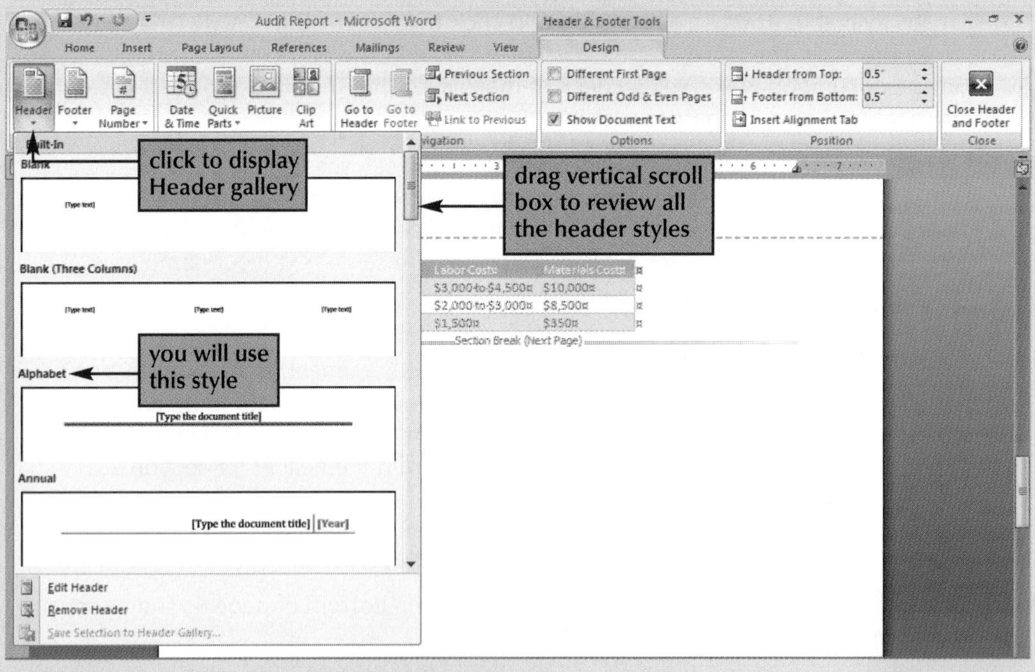

6. Scroll down and review the various header styles, and then click the **Alphabet style** (third from the top). A horizontal line is inserted in the document, along with the placeholder text "[Type the document title]." The placeholder text is actually contained within a document control, although right now you can't see anything that would indicate this is anything other than ordinary text.

7. Click the placeholder text **[Type the document title]**. The text is highlighted in blue, and a blue label with the word "Title" appears above the highlighted text. The blue highlighting and the blue label indicate that this is a document control. This particular document control is a text box; currently it contains the placeholder text "[Type the document title]." Now that the placeholder text is selected (as indicated by the blue highlight), you can replace it with something appropriate for Robin's report. See Figure 3-37.

Adding a header to section 1 | **Figure 3-37**

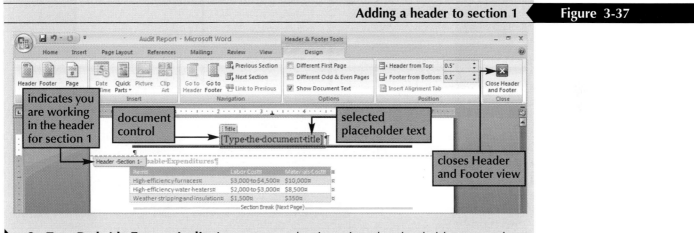

8. Type **Parkside Energy Audit**. As soon as you begin typing, the placeholder text and the blue highlight disappear. The new title, "Parkside Energy Audit," is displayed in the document control. You are finished creating the header and footer for Robin's report, so you can close Header and Footer view and return to Print Layout view.

9. In the Close group, click the **Close Header and Footer** button, save your work, and then zoom out until you can see all four pages of the document, including the header at the top of pages 1-3 and the footer at the bottom of pages 1–4. See Figure 3-38.

| Figure 3-38 | Document with new header and footer |

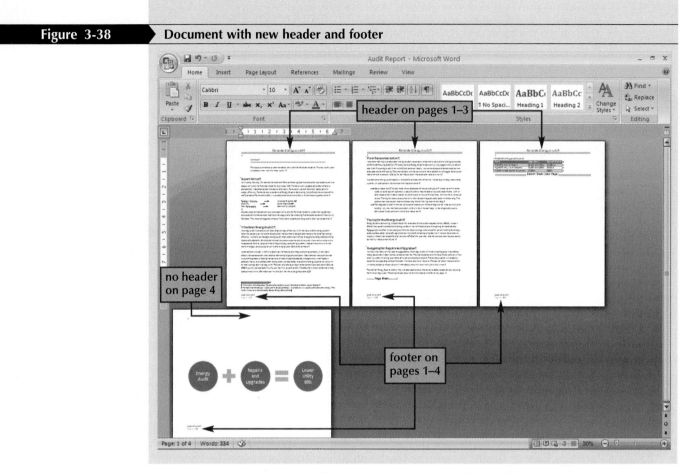

The header and footer will make it easier for Parkside board members to keep track of the pages of the printed report. This will be especially helpful as Robin adds more pages to the report. Your last job is to create an attractive cover page.

Inserting a Cover Page

A document's cover page typically includes the title and the author of the report. Some writers also prefer to include a summary on the cover page rather than on the first page of the report itself, as Robin chose to do. In addition, you might include the date, the name and possibly the logo of your company or organization, and a subtitle. A cover page should not include the document header or footer.

To create a simple cover page for a report, you can do the following: insert a Next Page section break at the beginning of the document, adjust the header and footer settings for the new section 1 so the header and footer do not appear on the cover page, type the title and other information, and, finally, format the text to add emphasis. To center cover page text between the top and bottom margins, click the Page Layout tab. In the Page Setup group, click the Dialog Box Launcher, click the Layout tab, click the Vertical alignment arrow, and then click Center.

To create a more elaborate cover page—one that includes design elements such as color, lines, and graphics—you can use the Cover Page button on the Insert tab. The Cover Page button inserts a predefined cover page at the beginning of the document.

As with Word's predefined headers and footers, a predefined cover page includes document controls in which you can enter the document title, the document's author, the date, and so on. These document controls are linked to any other document controls in the document. You already entered the document title into a control in the header of Robin's report. You'll see the advantages of that choice in the following steps, as you insert a cover page into Robin's report.

To insert a cover page at the beginning of the report:

▶ 1. Verify that the document is still zoomed so that you can see all four pages, and then press the **Ctrl+Home** keys. The insertion point moves to the beginning of the document. (You don't have to move the insertion point to the beginning of the document before you insert a cover page, but as a general rule it's a good idea to know where the insertion point is before you start a new task.)

▶ 2. Click the **Insert** tab, and then, in the Pages group, click the **Cover Page** button. A gallery of cover pages opens. Notice that the names of the cover page styles match the names of the preformatted header styles you saw earlier. For example, the list includes an Alphabet cover page, which is similar in design to the Alphabet header you inserted earlier. To give a document a coherent look, it's helpful to use elements (such as cover pages and headers) with the same name throughout. However, in this case, the Alphabet cover page is more complicated than Robin wants, so you will use the Stacks style instead.

▶ 3. Scroll down through the gallery to see the choice of cover pages and locate the Stacks cover page, in the left column, bottom row. See Figure 3-39.

Cover Page gallery   **Figure 3-39**

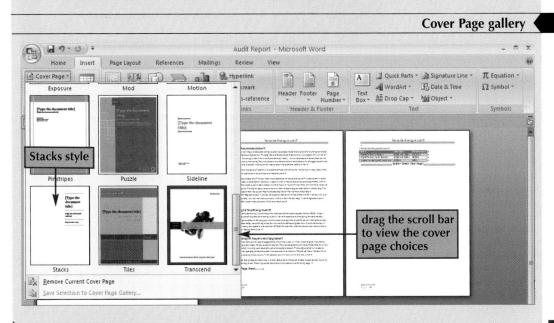

▶ 4. Click the **Stacks** cover page. The new cover page is inserted at the beginning of the document.

▶ 5. Zoom back in so you can read the document, and then scroll to view the new cover page. The insertion point is positioned in the upper-left corner of the document, just above a page break line. (In pages with complicated formatting, such as this one, a page break line sometimes appears in places you might not expect; you can ignore it.) On the right side of the document, you see controls for the title and the subtitle. Because you already entered "Parkside Energy Audit" in the Title document control in the header, the same text appears in the Title document control in the cover page. The Author document control (for entering the author's name) is located directly below the Subtitle document control. You might not be able to see the Author control. If you can see it, it probably contains a name inserted automatically by Word. See Figure 3-40.

Tip

To delete a cover page that you inserted from the Cover Page gallery, click the Cover Page button in the Pages group, and then click Remove Current Cover Page.

Trouble? If the header is on the new cover page, click the Cover Page button in the Pages group, click Remove Current Cover Page, and then repeat Steps 1 through 5.

Figure 3-40 ▶ **Newly inserted cover page**

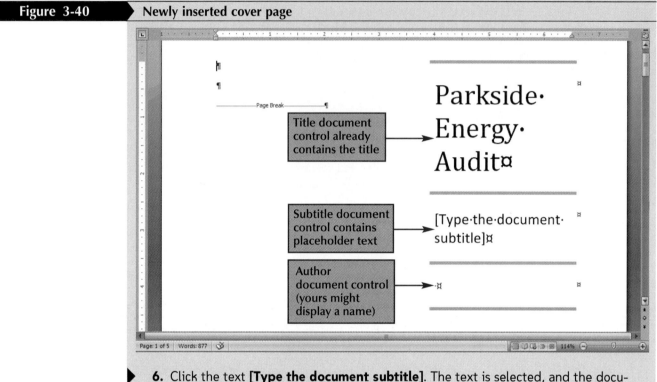

▶ **6.** Click the text **[Type the document subtitle]**. The text is selected, and the document control label "Subtitle" is visible. The Table Tools contextual tabs appear on the Ribbon because, although you can't tell by looking at them, the document controls are actually organized on the page in a table structure. When you clicked the Subtitle document control, you clicked within the table.

▶ **7.** Type **A Recommendation Report for the Parkside Housing Coalition Board of Directors**. Word formats the subtitle in a table cell below the title.

▶ **8.** Press the **Tab** key to display and select the Author control, and then type **Robin Kinsella**. The cover page now includes a title, a subtitle, and Robin's name.

▶ **9.** Save your work.

Your work on the report is finished. All that remains is to preview it and print it.

To preview and print the report:

▶ **1.** Click the **Office Button** ⊚, point to **Print**, and then click **Print Preview**. The document is displayed in the Print Preview window.

▶ **2.** On the Print Preview tab, in the Zoom group, click the **Two Pages** button to display the first two pages of the report side by side, and then use the **Next Page** and **Previous Page** buttons in the Preview group to move back and forth among the pages of the report. Make sure that the header is only visible on pages 2–4, and that the footer is visible on pages 2–5. Also, notice that Word renumbered the pages to account for the addition of the cover page, which is the new page 1.

▶ **3.** If you need to make any changes to the report, return to Print Layout view, edit the document, and then return to Print Preview.

▶ **4.** When you are satisfied with the document, click the **Print** button in the Print group, verify that the printer settings are correct, and then click the **OK** button.

▶ **5.** Close the document.

You now have a draft of the Parkside Housing Coalition report, including a cover page, the report text, a nicely formatted table, and the SmartArt graphic (printed in landscape orientation). Eventually, Robin will add more information to the report, including an introduction to the table.

Session 3.2 Quick Check | Review

1. True or False: There are default tab stops every one-half inch on the horizontal ruler.
2. Explain how to create a footnote.
3. What button do you use to insert a section break, and where is it located?
4. How do you know if a SmartArt graphic is selected?
5. Explain two ways to switch to Header and Footer view.
6. True or False: For page numbering purposes, a cover page inserted from the Cover Page gallery is considered page 1.

Review | **Tutorial Summary**

In this tutorial, you learned how to format headings with Quick Styles and insert a manual page break. Then you learned how to insert a table, select all or part of a table, sort the rows of a table, insert and delete rows or columns, change column widths, and format a table to improve its appearance. You also learned how to set tab stops, create footnotes and endnotes, and insert a section break. Finally, you learned how to create a SmartArt graphic, add headers and footers, and insert a cover page.

Key Terms

cell	handles	reference marker
character-level formatting	header	Shift+Enter key
document controls	Header and Footer view	combination
dot leader	header column	SmartArt
endnote	header row	section
first column	landscape orientation	section break
font color	manual line break	sort
footer	manual page break	tab
footnote	paragraph-level formatting	tab stop
graphic	portrait orientation	table
gridlines	Quick Styles	

| Practice | **Review Assignments** |

Apply the skills you learned in the tutorial using the same case scenario.

Data File needed for the Review Assignments: Class.docx

In conjunction with a local community college, Robin Kinsella has organized a series of computer training classes for Parkside residents to be held in the Parkside community center. She has begun work on a report for the board that outlines basic information about the classes and introduces the instructors. It's your job to format the report, add a table at the end containing a preliminary schedule, and create a sample graphic that Robin could use in a handout advertising the classes. When you are finished, Robin will expand each section of the report, adding more text to each. (*Note*: Text you need to type is shown in bold for ease of reference only; do not bold the text unless otherwise instructed.) Complete the following:

1. Open the file **Class** located in the Tutorial.03\Review folder included with your Data Files, and then save it as **Class Report** in the same folder.
2. Display the rulers and nonprinting characters and make sure the document is displayed in Print Layout view.
3. Format the document headings with the Heading 2 Quick Style. Use the Intense Quote style for the "Summary" heading and then indent the summary paragraph to match.
4. Click to the left of the heading "Schedule," insert a page break, move the insertion point to the end of the document, and then create the table shown in Figure 3-41.

Figure 3-41

Start Date	Topic
March 17	The Internet
April 21	Spreadsheets
January 13	Computer literacy
May 12	Simple database
June 9	HTML

5. Sort the table by the contents of the Start Date column in ascending order.
6. In the appropriate location, insert a new row for a word-processing class that starts on February 10.
7. Delete the HTML row at the bottom of the table.
8. Modify the widths of both columns to accommodate the widest entry in each.
9. Format the table with banded rows of pink and white and dark red shading for the header row, and then save your work.
10. On page 1, replace the text "[instructor names]" with the following list of instructors and their specialties. Insert a tab after each name, remembering that the list of specialties won't align properly until you complete Step 11. Remember to use the Shift+Enter key combination (instead of just the Enter key) to insert a new line for each name without adding extra space:

    Felicity J. Connelly-Porter   **Word processing**
    Antonio Morales   **Multimedia software**
    Jon Davis   **Web design**
    Amelia Guntz   **Database design and SQL programming**
11. Select the list of instructors and their specialties, and then insert a left tab stop 2.5 inches from the left margin.
12. Below the heading "Equipment Needs," locate the first sentence of the second paragraph, which begins "There are currently five...." At the end of that sentence, insert a footnote that reads **The computers should run either Windows Vista or Windows XP.**

13. Insert a Next Page section break after the table, format the new page 3 in landscape orientation, and then insert a SmartArt graphic that illustrates the advantages of computer classes. Use the Continuous Block Process graphic from the Process category, and, from left to right, include the following text: **Computer Education**, **Technological Advantage**, and **New Career Prospects**. Size the SmartArt graphic to fill the page.

14. Create a footer for sections 1 and 2 that aligns your name at the left margin. Insert the page number, without any design elements and without the word "Page," below your name.

15. Create a header for just section 1 using the Alphabet header style, enter **Parkside Computer Classes** as the document title, close Header and Footer view, and then save your work.

16. Insert a cover page using the Stacks style, verify that the document title is automatically inserted in the cover page, enter **An Informational Report** for the subtitle, and then enter your name for the author.

17. Save and preview the report, and then submit the finished document to your instructor, either in printed or electronic form, as requested.

| Apply | **Case Problem 1** |

Apply the skills you learned to create an annual report for a textile store.

Data File needed for this Case Problem: Textiles.docx

Noblewood Textiles, Inc. As an assistant manager of Noblewood Textiles in San Diego, California, you must help prepare an annual report for the board of directors. (*Note*: Text you need to type is shown in bold for ease of reference only; do not bold the text unless otherwise instructed.) Complete the following:

1. Open the file **Textiles** located in the Tutorial.03\Case1 folder included with your Data Files, and then save it as **Textiles Report** in the same folder.

2. Check your screen to make sure your settings match those in the tutorials, with the document displayed in Print Layout view.

3. Format the headings using the Heading 1 Quick Style. (There are 11 headings, beginning with "Introduction" and ending with "Sales Forecast.")

⊕ **EXPLORE**

4. Select the list of members under the heading "Board of Directors," and then click the Page Layout tab. In the Paragraph group, click the Dialog Box Launcher, click the Indents and Spacing tab if necessary, and then click the Tabs button at the bottom of the dialog box. To insert a tab stop with a dot leader at the 4-inch mark, type 4 in the Tab stop position text box, verify that the Left option button is selected in the Alignment section, and then click the 2..... option button in the Leader section. Click the Set button. (Notice the Clear button, which you can use to clear the tab stop you just set, and the Clear All button, which you can use to clear all the custom tab stops from a document.) Click the OK button to close the Tabs dialog box. Notice the tab setting and the dot leaders.

5. On page 2, at the end of the paragraph below the heading "Summer Fiber Art Festival," insert the following endnote: **The Noblewood Web site is currently hosted by NetMind Solutions, but that may change in the coming year.**

6. At the end of the paragraph below the heading "Company Philosophy," insert the following endnote: **Our major, statewide competitor continues to be Boardman Fabrics, which has five retail outlets.**

7. Move the insertion point to the blank paragraph at the end of the Sales Forecast section (above the endnote), and then insert a table consisting of three columns and four rows.

8. Enter the following column headers and data. Format the header row in bold.

Department	January–June	Projected July–December
Yarn	$150,000	$180,000
Quilting	$120,000	$140,000
Garment	$75,000	$100,000

9. Sort the table in ascending order by department.
10. Insert a row above the Garment row and enter the following information:

Embroidery	$100,000	$120,000

11. Adjust the column widths so each column accommodates the widest entry.
12. Format the table using the Light List - Accent 1 table style which applies blue shading to the header row, no shading in the other rows, and no column borders. Save the document.
13. Create a footer for the document that aligns your name at the left margin and the page number (in the Accent Bar 3 style) at the right margin. (*Hint*: Press the Tab key twice to move the insertion point to the right margin before inserting the page number.)

⊕ EXPLORE 14. Insert a cover page using the Sideline style. Enter the company name, **Noblewood Textiles**, and the title, **Annual Report**. In the subtitle document control, enter **Prepared by Student Name** (but replace "Student Name" with your first and last name). Click the date document control, click the arrow, and then click the current date in the calendar.
15. Save and preview the document, and then submit the finished document to your instructor, either in printed or electronic form, as requested.

Apply | Case Problem 2

Apply the skills you learned to create a report summarizing information on a municipal wireless network.

Data File needed for this Case Problem: WiFi.docx

Report on a Municipal Wireless Network   Like many communities, the town of Grand Island, Nebraska, is considering a citywide wireless (or WiFi) network to provide low-cost Internet access for all residents. A task force appointed by the mayor has investigated the issue and summarized its findings in a report. As you format the report in the following steps, you will focus on creating a cover page and a header from scratch, without relying on pre-defined elements provided by Word. You will also create and edit a SmartArt graphic to illustrate the process of creating the network. (*Note*: Text you need to type is shown in bold for ease of reference only; do not bold the text unless otherwise instructed.) Complete the following:

1. Open the file named **WiFi** located in the Tutorial.03\Case2 folder included with your Data Files, and then save it as **WiFi Report** in the same folder. Check your screen to make sure your settings match those in the tutorials.
2. Replace "Student Name" in the first page with your first and last name.
3. Divide the document into two sections. Begin the second section just before the heading "Summary" and have the second section begin a new page.
4. Position the insertion point somewhere in the page 1 text.

⊕ EXPLORE 5. Click the Page Layout tab. In the Page Setup group, click the Dialog Box Launcher, and then click the Layout tab. Click the Vertical alignment arrow, click Center, and then click the OK button. Zoom out so you can see the entire page and review the newly formatted cover page, with the text centered in the middle of the page.

6. Zoom in again so you can read the document text, and format the text of the title and the subtitle using the Title and Subtitle Quick Styles. Leave the line containing your name in Normal style.

7. Format the document headings using the Heading 1 Quick Style.

8. Insert a tab stop at the 2-inch mark in the list of task force members.

9. Change the section 2 header so it is no longer linked to section 1, move the insertion point to the center tab stop in the section 2 header, and then type the header **WiFi Network Report**. Format the header text in italic, 14-point Calibri.

10. Create a footer for just section 2 using the Alphabet style. Replace the placeholder text with your first and last name. Close Header and Footer view. Zoom out and verify that the header and footer appear only in section 2.

11. Move the insertion point to the end of the document, insert a page break, and insert a SmartArt graphic in the new page. In the Process category, select the Upward Arrow graphic. Enter the text **Hire Networking Firm**, **Construct Network**, and **Sell Broadband Rights**.

⊕ EXPLORE 12. In the Create Graphic group, click the Add Shape button (not the Add Shape button arrow), and then type **Sell Network Subscriptions**. Click anywhere in the white area of the SmartArt Graphic, inside the border, to deselect the text.

13. Save the document, preview it, and then submit the finished document to your instructor, either in printed or electronic form, as requested.

Challenge	Case Problem 3

Go beyond what you've learned to convert text into a table and then use other advanced table options to enhance the table.

Data Files needed for this Case Problem: Clients.docx and Expenses.docx

Contact List for Parson's Graphic Design   Amanda Parson recently launched a new graphic design firm that specializes in creating Web ads for small businesses in the Seattle area. A colleague has just e-mailed her a list of potential clients. The list consists of names, e-mail addresses, and phone numbers. Because it was exported from another program, the information is formatted as simple text, with the pieces of information separated by commas. Amanda asks you to convert this text into a table and then format the table to make it easy to read. When you're finished, she needs you to sum a column of numbers in her Office Expense table. (*Note:* Text you need to type is shown in bold for ease of reference only; do not bold the text unless otherwise instructed.) Complete the following:

1. Open the file named **Clients** located in the Tutorial.03\Case3 folder included with your Data Files, and then save it as **Potential Clients** in the same folder. Check your screen to make sure your settings match those in the tutorials.

⊕ EXPLORE 2. Use Word Help to learn how to convert text to a table. Use what you learned to convert the document to a table. Adjust the column widths to accommodate the widest entry in each column.

3. Insert a header row using the bold headers **Company**, **Contact**, **Phone**, and **E-Mail**.

4. Sort the list alphabetically by Company, and then replace the name "Katherine Shropshire" with your first and last name.

⊕ EXPLORE 5. Change the page orientation to landscape, and then drag the Table Resize handle (located just outside the lower-right corner of the table) until the table is 7 inches wide and 3 inches high. Notice that all the parts of the table increase proportionally.

6. Format the table using a Quick Style that includes row borders but not column borders.

7. Save and preview the document, and then submit the finished document to your instructor, either in printed or electronic form, as requested. Close the document.

8. Open the file named **Expenses** located in the Tutorial.03\Case3 folder included with your Data Files, and then save it as **Office Expenses** in the same folder.

✦ EXPLORE   9. Use Word Help to learn how to merge cells. Use what you learned to merge the cell containing the word "TOTAL" with the blank cell to its right.

✦ EXPLORE   10. In the Alignment group, click the Align Top Right button to align the word "TOTAL" on the right side of the new, larger cell. Select the four cells below the Expense header (including the blank cell at the bottom of the Expense column), and then click the Align Top Right button.

✦ EXPLORE   11. Click the blank cell at the bottom of the Expenses column and then, in the Data group, click the Formula button. The Formula dialog box opens. Make sure the formula "=SUM(ABOVE)" appears in the Formula text box, make sure the other two text boxes are blank, and then click the OK button. Word sums the costs in the Expense column and displays the total ($9587.00) in the selected cell.

12. Save and preview the document, and then submit the finished document to your instructor, either in printed or electronic form, as requested.

Create | **Case Problem 4**

Use your table skills to create the instruction sheet shown in Figure 3-42.

There are no Data Files needed for this Case Problem.

Hammond Astronomical Society   Sarah Vernon coordinates star-gazing tours for the Hammond Astronomical Society. To ensure that participants can see as well as possible in the night sky, they are asked to follow a set of rules that astronomers refer to as a dark sky protocol. You can use Word table features to create an instruction sheet describing the club's dark sky protocol. Figure 3-42 shows Sarah's sketch. (*Note*: Text you need to type is shown in bold for ease of reference only; do not bold the text unless otherwise instructed.)

Figure 3-42

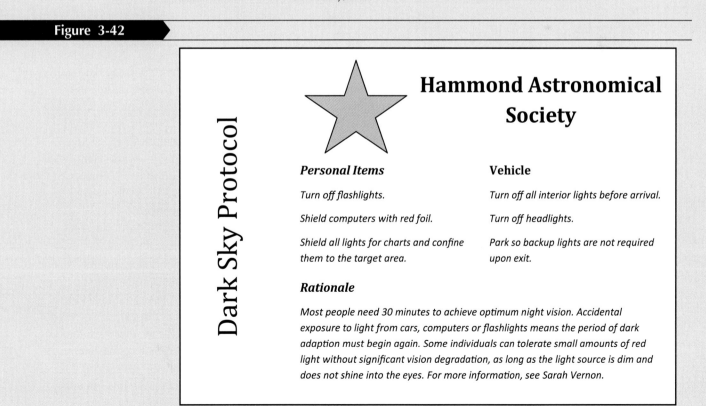

Complete the following steps:

1. Open a new, blank document, and save it as **Dark Sky Protocol** in the Tutorial.03\Case4 folder included with your Data Files.

2. If necessary, zoom out so you can see the entire page, switch to Print Layout view, and display the rulers.

3. Change the document's orientation to landscape.

⊕ **EXPLORE** 4. On the Insert tab, click the Table button, and then click Draw Table at the bottom of the Insert Table menu. The Draw Table pointer (which looks like a pencil) appears. You drag this pointer horizontally or vertically to create a straight line, and diagonally to create a rectangle.

⊕ **EXPLORE** 5. Click in the upper-left corner of the document (near the paragraph mark), and then drag down and to the right to draw a rectangle that stretches to the right and bottom margins. The rectangle should be a little less than nine inches wide and a little more than six inches high. If you make the rectangle too big, Word will insert a second page in the document. In that case, undo the change and redraw the rectangle.

⊕ **EXPLORE** 6. Use the Draw Table pointer to draw the columns and rows shown in Figure 3-42. For example, to draw the column border for the "Dark Sky Protocol" column, click the top of the rectangle where you want the column to begin, and drag down to the bottom of the rectangle. Use the same technique to draw rows. (If you make a mistake, use the Undo button. To delete a border, click the Eraser button on the Table Tools Design tab, click the border you want to erase, and then click the Eraser button again to turn it off. Click the Draw Table button to turn on the Draw Table pointer again.) Don't expect to draw the table perfectly the first time. You may have to practice until you become comfortable with the Draw Table pointer, but once you can use it well, you will find it a helpful tool for creating complex tables.

7. Press the Escape key to turn off the Draw Table pointer.

⊕ **EXPLORE** 8. In the left column, type the text **Dark Sky Protocol**. With the pointer still in that cell, click the Table Tools Layout tab, then in the Alignment group, click the Text Direction button twice to position the text vertically so that it reads from bottom to top. Using the formatting options on the Home tab, format the text in 36-point Cambria. Click the Table Tools Layout tab, and then, in the Alignment group, click the Align Center button. (*Hint*: You will probably have to adjust and readjust the row and column borders throughout these steps, until all the elements of the table are positioned properly.)

9. Type the remaining text, as shown in Figure 3-42. Replace "Sarah Vernon" with your own name. Use bold as shown in Figure 3-42 to draw attention to key elements. Change the font and font sizes as necessary to make your table look like the one in Figure 3-42. Likewise, use the Center Align button on the Table Tools Layout tab as necessary. (*Hint:* For the bottom three cells, use 16-point Cambria for the bold items and 14-point Calibri for the other text.)

⊕ **EXPLORE** 10. Switch to the Insert tab. In the Illustrations group, click the Shapes button and then, under "Stars and Banners," click the 5-Point Star shape. In the blank cell in the top row, position the mouse pointer over the upper-left corner, and then click and drag the mouse pointer down and to the right to draw a five-pointed star. If the star isn't centered neatly in the cell, click the Undo button, and try again until you draw a star that looks similar to the one in Figure 3-42. The star is selected, as indicated by the small squares (called selection handles) that surround it. A new tab, named Format, appears on the Ribbon with a label identifying it as a Drawing Tools contextual tab. On the Drawing Tools Format tab, in the Shape Styles group, click the Shape Fill button arrow and, under "Standard Colors," click the orange square. Click anywhere outside the star to deselect it.

⊕ **EXPLORE**

11. Now that you have organized the information using the Word table tools, you can remove the borders. Select the entire table, click the Table Tools Design tab, click the Borders button arrow (in the Table Styles group) and then click No Border. (You may still see dotted blue gridlines, which will not be visible in the printed document. If you would like to turn off the dotted blue gridlines, click the Table Tools Layout tab, and then click View Gridlines in the Tables group.)

12. Save your work, preview the document, make any necessary adjustments, and then submit the finished document to your instructor, either in printed or electronic form, as requested.

| Research | **Internet Assignments** |

Go to the Web to find information you can use to create documents.

The purpose of the Internet Assignments is to challenge you to find information on the Internet that you can use to work effectively with this software. The actual assignments are updated and maintained on the Course Technology Web site. Log on to the Internet and use your Web browser to go to the Student Online Companion for New Perspectives Office 2007 at **www.course.com/np/office2007**. Then navigate to the Internet Assignments for this tutorial.

| Assess | **SAM Assessment and Training** |

If you have a SAM user profile, you may have access to hands-on instruction, practice, and assessment of the skills covered in this tutorial. Log in to your SAM account (**http://sam2007.course.com**) to launch any assigned training activities or exams that relate to the skills covered in this tutorial.

| Review | **Quick Check Answers** |

Session 3.1

1. Click the paragraph containing the heading; on the Home tab in the Styles group, click the More button; and then click the Quick Style you want. (If the Quick Style you want is already visible in the Styles group, you don't have to click the More button.)
2. False
3. Click where you want to insert the table, click the Insert Tab, in the Tables group click the Tables button, drag the mouse pointer to select the desired number of rows and columns, and then release the mouse button.
4. Tab key
5. Select button on the Table Tools Layout tab
6. In the Data group on the Table Tools Layout tab, click the Sort button. Click the Sort by arrow, and select the header for the column you want to sort by. In the Type list box located to the right of the Sort by list box, select the type of information stored in the column you want to sort by. To sort in alphabetical, chronological, or numeric order, click the Ascending option button. To sort in reverse order, click the Descending option button. If you also want to sort by a second column, click the Then by arrow and click a column header. If the table includes headers, make sure the Header row option button is selected, and then click the OK button.
7. True

Session 3.2

1. True
2. Click where you want to insert a footnote, click the References tab, in the Footnotes group click the Insert Footnote button, and then type the text of the footnote in the bottom margin.
3. The Breaks button on the Page Layout tab
4. The SmartArt graphic appears with a blue border around it.
5. Click in the header area (in a page's top margin) or in the footer area (in a page's bottom margin); or click the Header button or the Footer button on the Insert tab.
6. False

Ending Data Files

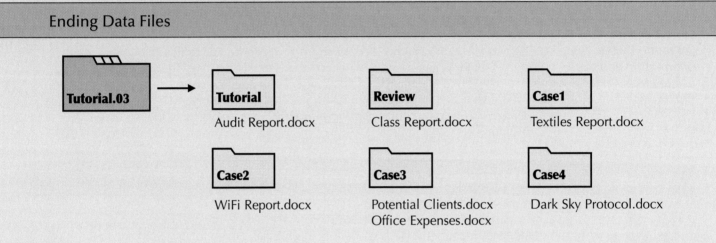

Tutorial.03 → Tutorial
Audit Report.docx

Review
Class Report.docx

Case1
Textiles Report.docx

Case2
WiFi Report.docx

Case3
Potential Clients.docx
Office Expenses.docx

Case4
Dark Sky Protocol.docx

Objectives

Session 4.1
- Identify desktop publishing features
- Create a title with WordArt
- Create newspaper-style columns
- Insert and edit graphics
- Wrap text around a graphic

Session 4.2
- Incorporate drop caps
- Use symbols and special typographic characters
- Add a page border
- Perform a mail merge
- Create a blog post

Desktop Publishing and Mail Merge

Creating a Newsletter, Cover Letter, and Blog Post

Case | Shepherd Bay Medical Center

Joel Conchola, a public outreach specialist at Shepherd Bay Medical Center, needs to create a one-page newsletter that explains the importance of exercise and diet in preventing type II diabetes. He has asked you to help him create the newsletter and a cover letter that will accompany the newsletter. He is also interested in creating a blog for Shepherd Bay Medical and needs your help to create a blog post.

Joel has already written the text of the newsletter. He wants you to transform this text into a publication that is neat, organized, and professional looking. He would like the newsletter to contain headings and an eye-catching headline. He also wants to include a picture that reinforces the newsletter content.

In this tutorial, you'll get acquainted with some desktop publishing features available in Word that you'll use to create the newsletter. You'll format the title as a prominent-looking headline and divide the document into newspaper-style columns to make it easier to read. To add interest and focus to the text, you'll include a graphic. You'll then fine-tune the newsletter layout, give it a more professional appearance with typographic characters, and you'll put a border around the page to give the newsletter a finished look. Next, you will use Word's mail merge feature to insert personalized information into the cover letter that will accompany the newsletter. Finally, you'll experiment with creating a blog post.

Starting Data Files

Tutorial.04 →	Tutorial	Review	Case1	Case2	Case3	Case4
	Addresses.docx	Addresses.docx	Audio.docx	Island.jpg	Hill.docx	(none)
	Letter.docx	Eating.docx		News.docx		
	Prevention.docx	Nutrition.docx				

Session 4.1

Elements of Desktop Publishing

Desktop publishing is the process of preparing commercial-quality printed material using a desktop computer system. In addition to newsletters, you can desktop-publish brochures, posters, and other documents that include text and graphics.

The following elements are commonly associated with desktop publishing:

- Columns and other page layout features—Columns of text, pull quotes (small portions of text pulled out of the main text and enlarged), drop caps (large initial letters at the beginning of paragraphs), page borders, and other special formatting features that you don't frequently see in letters and other documents distinguish desktop-published documents.
- Graphics—Clip art, horizontal or vertical lines (called **rules**), text boxes, and photographs help illustrate a concept or product, draw a reader's attention to the document, and make the text visually appealing.
- Multiple fonts—Two or three fonts, font sizes, and font colors provide visual interest, guide the reader through the text, and convey the tone of the document.
- High-quality printing—A laser printer or high-resolution inkjet printer produces the final output.

Although professional desktop publishers use software specially designed for desktop publishing, you can use Word to create basic desktop-published documents. You already know how to format text in multiple fonts and font sizes, and you know how to create a graphic using SmartArt. In this tutorial, you'll incorporate more of the desktop publishing elements listed to produce the newsletter shown in Figure 4-1.

Figure 4-1 ▶ **Shepherd Bay Medical Center newsletter**

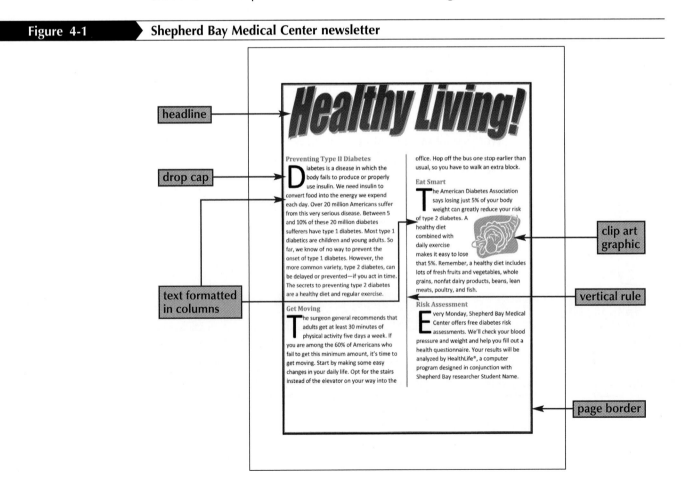

Before you can start creating the newsletter shown in Figure 4-1, you need to open Joel's document and review the text of the newsletter.

To open the newsletter document:

▶ **1.** Start Word and open the file **Prevention** from the Tutorial.04\Tutorial folder included with your Data Files.

▶ **2.** To avoid altering the original file, save the document as **Prevention Newsletter** in the same folder.

▶ **3.** Display nonprinting characters, switch to Print Layout view, display the rulers, and set the zoom so you can see the entire width of the newsletter. Throughout this tutorial, feel free to zoom in or zoom out if you prefer to see more or less of the newsletter.

▶ **4.** Read the document to familiarize yourself with its content.

▶ **5.** At the end of the document, replace "Shawn Kampa" with your first and last name. This will make it easier for you to find your copy of the newsletter when you print it.

Now that the newsletter contains all the necessary details, you can turn your attention to your first desktop publishing task—adding a headline.

Using WordArt to Create a Headline

Joel wants the title of the newsletter, "Healthy Living," to be eye-catching and dramatic. You can create such a headline using **WordArt**, a feature that allows you to create specially formatted text. You type the text for a piece of WordArt in the Edit WordArt Text dialog box and then insert it into the document. Unlike regular text, a WordArt headline is considered an **object**—that is, something that you can manipulate independently of the text. You can think of the WordArt object as a thing that lies on top of, or next to, the text in a document. This means that, for example, to alter its size you drag its handles, just as you would for a SmartArt graphic. A set of WordArt tools appears on the Ribbon when the WordArt is selected. You can use these tools to change its shape, size, and color and to add special effects such as 3-D and shadowing.

Creating WordArt | Reference Window

- Click the Insert tab, and then, in the Text group, click the WordArt button.
- In the WordArt gallery, click the style of text you want to insert.
- Type the text you want in the Edit WordArt Text dialog box.
- Click the Font and Size arrows to select the font and font size you want. If you want, click the Bold or Italic button, or both.
- Click the OK button.
- Use the tools on the WordArt Tools Format tab to format the WordArt.
- Drag any handle to resize and reshape the WordArt. To avoid altering the WordArt's proportions, press and hold down the Ctrl key while you drag a handle.

You're ready to use WordArt to create the newsletter title.

To create the title of the newsletter using WordArt:

▶ **1.** Press the **Ctrl+Home** keys to move the insertion point to the beginning of the document, and then click the **Insert** tab.

▶ **2.** In the Text group, click the **WordArt** button. The WordArt gallery opens. Joel wants to use the WordArt style in the middle row, second column from the left. See Figure 4-2.

Figure 4-2 ▶ WordArt gallery

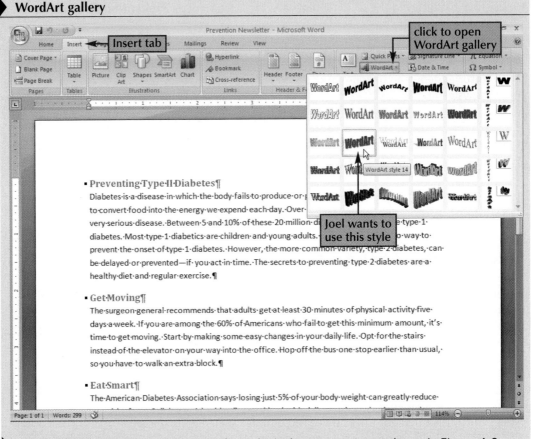

▶ **3.** Position the mouse pointer over the style Joel wants to use, as shown in Figure 4-2. A ScreenTip displays the name of this style: "WordArt style 14."

▶ **4.** Click **WordArt style 14**. The Edit WordArt Text dialog box opens, displaying the placeholder text "Your Text Here," which you will replace with the newsletter title. See Figure 4-3.

Edit WordArt Text dialog box | Figure 4-3

5. Type **Healthy Living** to replace the placeholder text with the newsletter title, and then click the **OK** button. The Edit WordArt Text dialog box closes, and the Word-Art is inserted as a graphic at the beginning of the newsletter. The "Preventing Type II Diabetes" heading moves to the right to accommodate the new headline. The WordArt Tools Format tab appears on the Ribbon. The border around the WordArt tells you that it is currently selected. The squares on the border are **sizing handles**, which you can drag to change the size of the WordArt. See Figure 4-4.

WordArt inserted into document | Figure 4-4

Eventually, you will position and resize the headline, so that it stretches from margin to margin. But for now, you can leave it in its current position.

Editing a WordArt Object

The WordArt object you have created is not regular text. You cannot edit it as you would other text. You can think of WordArt as an object that lies on top of or next to the text in a document. To edit WordArt, it must be selected. Then you can make changes using the tools on the WordArt Tools Format tab or by dragging its sizing handles.

The WordArt object you just created is already selected, so you can get to work modifying its appearance. First, Joel would like you to add an exclamation point at the end of the headline and format the headline in italic.

To edit the text and formatting of the WordArt object:

▶ **1.** Verify that the WordArt object is selected, as indicated by the border and the sizing handles. The WordArt Tools Format tab, which is visible only when a WordArt object is selected, contains tools for editing WordArt.

▶ **2.** In the Text group on the WordArt Tools Format tab, click the **Edit Text** button. The Edit WordArt Text dialog box opens. You used this dialog box earlier when you first created the WordArt object.

▶ **3.** Click at the end of the headline (to the right of the "g" in "Living"), and then type **!** (an exclamation point).

▶ **4.** Click the **Italic** button ⟨*I*⟩ in the Edit WordArt Text dialog box. The headline in the text box is now formatted in italic.

▶ **5.** Click the **OK** button. The Edit WordArt Text dialog box closes, and you can see the edited headline in the document. See Figure 4-5.

Figure 4-5 | **Edited WordArt headline**

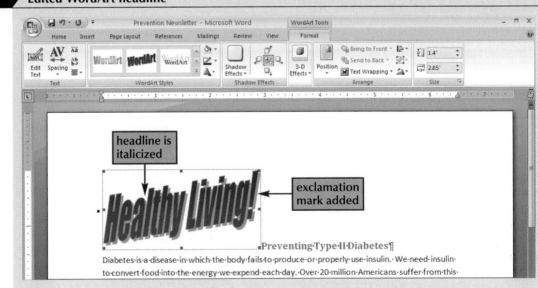

Changing the Shape of a WordArt Object

You can quickly change the shape of a WordArt graphic using the Change WordArt Shape button in the WordArt Styles group on the WordArt Tools Format tab. Right now, the WordArt headline has a straight shape, without any curve to it. Joel wants to use an arched shape.

To change the shape of the WordArt object:

▶ **1.** Verify that the WordArt object is selected, and then, in the WordArt Styles group, click the **Change WordArt Shape** button 🅰▾. A palette of shape options opens.

▶ **2.** Move the mouse pointer over each option in the palette to display a ScreenTip with the name of each shape and to see the live preview of each shape in the document.

▶ **3.** Point to (but don't click) the **Can Up** shape (top row in the Warp section, third column from the left), as shown in Figure 4-6.

Selecting a new WordArt shape | **Figure 4-6**

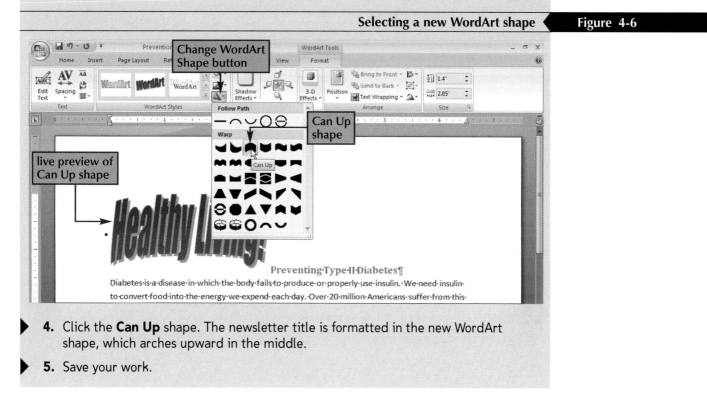

▶ **4.** Click the **Can Up** shape. The newsletter title is formatted in the new WordArt shape, which arches upward in the middle.

▶ **5.** Save your work.

The headline has the shape you want. Now you can position the WordArt object in relation to the text of the newsletter.

Wrapping Text Below a WordArt Object

At this point, the WordArt object is an **inline graphic**, which means it is located in a specific position in a specific line of the document (in this case, at the beginning of the first line). If you type text before an inline graphic, the graphic moves to accommodate the new text. You have more control over the position of a graphic, such as a WordArt object, if you change it to a floating graphic. A **floating graphic** is attached, or **anchored**, to a specific paragraph; however, you can drag a floating graphic to any location in the document. The text then flows, or **wraps**, around it. Adding or deleting text does not affect the position of a floating graphic.

To change an inline WordArt object to a floating graphic, you need to select a text wrapping style. You can wrap text around graphics many different ways. For example, you can have the text wrap above and below the graphic, or so the text follows the shape of the graphic, even if it has an irregular shape. The Arrange group on the WordArt Tools Format tab contains two useful tools for controlling the way text wraps around all graphics, including WordArt, pictures, and charts. First, there's the Position button, which allows you to position the WordArt or graphic in one of several locations on the page (top left, top middle, top right, and so on) and to wrap the document text around it. Second, there's the Text Wrapping button, which assumes the WordArt is already positioned where you want it and allows you to choose from a number of more refined wrapping options. Because the WordArt object is already located at the beginning of the document, where you want it, you'll use the Text Wrapping button in the Arrange group.

To wrap the newsletter text below the WordArt object:

► **1.** With the WordArt object selected, click the **Text Wrapping** button in the Arrange group. A menu of text wrapping options opens. See Figure 4-7.

| Figure 4-7 | Text Wrapping menu |

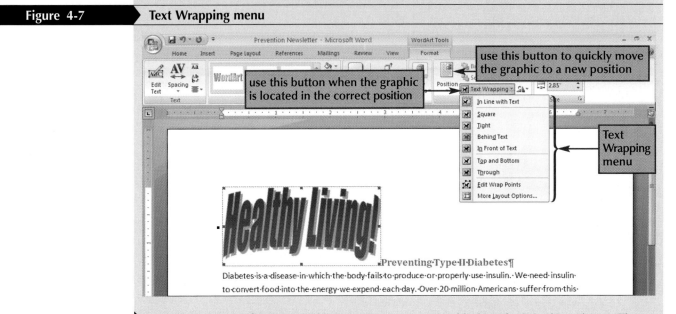

► **2.** Click **Top and Bottom**. The heading text is moved below the WordArt object. The WordArt is still selected, although now you see only the sizing handles, without the box. Also, there are more handles, and not all the handles are squares. Like the blue squares, the blue circles are sizing handles. However, the circle-shaped handles indicate that the graphic is a floating graphic. A number of other items appear around the WordArt object, as shown in Figure 4-8. The anchor symbol to the left of the heading "Preventing Type II Diabetes" tells you that the WordArt is attached, or anchored, to that paragraph.

WordArt after wrapping text | Figure 4-8

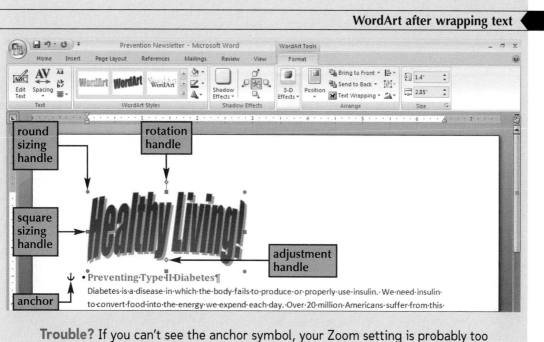

Trouble? If you can't see the anchor symbol, your Zoom setting is probably too high. Zoom out until you can see the full width of the page.

Positioning and Sizing the WordArt Object

After you choose a text wrapping style for a WordArt object, you can adjust its position in the document by dragging it with the mouse pointer. To change the size of a WordArt object, drag one of its sizing handles. To keep the headline the same proportion as the original, hold down the Ctrl key as you drag the sizing handle. This prevents "stretching" the headline more in one direction than the other.

Joel asks you to widen the headline so it stretches neatly across the margins. Before you enlarge the headline, you will drag it to a new position.

To position and enlarge the WordArt object:

▶ **1.** Move the mouse pointer over the headline.

▶ **2.** Use the 🔧 pointer to drag the WordArt object to the right until it is centered below the 3-inch mark on the horizontal ruler. Release the mouse button.

▶ **3.** With the WordArt object still selected, position the pointer over the lower-right sizing handle. The pointer changes to ↘ .

▶ **4.** Press and hold the **Ctrl** key while you drag the sizing handle almost to the right margin. Use the horizontal ruler as a guide. As you drag the handle, the pointer changes to ＋ and a dotted outline appears to show you how big the WordArt will be when you release the mouse button. Take care not to drag the handle down too far, or the WordArt object will be too tall. See Figure 4-9.

Figure 4-9 **Resizing the WordArt**

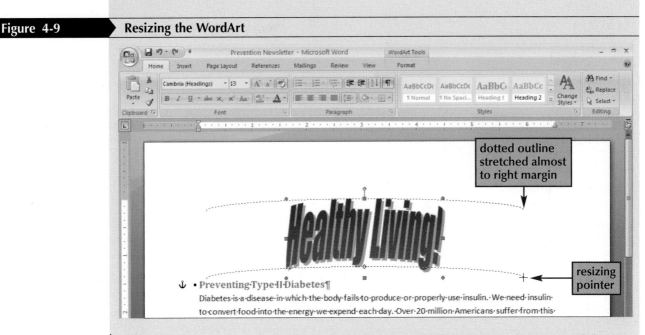

▶ **5.** Release the mouse button when the dotted horizontal line stretches almost from the left to the right margin. The WordArt heading should be about 5.5 inches wide and a little less than 1.5 inches high at its tallest.

Trouble? If the WordArt heading spans the margins, but is not tall enough to read easily, you probably didn't hold down the Ctrl key when you dragged the mouse pointer. Undo the change and repeat Steps 4 and 5.

▶ **6.** If necessary, drag the headline down slightly, so that the top of the headline does not extend into the top margin.

Trouble? If the headline jumps to the middle of the first paragraph of text, you dragged it too far. Undo the change, and then repeat Step 6.

Next, you need to turn your attention to the anchor symbol located by the lower-left corner of the WordArt headline.

Anchoring the WordArt Object to a Blank Paragraph

The text wrapping that you applied earlier changed the WordArt object into a floating graphic that is anchored to the paragraph containing the heading "Preventing Type II Diabetes." Later in this tutorial, you will format the newsletter text in narrow, newspaper-style columns. To prevent the column format from affecting the WordArt object, you need to anchor it to its own, blank paragraph. Then you can format that paragraph as a separate section.

At this point, the anchor symbol is probably located to the left of, and just above, the first paragraph (the heading "Preventing Type II Diabetes"). However, yours may be in a different position—for instance, it might be positioned above and to the left of the WordArt. In the next set of steps, you will move the anchor to a new, blank paragraph at the beginning of the document.

To anchor the WordArt object to a blank paragraph:

▶ **1.** Press the **Ctrl+Home** keys. The insertion point moves to the left of the "P" in the heading "Preventing Type II Diabetes," where you need to insert a blank paragraph. The WordArt object is no longer selected, so you cannot see the anchor at this point.

▶ **2.** Press the **Enter** key. A new paragraph symbol is inserted just above the Preventing Type II Diabetes heading.

▶ **3.** If the new paragraph symbol is inserted above the WordArt heading, drag the WordArt heading up slightly until the paragraph mark moves below the WordArt heading.

▶ **4.** Click the **WordArt** object. The selection handles and the anchor symbol appear. The anchor symbol is probably positioned to the left of, and just above, the new paragraph, although it might be positioned to the left of the "Preventing Type II Diabetes" paragraph instead.

▶ **5.** If necessary, click the anchor and drag it up to position it to the left of the new, blank paragraph, as shown in Figure 4-10, if it is not already positioned there.

Properly anchored WordArt ◀ **Figure 4-10**

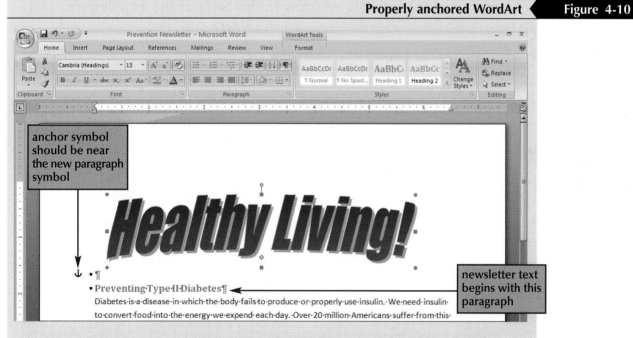

Trouble? If you notice any other differences between your headline and the one shown in Figure 4-10, edit the headline to make it match the figure. For example, you may need to drag the WordArt left or right slightly, or you may need to adjust its size by dragging one of its sizing handles.

▶ **6.** Click anywhere in the newsletter to deselect the WordArt, and then save your work.

Your WordArt is finished. The headline draws attention to the newsletter and makes it visually appealing.

Formatting Text in Newspaper-Style Columns

Because newsletters are meant for quick reading, they are usually laid out in newspaper-style columns. In **newspaper-style columns**, a page is divided into two or more vertical blocks, or columns. Text flows down one column, continues at the top of the next column, flows down that column, and so forth. The columns allow the eye to take in a lot of text and to scan a newspaper quickly for interesting information.

To quickly format a document in columns, click the Columns button on the Page Layout tab, and then select the number of columns you want on the Columns menu. If your document is already divided into sections, the column format is applied only to the section that currently contains the insertion point. For more detailed options, use the More Columns command (at the bottom of the Columns menu), which opens the Columns dialog box. In the Columns dialog box, you can insert a vertical line between columns, select a specific column width, and insert a section break at the same time you apply the column formatting, so that only part of a document is formatted in columns.

Joel wants you to format the text below the WordArt object into two columns and add a vertical line between them. To accomplish this, you need to use the Columns dialog box.

To apply newspaper-style columns to the body of the newsletter:

▶ **1.** Click to the left of the "P" in "Preventing Type II Diabetes."

▶ **2.** Click the **Page Layout** tab, and then, in the Page Setup group, click the **Columns** button. The Columns menu opens. You could click an option on the menu to format the entire document, including the paragraph containing the WordArt, in columns. However, you don't want the WordArt to be part of a column, so you need to start the columns below the paragraph to which the WordArt object is anchored. To do this, you need to use the More Columns command at the bottom of the menu.

▶ **3.** Click **More Columns**. The Columns dialog box opens.

▶ **4.** In the Presets section, click the **Two** icon, and then verify that the Equal column width check box (in the lower-left corner of the dialog box) is selected.

▶ **5.** Click the **Line between** check box to select it. The text in the Preview box changes to a two-column format with a vertical rule between the columns.

You don't want the WordArt object to be included in the columns; you want the columns to start at the current location of the insertion point and to continue through the rest of the document.

▶ **6.** Click the **Apply to** arrow, and then click **This point forward**. This tells Word to insert a section break at the insertion point and format the columns starting there. See Figure 4-11.

Correct settings in Columns dialog box ◀ **Figure 4-11**

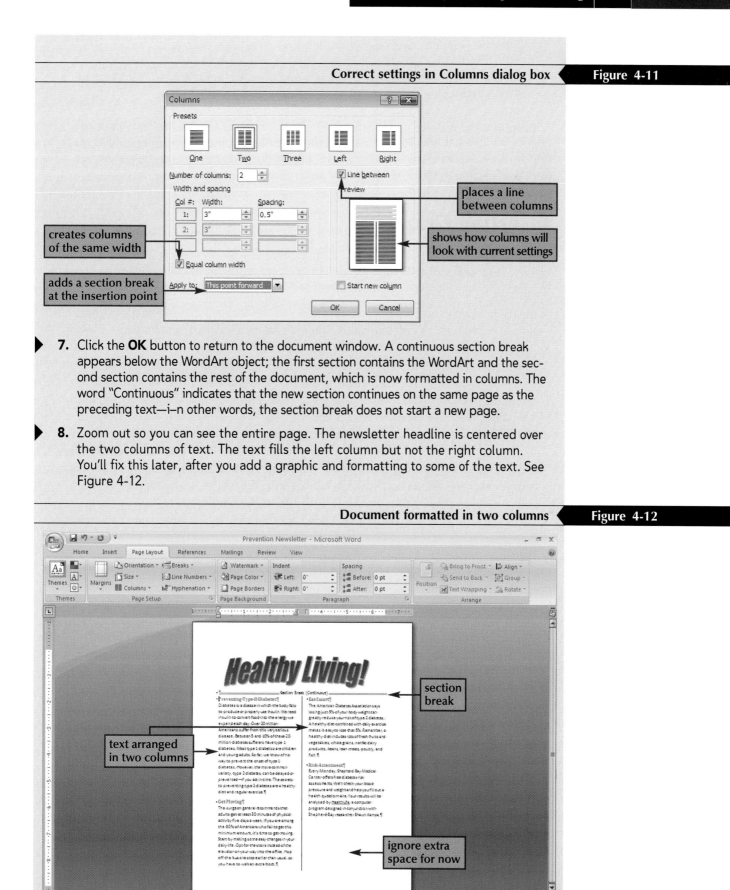

creates columns of the same width

adds a section break at the insertion point

places a line between columns

shows how columns will look with current settings

▶ **7.** Click the **OK** button to return to the document window. A continuous section break appears below the WordArt object; the first section contains the WordArt and the second section contains the rest of the document, which is now formatted in columns. The word "Continuous" indicates that the new section continues on the same page as the preceding text—i–n other words, the section break does not start a new page.

▶ **8.** Zoom out so you can see the entire page. The newsletter headline is centered over the two columns of text. The text fills the left column but not the right column. You'll fix this later, after you add a graphic and formatting to some of the text. See Figure 4-12.

Document formatted in two columns ◀ **Figure 4-12**

▶ **9.** Save your work.

   Trouble? Your columns may break at a slightly different line of text from those shown in the figure. This is not a problem.

Keep in mind that you can modify columns as you work on a document; you can change the number of columns or return the document to its original format by formatting it as one column. You can also insert column breaks to control where text moves from one column to the next.

Inserting Graphics

Word makes it easy to insert graphics, or illustrations, in your documents. The term **graphic** can refer to a drawing, a photograph, clip art, a chart, and so on. The Illustrations group on the Insert tab contains five buttons, for five types of graphics, as described below:

Tip

To search for clip art on the Microsoft Web site, click Clip art on Office Online at the bottom of the Clip Art task pane.

- The Picture button opens a dialog box where you can locate and insert an image that already exists, such as a picture taken with a digital camera or a scan of a paper drawing.
- The Clip Art button opens the Clip Art task pane on the right side of the Word window, where you can select from premade images known as **clip art**. A collection of clip art images is installed with Word, and you are free to use them in your documents. You can also search the Web for free clip art, available from the Microsoft Web site and from other Web sites devoted to clip art.
- The Shapes button opens a gallery where you can select from over a hundred basic shapes, such as arrows, stars, and banners. You click the shape you want in the gallery, and then drag the mouse pointer in the document to draw the shape. When the shape is selected in the document, you can change its color, shape, text wrapping settings, and so on using the options on the Drawing Tools Format tab.
- The SmartArt button, as you already know, opens a dialog box where you can create diagrams.
- The Chart button opens the Insert Chart dialog box, where you can create a variety of charts similar to the charts you can create in a spreadsheet program such as Microsoft Excel. You can choose from bar charts, pie charts, and line charts, to name a few. After you select a chart type, a spreadsheet window opens where you can enter the chart data. When the chart is selected in the document, you can edit it using the three tabs that appear under the label "Chart Tools."

| Working with Graphics Files | | InSight |

There are several types of graphics files, many of which were developed for use in Web pages. In desktop publishing, you will often work with **bitmaps**. The most common types of bitmaps are:

- BMP—Used by Microsoft Paint and other graphics programs to store graphics you create. These files, which have the .bmp file extension, tend to be very large.
- TIFF—Commonly used for photographs or scanned images. TIFF files are usually much larger than GIF or JPEG files, but smaller than BMP files. A TIFF file has the file extension .tif.
- GIF—Suitable for most types of simple art. A GIF file is compressed, so it doesn't take up much room on your computer. A GIF file has the file extension .gif.
- JPEG—Suitable for photographs and drawings. Files stored using the JPEG format are even more compressed than GIF files. A JPEG file has the file extension .jpg.

A document containing graphics can take up a lot of memory, making it difficult to work with. To save file space, use JPEG graphics as much as possible.

You'll have a chance to work with graphics files in the Case Problems at the end of this tutorial. You'll also have a chance to work with text boxes, which are similar to graphics. A **text box**, as its name implies, is a box in which you can type text. The box sets off the text and draws special attention to it. You can use a text box to create a **pull quote**—a brief quotation from the main document.

Joel wants you to insert a clip art image in the newsletter. He asks you to use one of the food-related images that are installed with Word.

To insert the clip art image into the newsletter:

▶ 1. With the document still zoomed out so you can see the whole page, and the insertion point located anywhere in the document, click the **Insert** tab, and then in the Illustrations group, click the **Clip Art** button. The Clip Art task pane opens, as shown in Figure 4-13. You use the top part of the Clip Art task pane to search for graphics related to a specific topic. The Search for text box on your computer may contain text left from a previous search. You can click the Organize clips option (near the bottom) to open the Microsoft Clip Organizer window, where you can browse among the various clip art images stored on your computer. You'll use the Microsoft Clip Organizer to insert an image into the newsletter.

Figure 4-13 **Clip Art task pane**

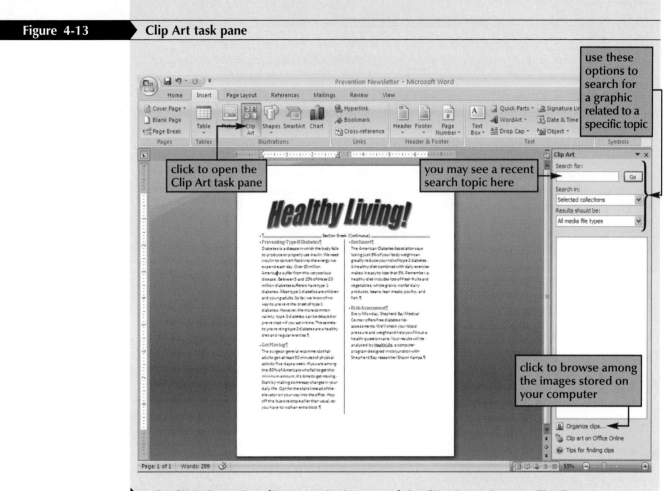

> **2.** Click **Organize clips** near the bottom of the Clip Art task pane. The Favorites - Microsoft Clip Organizer window opens. This window is similar to Windows Explorer. For example, you click the plus sign next to a folder to display its subfolders. You select a subfolder to display its contents in the right pane. The default Microsoft Office clip art is stored in subfolders within the Office Collections folder. See Figure 4-14. You might see different folders from those shown in Figure 4-14, but you should see the Office Collections folder.

Microsoft Clip Organizer ◄ Figure 4-14

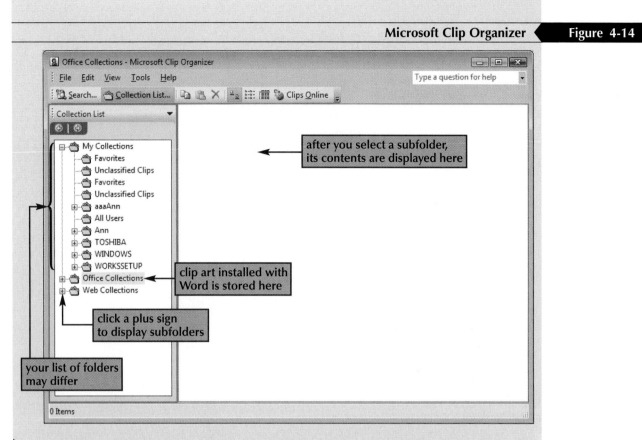

3. If necessary, scroll down to display the Office Collections folder in the left pane, and then click the **plus sign** next to the Office Collections folder. A list of subfolders within the Office Collections folder appears. This list of folders, which is created when you install Word, organizes clip art images into related categories. The folders with plus signs next to them contain subfolders and clip art images.

4. Scroll down and examine the list of folders. Click any plus signs to open subfolders, and then click folders to display clip art images in the right pane.

5. Click the **Food** folder to select it. Four images stored in the Food folder are displayed in the right pane.

6. Move the pointer over the image of the cornucopia (the second image from the left). An arrow button appears on the right side of the image. You might also see a ScreenTip with information about the file.

7. Click the **arrow button** that appears when your pointer is over the image. A menu of options opens, as shown in Figure 4-15.

Figure 4-15 ▶ Selected image in Food folder

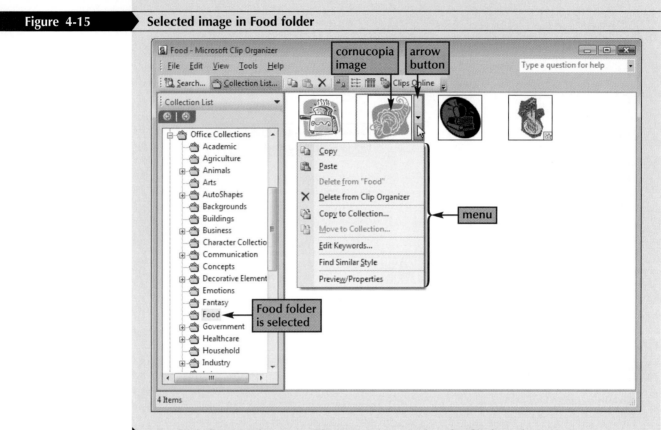

8. Click **Copy** in the menu. The image is copied to the Clipboard.

Now that you have copied the image to the Clipboard, you can paste it into the document at the insertion point. Joel asks you to insert the graphic in the paragraph below the heading "Eat Smart." Before you insert the image, you will close the Clip Art task pane.

To paste the clip art into the document:

1. Click the **Close** button ▣✕▣ in the Microsoft Clip Organizer title bar, and then click **Yes** when you see a dialog box asking if you want the item to remain on the Clipboard. You return to the document window.

2. Click the **Close** button ☒ on the Clip Art task pane.

3. Zoom back in so you can read the document, and then position the insertion point to the left of the word "The" below the heading "Eat Smart." At this point, you could switch to the Home tab and click the Paste button, but it's faster to use a keyboard shortcut.

4. Press the **Ctrl+V** keys. The cornucopia clip art is inserted into the document at the insertion point. The text moves right to accommodate the image, which nearly fills the right column.

5. Save the document.

6. Click the **cornucopia** image. A border with sizing handles appears, indicating that the image is selected. The Picture Tools Format tab also appears, containing tools related to working with graphics. The Insert tab is still selected, however, so at this point you can't actually see the tools on the Picture Tools Format tab. See Figure 4-16.

Tip

To delete a graphic (clip art, WordArt, etc.), click it to select it, and then press the Delete key.

Newsletter with the clip art graphic selected ◄ **Figure 4-16**

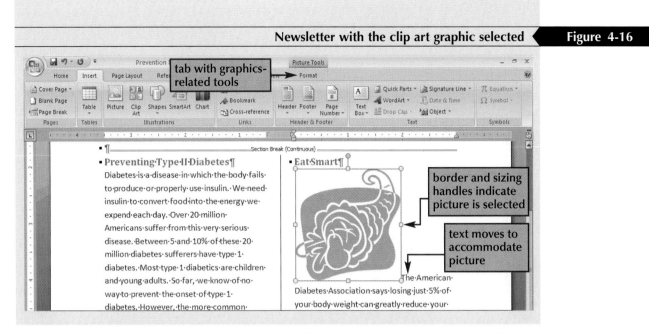

Joel would like the image to be smaller so it is better balanced with the text. You'll make that change in the next section.

Resizing a Graphic

It's often necessary to change the size of a graphic to make it fit into a document. This is sometimes called **scaling** the image. You can resize a graphic either by dragging its sizing handles or, for more precise control, by specifying an exact height and width in the Size group on the Picture Tools Format tab. For Joel's newsletter, the dragging technique will work well. You can then use the height and width controls on the Picture Tools Format tab to check the exact size of the graphic.

To resize the clip art graphic:

▶ **1.** Make sure the clip art graphic is selected, click the **Picture Tools Format** tab, and then locate the Shape Height and Shape Width boxes in the Size group on the right edge of the Picture Tools Format tab. These boxes tell you that the cornucopia graphic is currently 1.98 inches high and 1.95 inches wide.

▶ **2.** Move the mouse pointer over the lower-right sizing handle of the clip art. The pointer changes to ⤡ . When you drag the pointer in the next step, a faint copy of the cornucopia image will resize accordingly, allowing you to see how the image will alter when you release the mouse button.

▶ **3.** Drag the handle up and to the left until the faint copy of the cornucopia image is approximately 1.5 inches wide. Use the horizontal ruler as a guide. The measurements in the Shape Height and Shape Width boxes will not change until you release the mouse button, in the next step. See Figure 4-17.

Figure 4-17 | **Resizing the graphic**

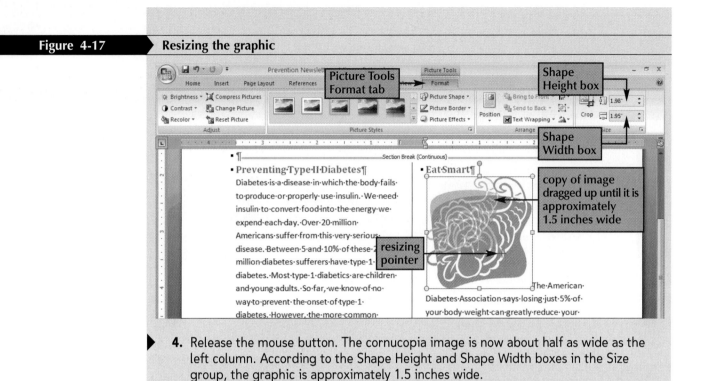

▶ **4.** Release the mouse button. The cornucopia image is now about half as wide as the left column. According to the Shape Height and Shape Width boxes in the Size group, the graphic is approximately 1.5 inches wide.

Trouble? If the measurement in your Shape Width box is greater than 1.53 inches, or less than 1.45 inches, resize the graphic until its width is closer to 1.5 inches.

Joel wonders if the graphic would take up less space if you deleted the tip of the cornucopia at the top of the image. You'll make that change in the next section.

Cropping a Graphic

You can **crop** a graphic—that is, cut off one or more of its edges—using the Crop button on the Picture Tools Format tab. Once you crop a graphic, the part you cropped is hidden from view. It remains a part of the graphic, which means you can change your mind and restore a cropped graphic to its original form.

To crop the graphic:

▶ **1.** If necessary, click the clip art to select it. The sizing handles appear.

▶ **2.** Click the **Crop** button in the Size group on the Picture Tools Format tab. The Crop button turns orange, indicating that it is currently selected; it stays selected until you click it again. The graphic is surrounded by a broken black box, and the pointer changes to ⁺ᚴ when you move it over the text.

▶ **3.** Position the pointer directly over the middle sizing handle on the top of the picture. The pointer changes to ⊥.

▶ **4.** Press and hold down the mouse button. The pointer changes to ┼.

▶ **5.** Drag the handle down. As you drag, a solid outline appears to indicate the new shape of the graphic.

6. Position the top edge of the solid outline along the top of the cornucopia's orange background. See Figure 4-18.

Cropping the graphic **Figure 4-18**

drag the pointer down to the top of the orange background

Crop button is selected

7. Release the mouse button. The tip of the cornucopia is cropped from the image. The Crop button is still selected. The cropping pointer and the broken black box around the graphic remain visible, in case you want to crop the graphic some more. You are finished cropping the graphic, so you can turn off the cropping feature.

8. Click the **Crop** button in the Size group to deselect it. The broken black box around the graphic is replaced with the solid box with the round and square selection handles (shown earlier in Figure 4-16).

In the next session you will wrap the newsletter text around the graphic and move the graphic to a new location. Then you'll finalize the newsletter and turn your attention to creating the cover letter with mail merge.

Session 4.1 Quick Check | Review

1. List four elements you might see in a desktop-published document.
2. Explain how to change the text of a WordArt object after you've already inserted it into the document.
3. True or False: To avoid altering the proportions of a WordArt object, you press and hold down the Alt key while you drag a handle.
4. What button should you use to change the way text flows around a WordArt object? Where is this button located?
5. Suppose you want to format only part of a document in columns, and you haven't inserted any section breaks. Should you use the Columns menu or the Columns dialog box?
6. Name four types of bitmap files.
7. On what tab are the buttons for inserting graphics located?

Session 4.2

Wrapping Text Around a Graphic

Earlier in this tutorial, you used Top and Bottom text wrapping with the WordArt object so the WordArt would appear above the columns of text. Now you'll apply Tight text wrapping to make the text follow the shape of the cornucopia.

To wrap text around the graphic:

▶ 1. If you took a break after the previous session, make sure Word is still running and that the Prevention Newsletter file is open with the document in Print Layout view and with the nonprinting characters and rulers displayed.

▶ 2. If necessary, click the cornucopia graphic to select it, and, if necessary, click the Picture Tools Format tab to display it.

▶ 3. In the Arrange group on the Picture Tools Format tab, click the **Text Wrapping** button. A menu of text wrapping options appears.

▶ 4. Click **Tight**. The text wraps to the right of the cornucopia, roughly following its shape. See Figure 4-19.

Figure 4-19 ▶ Text wrapped around the graphic

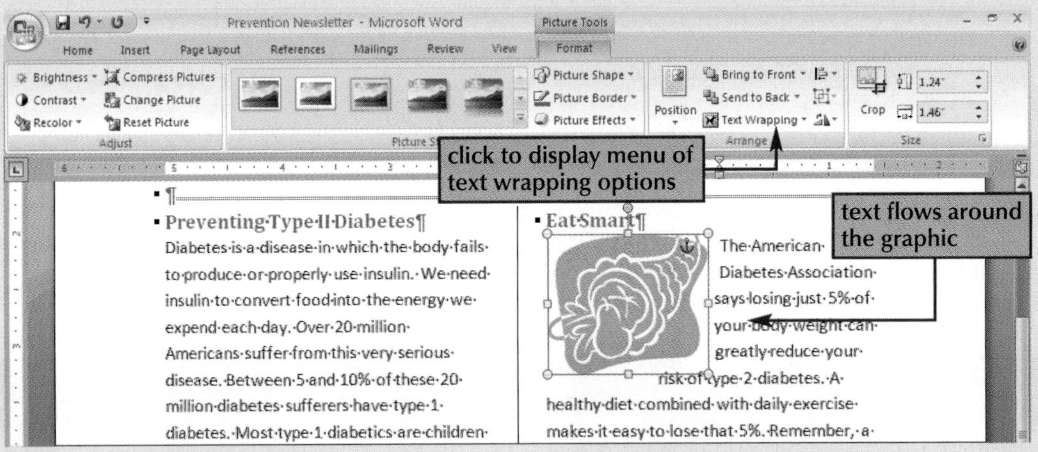

▶ 5. Click anywhere in the newsletter text to deselect the graphic, and then save the newsletter. Don't be concerned if the heading "Eat Smart" wraps to the right of the graphic. You will move the graphic away from the heading in the next section. If the heading does not wrap around the graphic, that's fine too.

Trouble? If the heading "Eat Smart" moves back down to the bottom of the left column, you probably didn't make the WordArt object tall enough. Undo the insertion of the graphic, increase the height of the WordArt object so that it is about 1.5 inches tall at its highest point, drag it down if necessary so it doesn't overlap the top margin, click at the beginning of the paragraph under the heading "Eat Smart," and begin again with Step 2.

You are almost finished with the graphic. You just need to move it to the middle of the paragraph, so that it is not so close to the heading.

Moving and Aligning a Graphic

You can move a graphic by dragging it, just as you dragged the WordArt object. Like WordArt, a clip art graphic is anchored to a specific paragraph in a document. When you drag a graphic to a new paragraph, the anchor symbol moves to the beginning of that paragraph. When you drag a graphic to a new position within the same paragraph, the anchor symbol remains in its original position and only the graphic moves. You'll see how this works when you move the cornucopia clip art to the middle of its current paragraph, next to the right margin.

When you move a graphic, it's a good idea to specify exactly where you want to align it. For example, you can choose to align a graphic along any one of the page margins, or you can choose to align it along the edge of the page. Specifying an alignment option prevents the graphic from moving if you make changes to the document later. The Align button in the Arrange group on the Picture Tools Format tab provides some preset alignment options that are appropriate for most documents. You'll see how this works in the following steps.

To move the graphic:

▶ **1.** Click the graphic to select it if necessary. You should see an anchor symbol either within the graphic or to the left of the heading "Eat Smart."

▶ **2.** Move the mouse pointer ⌖ over the graphic.

▶ **3.** Click and slowly drag the pointer down. As you move the mouse, a faint copy of the image moves too, so that you can see where you're moving the image.

▶ **4.** Position the image near the middle of the paragraph, next to the right margin, and then release the mouse button. The graphic moves to its new position, with the text wrapped to its left. The anchor is probably located to the left of the first line under the heading "Eat Smart," although it may have moved to somewhere else near the top of the newsletter. In the next few steps, you'll make some adjustments to make sure the position of your graphic and anchor matches Figure 4-20. First, you'll align the graphic along the right margin.

Trouble? If paragraph text wraps to the right of the graphic, you need to drag the graphic farther to the right.

Tip
To move a graphic to one of several preset positions on the page, click the Position button in the Arrange group on the Picture Tools Format tab.

Graphic in new position ◄ **Figure 4-20**

5. On the Picture Tools Format tab in the Arrange group, click the **Align** button. A menu of alignment options opens. You want to align the graphic along the right margin. It's possible to align the graphic along the edge of the page, so first you have to make sure the Align to Margin option is selected.

6. Verify that you see a check mark before "Align to Margin." Now you can specify what margin you want to align the graphic to.

7. Near the top of the Align menu, click **Align Right**.

8. If necessary, drag the anchor up or down slightly until it is positioned as in Figure 4-20, with three lines of text wrapped above it. If the anchor is not located next to the first line under the heading "Eat Smart," click it and drag it there now. When you are finished, your newsletter should match Figure 4-20.

   Trouble? If you can't get the text to wrap properly around the graphic (for example, if individual words wrap to the right of the graphic), try reducing the size of the graphic slightly by dragging the lower-right sizing handle.

9. Click anywhere outside the graphic to deselect it and save your work.

The graphic helps draw the reader's attention to the newsletter, but the rest of the text looks plain. Joel suggests adding a drop cap at the beginning of each section.

Inserting Drop Caps

A **drop cap** is a large, capital letter that begins the text of a paragraph, chapter, or some other document section. You can place a drop cap in the margin, next to the paragraph, or you can have the text of the paragraph wrap around the drop cap. In the following steps, you will create a drop cap for each of the four paragraphs that follow each heading in the newsletter. The drop cap will extend three lines into the paragraph, with the text wrapping around it.

To insert drop caps in the newsletter:

1. Click in the paragraph below the heading "Preventing Type II Diabetes."

2. Click the **Insert** tab, and then, in the Text group, click the **Drop Cap** button. The Drop Cap menu opens.

3. Move the mouse pointer over the In margin option and then the Dropped option, and observe the live preview of the two types of drop caps in the document. The default settings applied by these two options are fine for most documents. Clicking Drop Cap Options, at the bottom of the menu, opens the Drop Cap dialog box, where you can select more detailed settings. See Figure 4-21.

Figure 4-21 ▶ Drop Cap menu

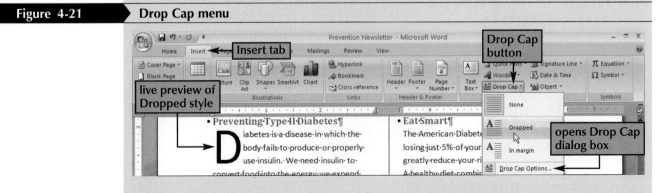

4. Click **Dropped** in the Drop Cap menu. The Drop Cap menu closes, and Word formats the first character of the paragraph as a drop cap, just as in the live preview in Figure 4-21. The blue box with square selection handles around the drop cap tells you the drop cap is selected.

5. Click in the paragraph following the heading "Get Moving," and then repeat Steps 3 and 4 to insert a drop cap in that paragraph.

6. Insert a drop cap in the paragraph following the heading "Eat Smart." Word adjusts the text wrapping around the graphic.

   Trouble? If a drop cap does not appear after you perform Step 6, there might be a blank space at the beginning of the paragraph that is left over from when you inserted the graphic. Delete the space and repeat Step 6.

7. Insert a drop cap in the paragraph following the last heading, click anywhere in the text to deselect the drop cap, and scroll so you can see the drop caps.

Tip

To change the size of the drop cap, you can drag one of the sizing handles.

The drop caps are a nice, eye-catching detail. Next, you turn your attention to inserting a registered trademark symbol (®) next to a registered trademark name.

Inserting Symbols and Special Characters

In printed publications, it is customary to change some of the characters available on the standard keyboard into more polished-looking characters called **typographic characters**. Word's AutoCorrect feature automatically converts some standard characters into typographic characters as you type. For instance, as Joel typed the paragraph under the heading "Preventing Type II Diabetes," he typed two hyphens after the phrase "be delayed or prevented." As he began to type the rest of the sentence, "if you act in time," Word automatically converted the two hyphens into a single, longer character called an em dash.

Figure 4-22 lists some of the other character combinations that AutoCorrect automatically converts to typographic characters. In most cases you need to press the spacebar and type more characters before Word inserts the appropriate typographic character. If you don't like the typographic character inserted by Word, click the Undo button to revert to the characters you originally typed.

Common typographic characters **Figure 4-22**

To insert this symbol or character	Type	After you press the spacebar, Word converts to
Em dash	word--word	word—word
Smiley	:)	☺
Copyright symbol	(c)	©
Trademark symbol	(tm)	™
Ordinal numbers	1st, 2nd, 3rd, etc.	1st, 2nd, 3rd, etc.
Fractions	1/2, 1/4	½, ¼
Arrows	--> or <--	← or →

In addition to characters inserted by AutoCorrect, Word also has many typographic characters that you can insert into a document. You can access these with the Symbol button on the Insert tab.

Reference Window | **Inserting Symbols and Special Characters**

- Move the insertion point to the location where you want to insert a particular symbol or special character.
- Click the Insert tab, and then, in the Symbols group, click the Symbol button.
- If you see the symbol or character you want in the Symbol gallery, click it. For a more extensive set of choices, click More Symbols to open the Symbol dialog box.
- In the Symbol dialog box, locate the symbol or character you want on either the Symbols tab or the Special Characters tab.
- Click the symbol or special character you want, click the Insert button, and then click the Close button.

Joel needs to include a registered trademark symbol (®) after "HealthLife" in the last paragraph of the newsletter.

To insert the registered trademark symbol:

1. Scroll down to display the paragraph below the heading "Risk Assessment" at the bottom of the right column, and then click to the right of the word "HealthLife." (Take care to click between the final "e" and the comma.)

2. Click the **Insert** tab, if necessary, click the **Symbol** button in the Symbols group, and then click **More Symbols**. The Symbol dialog box opens.

3. If necessary, click the **Special Characters** tab. See Figure 4-23.

Figure 4-23 ▶ Symbol dialog box

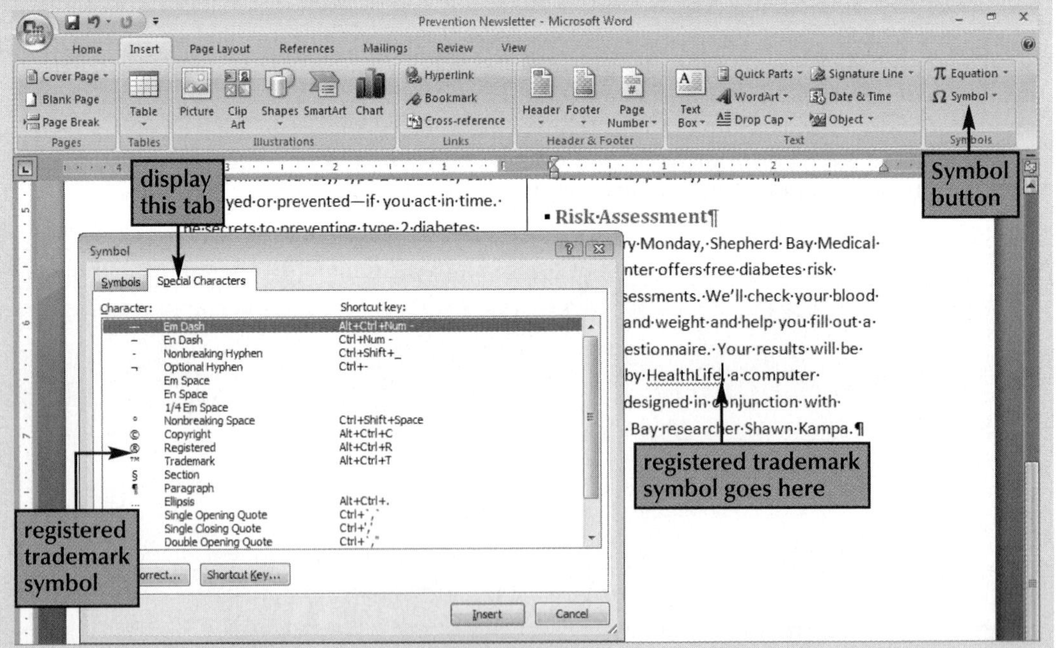

4. Click **Registered** to select it, and then click the **Insert** button.

5. Close the Symbol dialog box. Word inserts an ® immediately after and slightly above the word "HealthLife."

Next, you need to adjust the columns of text, so they are approximately the same length.

Balancing the Columns

You can shift text from one column to another by adding blank paragraphs to move the text into the next column or by deleting blank paragraphs to shorten the text, so it will fit into one column. The problem with this approach is that any edits you make later could throw off the balance. Instead, you can insert a continuous section break at the end of the document. This tells Word to automatically **balance** the columns, or make them of equal length. You'll balance the columns in the newsletter next.

To balance the columns:

▶ **1.** Press the **Ctrl+End** keys to move the insertion point to the end of the text in the right column, just after the period following your name.

▶ **2.** Zoom out, so you can see the entire newsletter at once.

▶ **3.** Click the **Page Layout** tab, and then, in the Page Setup group, click the **Breaks** button. The Breaks menu opens.

▶ **4.** Below "Section Breaks," click **Continuous**. Word inserts a continuous section break at the end of the text. As shown in Figure 4-24, Word balances the text between the two columns, so they are approximately the same length.

Newsletter with balanced columns ◀ Figure 4-24

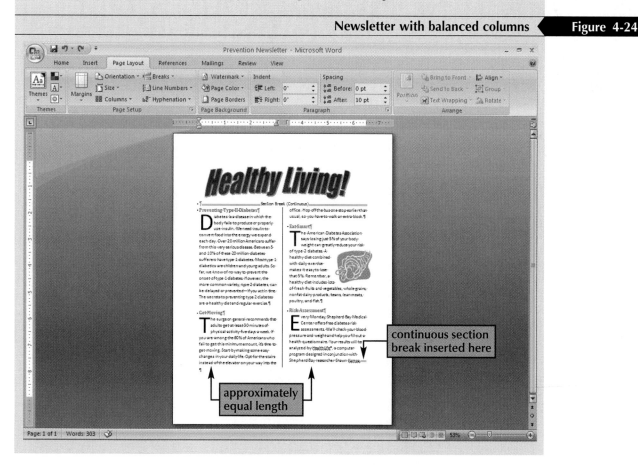

Inserting a Border Around a Page

You can add definition to a paragraph or an entire page by adding a border. Borders can be simple lines or they can be elaborate artwork. You can also emphasize pages and paragraphs by adding shading (a colored background). In both cases, you use the Page Borders button on the Page Layout tab, which opens the Borders and Shading dialog box. Right now, Joel wants to add a border around the entire newsletter page.

To insert a border around the newsletter:

▶ 1. Make sure the document is still zoomed out, so you can see the whole page and that the Page Layout tab is selected.

▶ 2. In the Page Background group, click the **Page Borders** button. The Borders and Shading dialog box opens.

▶ 3. If necessary, click the **Page Border** tab. (Take care not to click the Borders tab by mistake.) You use the Setting options on the left side of this tab to specify the type of border you want. In this case, you want a simple box.

▶ 4. In the Setting section, click the **Box** option. Now that you have selected the type of border you want, you can choose the style of line that will be used to create the border.

▶ 5. In the Style list box, scroll down and select the ninth style down from the top (the thick line with the thin line underneath), and then verify that the Apply to option is set to **Whole document**. See Figure 4-25. While the Borders and Shading dialog box is open, notice the Art arrow, which you can use to select a border consisting of graphical elements such as lightening bolts, boxes, or specially designed borders.

Tip

Use the Borders tab in the Borders and Shading dialog box to add a border around a selected paragraph. Use the Shading tab to add a colored background to a page or a selected paragraph.

Figure 4-25 ▶ Adding a border to the newsletter

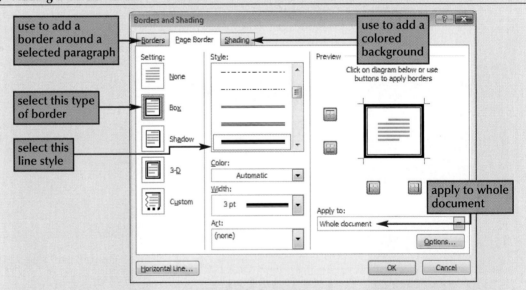

6. Click the **Options** button in the lower-right corner of the Borders and Shading dialog box. The Border and Shading Options dialog box opens. Here you can change settings that control where the border is positioned on the page. By default, the border is positioned 24 points from the edges of the page. To ensure that your printer will print the entire border, you need to change the Measure from setting so that it is positioned relative to the outside edge of the text rather than the edge of the page.

7. Click the **Measure from** arrow, and then click **Text**. The settings in the Top and Bottom boxes change to 1 pt, and the settings in the Left and Right boxes change to 4 pt, indicating the border's position relative to the edge of the text. You can leave the other settings as they are. See Figure 4-26.

Border and Shading Options dialog box ◄ Figure 4-26

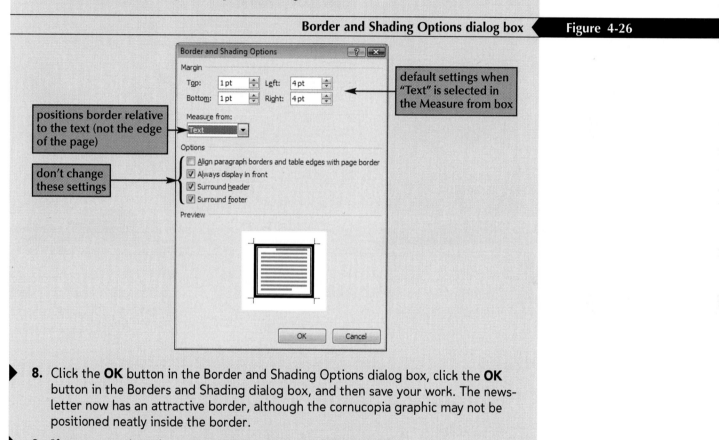

positions border relative to the text (not the edge of the page)

don't change these settings

default settings when "Text" is selected in the Measure from box

8. Click the **OK** button in the Border and Shading Options dialog box, click the **OK** button in the Borders and Shading dialog box, and then save your work. The newsletter now has an attractive border, although the cornucopia graphic may not be positioned neatly inside the border.

9. If necessary, drag the cornucopia graphic to position it inside the border, as shown in Figure 4-27. You may also need to drag the graphic up or down, so that the text wraps neatly around it. When you are finished, save the document.

Figure 4-27 ▶ **Newsletter with border**

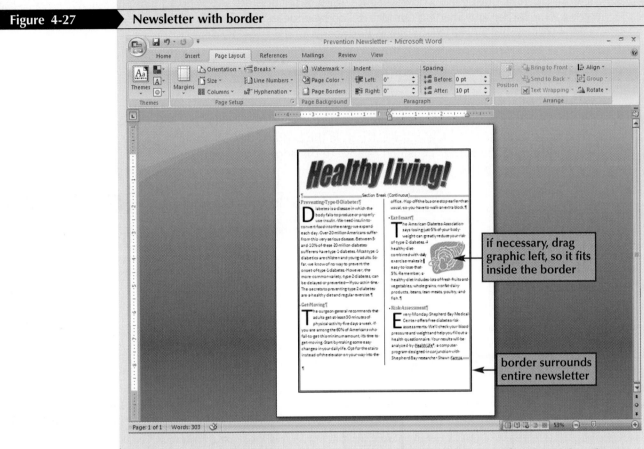

10. Print the newsletter, and then close the document, saving it if prompted to do so.

Joel will print the newsletter later on a high-quality color printer. But first, he asks you to use Word's mail merge feature to insert customer names and addresses into a cover letter he's written. He plans to send the cover letter with the newsletter.

Performing a Simple Mail Merge

The term **mail merge** refers to the process of combining information from two separate documents to create many final documents, each containing customized information. The two separate documents are called a main document and a data source. A **main document** is a document that contains text, such as a business letter, as well as placeholders called **merge fields**. The merge fields tell Word where to insert customized information such as a name or an address. You can distinguish merge fields from the text of the main document because each merge field name is enclosed by pairs of angled brackets like this: << >>.

Joel's main document is a letter that contains the text shown in Figure 4-28. You will replace the text in brackets with merge fields.

Joel's main document ◄ **Figure 4-28**

June 26, 2010

[INSERT ADDRESS FIELDS]

Dear [INSERT FIRST NAME FIELD]:

Enclosed you will find an informational newsletter published by Shepherd Bay Medical Center. We would like to make this a regular publication that focuses on health-related topics. To ensure that it is as helpful as possible, we are soliciting feedback from potential readers. Would you have a moment to give me your opinion regarding the newsletter's content and layout? My office is located at the South Clinic. You can reach me everyday from noon to 5 P.M. at 555-5555.

Sincerely,

Joel Conchola

Public Outreach Specialist

A **data source** is a document that contains the data, such as clients' names and addresses, that you can insert into the main document. Joel plans to send the newsletter to a small test group of clients. His data source is a table in a Word document that contains the names and addresses of five Shepherd Bay Medical Center clients. This table is shown in Figure 4-29. The header row in the table contains the names of the merge fields. Each row in the table contains information about an individual client. In mail merge terminology, all of the information about one person or one object is called a **record**.

Joel's data source ◄ **Figure 4-29**

a merge field name

header row includes all merge field names for this data source

First Name	Last Name	Street Address	City	State	ZIP
Rhoda	Carey	3545 Route 14	Brandon	MS	39875
Marley	Delisle	1234 E. Pascagoula	Jackson	MS	39204
Catherine	Larke	36 Capers Avenue	Jackson	MS	39211
Luca	Peters	3453 River Lane	Richland	MS	39345
Daniel	Shorba	4533 Terry Road	Jackson	MS	39298

record for individual client

During a mail merge, the merge fields in the main document instruct Word to retrieve information from the data source. For example, one merge field in the main document might retrieve a first name from the data source; another merge field might retrieve a street address. For each record in the data source, Word will create a separate letter in the final document, which is called the **merged document**. Thus, if the data source contains five sets of client names and addresses, the merged document will contain five separate letters, each one containing a different client name and address in the appropriate places.

The Mailings tab contains all the options you need for performing a mail merge. However, when you're just getting started with mail merge, it's helpful to use the Mail Merge task pane, which walks you through the process.

In the following steps, you'll open the Word document that you'll use as the data source, so you can see how it's set up. Then you'll open the Mail Merge task pane and start the mail merge.

To begin the mail merge process:

▶ 1. Open the document named **Addresses** from the Tutorial.04\Tutorial folder included with your Data Files. Review the table, which contains addresses for five clients of Shepherd Bay Medical Center.

▶ 2. Close the Addresses document without making any changes, and then open the document named **Letter** from the Tutorial.04\Tutorial folder included with your Data Files. When he typed this letter, Joel included text in brackets as placeholders to indicate where he wants to insert the merge fields.

▶ 3. Near the end of the letter, replace "Joel Conchola" with your first and last name, and then save the document as **Cover Letter** in the Tutorial.04\Tutorial folder included with your Data Files.

▶ 4. Click the **Mailings** tab, and then, in the Start Mail Merge group, click the **Start Mail Merge** button. The Start Mail Merge menu opens.

▶ 5. In the Start Mail Merge menu, click **Step by Step Mail Merge Wizard**. The Mail Merge task pane opens, displaying the first of six steps related to completing a mail merge. See Figure 4-30. Your first task is to specify the type of main document you want to use for the merge.

Figure 4-30	Mail Merge task pane

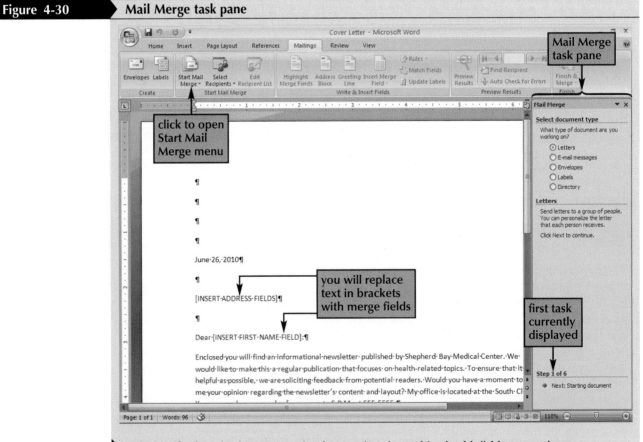

▶ 6. Verify that the **Letters** option button is selected in the Mail Merge task pane.

▶ 7. At the bottom of the Mail Merge task pane, click **Next: Starting document**. The Mail Merge task pane now displays information and options that you can use to select a starting document—that is, to select a main document. In this case, you want to use the current document, Cover Letter.

▶ **8.** Verify that the **Use the current document** option button is selected.

▶ **9.** At the bottom of the Mail Merge task pane, click **Next: Select recipients**. You'll continue working with the Mail Merge task pane in the next set of steps.

You've finished the first two tasks, which relate to selecting the main document. Now you are ready to tell Word where to find the list of recipients for Joel's letter.

Selecting a Data Source

You can use many kinds of files as data sources for a mail merge, including Word tables, Excel worksheets, Access databases, or Contacts lists from Microsoft Outlook. You can select a preexisting file or you can create a new data source. In this case, you will use the table in the Addresses document, which you examined earlier.

To select the data source:

▶ **1.** In the Mail Merge task pane, verify that the **Use an existing list** option button is selected.

▶ **2.** Click **Browse** in the Mail Merge task pane. The Select Data Source dialog box opens. This dialog box works similarly to Word's Open dialog box.

▶ **3.** Navigate to the Tutorial.04\Tutorial folder, select the **Addresses** document, and then click the **Open** button. The table from the Addresses document is displayed in the Mail Merge Recipients dialog box. See Figure 4-31.

Mail Merge Recipients dialog box ◀ **Figure 4-31**

▶ **4.** Click the **OK** button. The Mail Merge Recipients dialog box closes, and you return to the Cover Letter document with the Mail Merge task pane open. Under "Use an existing list," you see the name of the file selected as the data source—or, depending on where you store your Data Files, you may see only the beginning of a directory path, which identifies the location where the data source file is stored.

▶ **5.** Click **Next: Write your letter** at the bottom of the Mail Merge task pane. The task pane displays options related to inserting merge fields in the main document, which you'll learn about next.

Inserting Merge Fields

Joel's letter is a standard business letter, so you'll place the recipient's name and address below the date. You could insert individual merge fields for the client's first name, last name, address, city, and ZIP code. But it's easier to use the **Address block** link in the Mail Merge task pane, which inserts a merge field for the entire address with one click.

To insert an Address Block merge field:

▶ **1.** Select the text **[INSERT ADDRESS FIELDS]**, and then delete it. Remember to delete the opening and closing brackets. Do not delete the paragraph mark following the text.

▶ **2.** Verify that there are three blank paragraphs between the date and the salutation and that the insertion point is positioned in the second blank paragraph below the date.

▶ **3.** Click **Address block** in the Mail Merge task pane. The Insert Address Block dialog box opens. See Figure 4-32. The options in this dialog box allow you to fine-tune the way the address will be inserted in the letter. The Preview box shows you how the address will look in the document after the merge is complete.

Figure 4-32 ▶ **Insert Address Block dialog box**

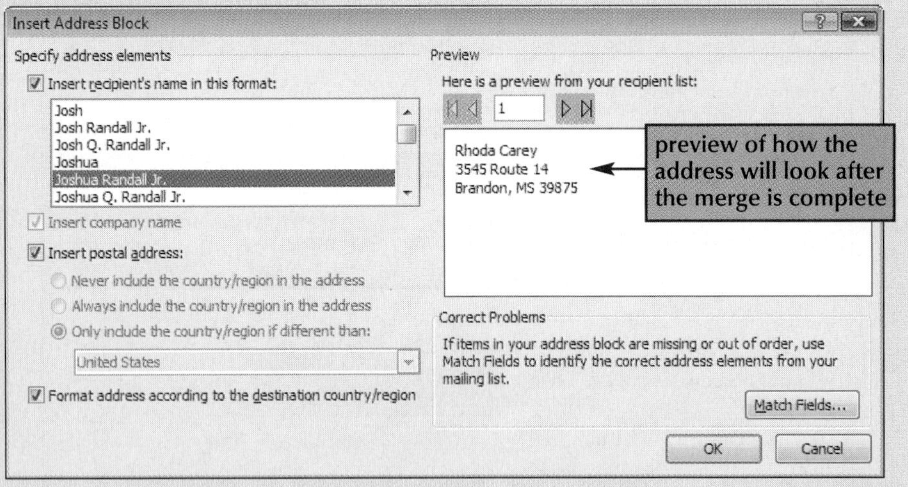

▶ **4.** Verify that the **Insert recipient's name in this format** check box is selected, and also verify that **Joshua Randall Jr.** is selected in the list box. This ensures that Word will insert each recipient's first and last name. (The other options in this list are useful with more complicated data sources.)

▶ **5.** Verify that the **Insert postal address** check box is selected. It doesn't matter whether the other check box and option buttons are selected; you only need to be concerned with them when working with more complicated data sources.

▶ **6.** Click the **OK** button. An Address Block merge field is inserted in the letter. See Figure 4-33. Depending on how your computer is set up, you might see a gray background behind the merge field. Notice the angled brackets that surround the merge field. The angled brackets are automatically inserted when you insert a merge field. It is important to note that you cannot type the angled brackets and merge field information—you must enter it via a dialog box selection.

Address Block merge field in letter ◀ **Figure 4-33**

Later, when you merge the main document with the data source, Word will replace the Address Block merge field with the address information for each record in the data source. Your next job is to insert a merge field that will include each client's first name in the salutation. To insert an individual merge field (rather than a field for the entire address), you need to use the More items option in the Mail Merge task pane.

To insert the merge field for the salutation:

▶ **1.** Select and delete **[INSERT FIRST NAME FIELD]** in the salutation. Remember to delete the opening and closing brackets. Do not delete the colon.

▶ **2.** If necessary, insert a space to the left of the colon. When you finish, the insertion point should be positioned between the space and the colon.

▶ **3.** In the Mail Merge task pane, click **More items**. The Insert Merge Field dialog box opens. The Fields list shows all the merge fields in the data source. See Figure 4-34. Note that merge fields cannot contain spaces, so Word replaces any spaces in the merge field names with underlines. You want to insert the client's first name into the main document, so you need to make sure the First_Name merge field is selected.

Figure 4-34 ▷ **Insert Merge Field dialog box**

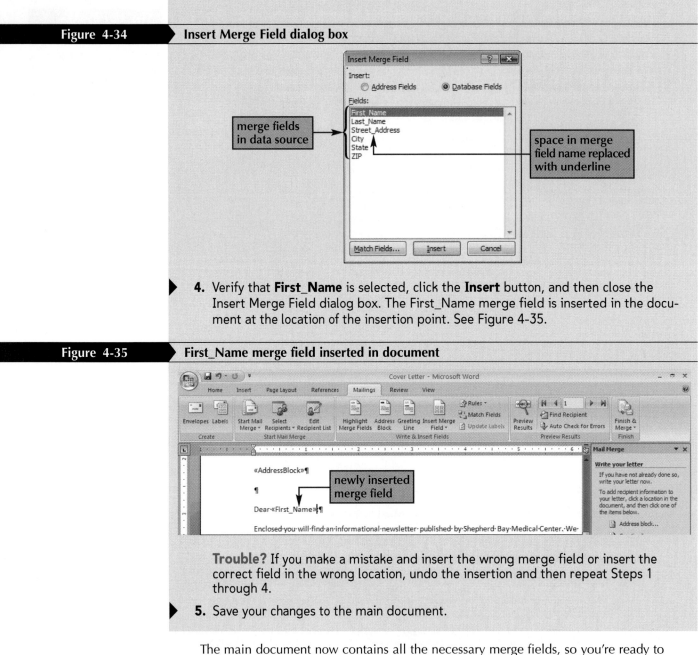

▷ **4.** Verify that **First_Name** is selected, click the **Insert** button, and then close the Insert Merge Field dialog box. The First_Name merge field is inserted in the document at the location of the insertion point. See Figure 4-35.

Figure 4-35 ▷ **First_Name merge field inserted in document**

Trouble? If you make a mistake and insert the wrong merge field or insert the correct field in the wrong location, undo the insertion and then repeat Steps 1 through 4.

▷ **5.** Save your changes to the main document.

The main document now contains all the necessary merge fields, so you're ready to merge the main document with the data source. First, however, you should preview the merged document.

Previewing the Merged Document

When you preview the merged document, you see the main document with the customized information inserted in place of the merge fields. Previewing a merged document allows you to check for errors or formatting problems before you perform the merge.

To preview the merged document:

▶ **1.** In the Mail Merge task pane, click **Next: Preview your letters**. The data for the first client in the data source (Rhoda Carey) replaces the merge fields in the cover letter. The top of the task pane indicates which record is currently displayed in the document. As shown in Figure 4-36, Word's default paragraph and line spacing results in too much space between the lines of the address. You can fix this by adjusting the spacing for the paragraph containing the Address Block merge field.

Trouble? If the address is highlighted with a gray background, the merge field is selected. Click anywhere in the document outside the address to deselect the merge field.

Previewing the merge document   Figure 4-36

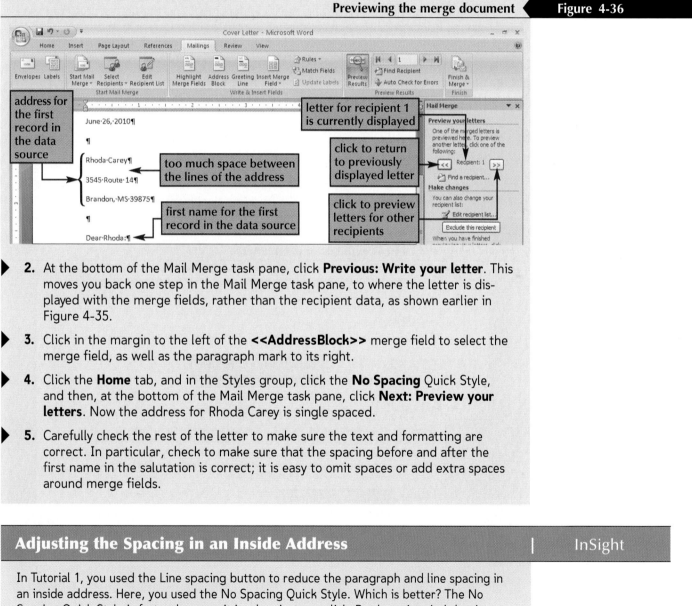

▶ **2.** At the bottom of the Mail Merge task pane, click **Previous: Write your letter**. This moves you back one step in the Mail Merge task pane, to where the letter is displayed with the merge fields, rather than the recipient data, as shown earlier in Figure 4-35.

▶ **3.** Click in the margin to the left of the **<<AddressBlock>>** merge field to select the merge field, as well as the paragraph mark to its right.

▶ **4.** Click the **Home** tab, and in the Styles group, click the **No Spacing** Quick Style, and then, at the bottom of the Mail Merge task pane, click **Next: Preview your letters**. Now the address for Rhoda Carey is single spaced.

▶ **5.** Carefully check the rest of the letter to make sure the text and formatting are correct. In particular, check to make sure that the spacing before and after the first name in the salutation is correct; it is easy to omit spaces or add extra spaces around merge fields.

Adjusting the Spacing in an Inside Address | InSight

In Tutorial 1, you used the Line spacing button to reduce the paragraph and line spacing in an inside address. Here, you used the No Spacing Quick Style. Which is better? The No Spacing Quick Style is faster, because it involves just one click. But keep in mind that it adjusts the line spacing and paragraph spacing at the same time. If you want more control over your spacing selections, use the Line spacing button instead.

You are ready for the final step—completing the merge.

Merging the Main Document and Data Source

Because your data source consists of five records, merging the main document with the data source will result in five copies of the letter to five different clients of Shepherd Bay Medical Center. Each letter will appear on its own page. Keep in mind that mail merges often involve hundreds or even thousands of records. As a result, the resulting document can be extremely long, with one page for every record in the data source.

To complete the mail merge:

▶ **1.** In the Mail Merge task pane, click **Next: Complete the merge**. The task pane displays options related to merging the main document and the data source. You can use the Print option to have Word print the customized letters immediately, without displaying them on the screen. Instead, you'll use the Edit individual letters option to merge to a new document.

▶ **2.** Click **Edit individual letters** in the Mail Merge task pane. The Merge to New Document dialog box opens. Here, you need to specify which records you want to include in the merge. You want to include all the records in the data source.

▶ **3.** Verify that the **All** option button is selected, click the **OK** button, and then scroll as needed to display the entire first letter. Word creates a new document (the merged document) called Letters1, which contains five pages, one for each record in the data source. Each letter is separated from the one that follows it by a Next Page section break. See Figure 4-37. The main document with the merge fields (Cover Letter) remains open, as indicated by its button on the taskbar.

Figure 4-37	Newly merged document with customized letters

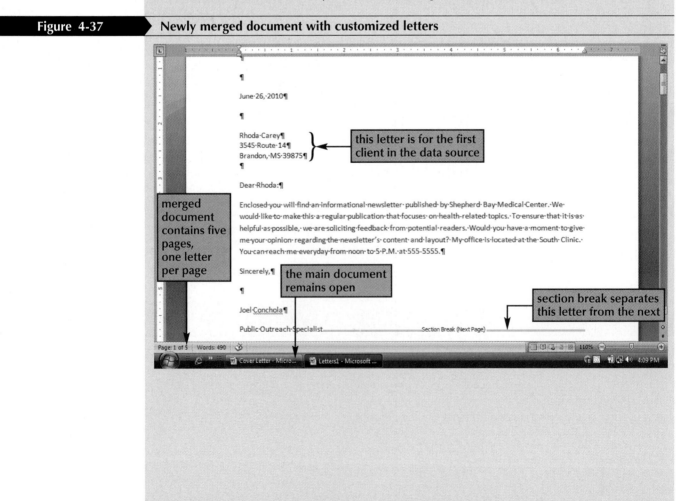

> **4.** Save the merged document in the Tutorial.04\Tutorial folder, using the filename **Merged Cover Letters**.

> **5.** Scroll down and review the five letters. Note the different address and salutation in each.

> **6.** Close the Merged Cover Letters document. The document named Cover Letter reappears, along with the Mail Merge task pane.

> **7.** Save the document and then close it.

You have completed a mail merge and generated a merged document. Joel will send the cover letters out with sample copies of his newsletter. Next, he wants to explore another means of communicating with the public—a blog.

Creating a Blog Post

A **blog** is an online journal that other people can read via the World Wide Web. The word "blog" is short for "Web log." Blogs typically include headings, paragraphs of text, pictures, and links to other blogs or Web sites. Although individuals often use blogs for personal reasons, in the business world a blog can serve the same function as a printed newsletter—providing news, product updates, and schedules of events. Because it can be updated instantly, and because the business doesn't incur printing costs, a blog is an effective way for a business or organization to communicate with the public.

A **blog post** is an addition to a blog, similar to an entry in a journal. When you create a blog post in Word, the file is a regular .docx file like an ordinary Word document, except that it doesn't have any of the formatting that controls the way a document looks on a printed page. It doesn't need that kind of formatting, because a blog is meant to be read on a computer screen. For example, the margins of a blog post are not fixed; instead, the margins change to accommodate the current zoom setting, with the text rewrapping as necessary. When it's finished, you can **post** it, or publish it—that is, add it to your online blog. At that point, the file is changed to an HTML file, so that it can easily be transferred over the Web.

Before you can post material to a blog, you need to create an account with a service that manages blogs and makes them available on the Web. Joel hasn't yet set up an account, but he wants to experiment with creating a blog post in Word. You can take an existing document and save it as a blog post, or you can start with a new, blank blog post. Joel wants to create a blog post from scratch. In the Case Problems at the end of this tutorial you'll save an existing document as a blog post.

To create a new blog post:

> **1.** If necessary, start Word.

> **2.** Click the **Office Button** (), and then click **New**. The New Document dialog box opens. The middle pane contains an option for creating a new blog post. (Note that your New Document dialog box may not include the Recently Used Templates section.) See Figure 4-38.

Figure 4-38 Selecting a blog post in the New Document dialog box

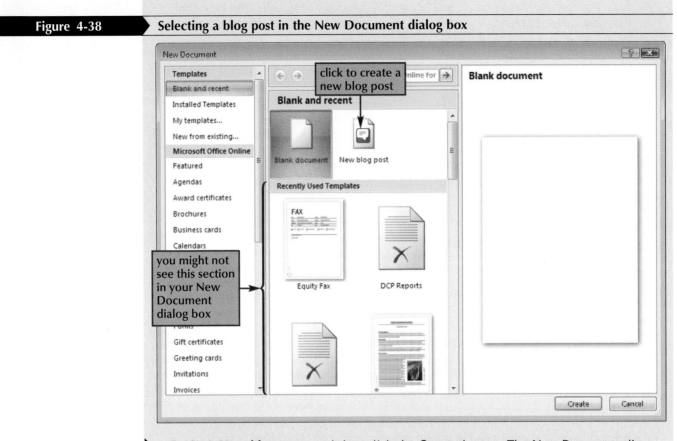

3. Click **New blog post**, and then click the **Create** button. The New Document dialog box closes and the Register a Blog Account dialog box opens. You don't need to create a blog account in order to create a blog post, so you'll skip this step. Later, if you decide to start an online blog, you could use this dialog box to register with a blog provider.

4. Click **Register Later**. The Register a Blog Account dialog box closes. A blank blog post opens. It includes some placeholder text, which you can replace with a title for the new post. Notice that the Ribbon has only two tabs, both containing tools related to working with blog posts. See Figure 4-39.

Figure 4-39 Blank blog post

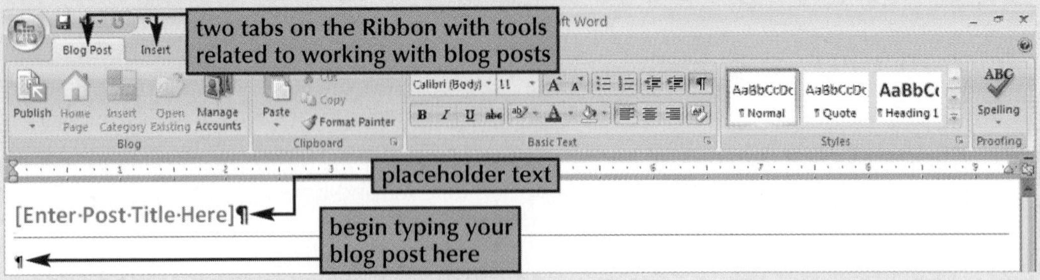

5. Click the placeholder text **[Enter Post Title Here]** and type **Shepherd Bay Medical Center's New Blog**. The placeholder text is replaced with the new post title.

6. Click in the blank paragraph below the horizontal line and type **This is a sample blog post for Shepherd Bay Medical Center.** See Figure 4-40. A typical blog post is at least several lines long, and may contain graphics, tables, and links to other information on the Web. The Insert tab simplifies the process of adding this type of material. If you had registered with a blog provider, you could click the Publish button in the Blog group to post this to your online blog. Because you have not registered with a blog provider, you will simply save the blog post instead. Even if you publish a blog post, you should always save a copy on your computer, so you have a complete record of all your posts.

Sample blog post   Figure 4-40

if you had registered with a blog provider, you could click here to add this post to your online blog

Shepherd·Bay·Medical·Center's·New·Blog¶

This·is·a·sample·blog·post·for·Shepherd·Bay·Medical·Center.¶

7. Click the **Save** button on the Quick Access Toolbar, and then save the blog post as **Sample Blog Post** in the Tutorial.04\Tutorial folder included with your Data Files.

8. Print the blog post just as you would print an ordinary Word document, and then close the blog post.

Now that Joel understands how easy it is to create a blog post in Word, he will look into registering with a blog provider. A blog, along with the newsletter and the mass mailings he can create in Word, will help him communicate important information to the clients of Shepherd Bay Medical Center.

Session 4.2 Quick Check | Review

1. What type of text wrapping makes text follow the shape of the graphic?
2. True or False: When inserting a drop cap, you can specify the number of lines you want the drop cap to extend into the paragraph.
3. Explain how to open the Borders and Shading dialog box.
4. Name the two types of documents you need in a mail merge.
5. Define "record" as a mail merge term.
6. List the steps in performing a mail merge.
7. Explain how to open a new, blank blog post.

In this tutorial, you planned a newsletter and learned about the elements of desktop publishing. You created a headline using WordArt, anchored the WordArt object, and formatted text in newspaper-style columns. You also inserted a graphic into a document, edited the graphic, inserted drop caps, and inserted symbols and special characters. Next, you balanced the newsletter columns, drew a border around the page, and used mail merge to create customized cover letters to accompany the newsletter. Finally, you created a blog post.

Key Terms

anchoring	floating graphic	pull quote
balance	graphic	record
bitmap	inline graphic	rules
blog	mail merge	scaling
blog post	main document	sizing handles
clip art	merge fields	template
crop	merged document	text box
data source	newspaper-style column	typographic symbols
desktop publishing	object	WordArt
drop cap	post	wrap

Practice	**Review Assignments**

Apply the skills you learned in the tutorial using the same case scenario.

Data Files needed for the Review Assignments: Addresses.docx, Eating.docx, and Nutrition.docx

Joel's Healthy Living newsletter was well received. Now the Nutrition Department of the Shepherd Bay Medical Center has asked him to create a newsletter providing information and encouragement for Shepherd Bay clients to eat well. Joel has already written the text of the newsletter and asks you to transform it into a professional-looking newsletter. He asks you to create an accompanying cover letter using Word's mail merge feature, and then to create the first blog post for a new nutrition blog. (Note: Text you need to type is shown in bold for ease of reference only; do not bold the text unless otherwise instructed.) Complete the following:

1. Open the file **Eating** from the Tutorial.04\Review folder included with your Data Files, and then make sure your Word document is displayed in Print Layout view and that the nonprinting characters and rulers are displayed.
2. Save the document as **Eating Well** in the same folder.
3. In the last paragraph, replace "STUDENT NAME" with your first and last name.
4. At the top of the document, create the headline **Healthy Servings** using WordArt. In the WordArt Gallery, choose the fourth style from the left in the third row down from the top (the rainbow style with the shadow—WordArt style 16).
5. Change the shape of the WordArt object to Double Wave 2, and then italicize the WordArt text.
6. Apply the Top and Bottom text wrapping style to the WordArt object.
7. Drag the WordArt object to center it at the top of the page, then enlarge the WordArt object to span the width of the page. When you are finished, the WordArt object should be slightly less than one inch high and a little more than six inches wide.
8. Insert a blank paragraph at the beginning of the document, anchor the WordArt object to the new blank paragraph, and then save your work. If the WordArt moves below the new paragraph symbol, drag it up above the new paragraph. When you are finished, the anchor symbol should be positioned to the left of, and just above, the new paragraph symbol, with the WordArt object positioned above the new paragraph symbol.
9. Position the insertion point at the beginning of the newsletter text (to the left of the heading "Eat Light, Eat Right"), and then format the newsletter text in two columns. Insert a section break so that the two-column formatting is applied below the insertion point and insert a line between the two columns.
10. Click at the beginning of the paragraph below the heading "Eating Well in a Busy World."
11. At the insertion point, insert the clip art graphic of the running person with the cell phone from the Business folder in the Office Collections folder. (The image is black and blue.)
12. Close the Clip Art task pane, and then resize the graphic, so it is approximately 1.5 inches square.
13. Crop the image slightly on the top to remove most of the dotted blue line. Make sure not to crop any part of the satellite dish or the black and blue background behind the running figure.
14. Wrap text around the graphic using Tight text wrapping, and then drag the graphic down to position it near the middle of the paragraph, next to the left margin. Three lines of the paragraph text should wrap below the graphic. Use the Align button to align the graphic at the left margin. You may have to move the graphic around a bit until you find a location that allows the text to wrap neatly around it.

15. Create a drop cap in the first paragraph under each heading. When you are finished, adjust the position of the graphic if necessary, so the text wraps neatly around it, without excessive space between words.

16. In the paragraph below the heading "Eating Well in a Busy World," insert the trademark symbol after "20 Fast Food Friends."

17. Check to make sure the document is still only one page long. If the text has flowed to the second page, then you probably made the WordArt headline too tall. Resize the WordArt object (and the graphic, if necessary) until the document is only one page long.

18. If you think it's necessary, balance the columns by inserting a Continuous section break at the bottom of the document. If you do insert a Continuous section break, and a new page is added at the end of the document, delete the section break. You probably sized the WordArt object and the graphic in a way that makes the section break unnecessary.

19. Add a border around the page using the Box setting and the border style with three thin lines (eighth from the top). Remember to position the border relative to the text, and not the edge of the page. Adjust the position of the clip art graphic if necessary.

20. Preview, save, and print the newsletter. When you are finished, close the document.

21. Open the file **Nutrition** located in the Tutorial.04\Review folder, replace "Joel Conchola" at the end of the letter with your name, and then save the document as **Nutrition Letter** in the same folder.

22. Merge the Nutrition Cover Letter document with the Addresses file found in the Tutorial.04\Review folder. Use the Address Block merge field for the inside address. Next, include a merge field that will insert the customer's first name in the salutation. Preview the merged letters and make any necessary changes before completing the merge. Remember to adjust the spacing for the Address Block field, so the inside address is single spaced.

23. Save the merged document as **Merged Nutrition Letters** and close it. Save your changes to the main document and close it. Close the task pane if necessary.

24. Create a new blog post. Use "Eating Right for Life" as the post title. For the blog post, type two sentences introducing a health and nutrition blog sponsored by the Nutrition Department at Shepherd Bay Medical Center. Save the blog post as **Nutrition Blog** in the Tutorial.04\Review folder included with your Data Files, and then close it.

25. Submit the finished documents to your instructor, either in printed or electronic form, as requested.

Apply | **Case Problem 1**

Apply the skills you learned to create a newsletter and a blog post for a public library.

Data File needed for this Case Problem: Audio.docx

Florentina, Arizona, Public Library Michaela Novoa is the director of the Florentina, Arizona, Public Library. She and her staff have developed a new program that makes it possible for library patrons to download audio books over the Web as MP3 files. Michaela has written the text of a newsletter explaining the download system. She asks you to finalize the newsletter and then create a blog post from the formatted newsletter. (Note: Text you need to type is shown in bold for ease of reference only; do not bold the text unless otherwise instructed.) Complete the following:

1. Open the file **Audio** located in the Tutorial.04\Case1 folder included with your Data Files. Make sure your document is displayed in Print Layout view at Page width zoom and that the ruler and the nonprinting characters are displayed.

2. At the end of the document, replace "STUDENT NAME" with your first and last name. Save the document as **Audio Books** in the same folder.

3. At the top of the document, create the headline **Downloading Audio Books** using WordArt. In the WordArt Gallery, choose WordArt style 11, in the second column from the right, second row from the top (blue block letters).

4. Set the text wrapping style to Top and Bottom.

5. Drag the WordArt object to center it at the top of the page, and then enlarge the WordArt object to span the entire width of the page. When you are finished, the WordArt object should be a little less than 1 inch high and about 6.5 inches wide.

6. Edit the WordArt object to set the font to Arial and to apply bold to it. Then apply the Inflate Top shape to the headline and save your work.

7. Make sure the WordArt is anchored to the paragraph containing the subtitle of the newsletter, "Florentina, Arizona, Public Library." (The anchor should be located in the margin, on the same line as the subtitle.) In this newsletter, you don't need to insert a blank paragraph and anchor the WordArt to it, because the columns will begin below the subtitle, not directly below the WordArt.

✛ EXPLORE

8. Select the paragraph containing the subtitle and center and italicize it. Open the Borders and Shading dialog box, click the Borders tab, and apply a Box border with the default line style. Make sure the Apply to box shows Paragraph. Click the Shading tab, click the Fill arrow, and click the pink box in the second row from the top. Be sure Paragraph is still selected in the Apply to list box, and then click the OK button.

9. Format all the text below the subtitle in two newspaper style columns, without a line between them. The subtitle should be centered over the two columns.

10. Open the Clip Art task pane and use the Clip Organizer to locate the image of a man in a brown suit typing on a keyboard. The image is stored in the Business folder within the Office Collections folder. Paste the image at the beginning of the first paragraph under the heading "How do I Listen to a Downloaded Book?" Close the Clip Art task pane.

11. Resize the picture, so that it is 1.5 inches wide.

12. Apply the Square text wrapping option. Drag the graphic down to the middle of the paragraph, next to the right column border. Align the graphic using the Align Right option in the Align menu.

13. Balance the columns, then zoom out, so you can see the whole page and review your work. If the newsletter text flows to a second page, reduce the height of the WordArt object until the newsletter is again only one page long.

14. Save and print the newsletter.

✛ EXPLORE

15. Click anywhere in the document text to make sure the graphic and the WordArt object are not selected. Click the Office Button, point to Publish, and then click Blog. If you are asked to register a blog account, click Register Later. Save the new blog post as **Audio Books Blog** in the Tutorial.04\Case1 folder included with your Data Files. When saved as a blog post, the document loses the two-column formatting. You can format a blog in columns, but you need to do it through the blog provider, not when you create individual blog posts in Word.

16. Increase the zoom setting to at least 130%, so you can easily read the text. Notice how, in a blog post, the text wraps to fit the zoom size.

17. Click the WordArt title and delete it. Enter **Downloading Audio Books** as the post title. Select the subtitle in the pink box, and align it on the left margin. Delete the section break, as it is no longer necessary. If necessary, drag the clip art down to the paragraph below the heading "How do I download a book from ListenBooks?" Note that the final position of graphics in an online blog is often determined by the blog service provider.

18. Save your work, submit the finished documents to your instructor, either in printed or electronic form, as requested, and then close the files.

Apply | **Case Problem 2**

Apply the skills you learned to create an employee newsletter.

Data Files needed for this Case Problem: Island.jpg and News.docx

Flannery Investments You work in the Personnel Department for Flannery Investments, a national investment company with headquarters in Minneapolis, Minnesota. You've been assigned the task of preparing the monthly newsletter *Flannery News*, which provides news about employees of Flannery Investments. You will use text written by other employees for the body of the newsletter. The newsletter will ultimately be three pages long, but at this point you have enough text to fill only one page and part of another. Complete the following:

1. Open the file **News** located in the Tutorial.04\Case2 folder included with your Data Files, and then save it as **Flannery Newsletter** in the same folder.

2. Use the Find and Replace command to replace all instances of the name "Daniela" with your first name. Then replace all instances of "Alford" with your last name.

3. At the top of the newsletter, create a **Flannery News** WordArt headline. Use the WordArt style in the second row down, third column from the left (WordArt style 9), select Arial as the font, and apply bold formatting. Set the wrapping style to Top and Bottom, and then anchor the WordArt to the blank paragraph at the top of the document, if it isn't already.

4. Center the WordArt if necessary, and resize the WordArt proportionally, so that it spans the width of the page and is about 1 inch high and 6 inches wide.

5. Make sure the WordArt object is positioned above the blank paragraph and anchored to the blank paragraph. Format the body of the newsletter into three newspaper-style columns. Place a vertical rule between the columns.

⊕ **EXPLORE** 6. Position the insertion point at the beginning of the paragraph below the heading "Win a Vacation Get-Away." Click the Insert tab, and then, in the Illustrations group, click the Picture button. In the Picture dialog box, navigate to the Tutorial.04\Case2 folder, select the **Island** file, and then click the Insert button.

7. Crop about a third of the photo from the left and right sides, so that you only see the pier stretching out into the water. When you are finished, the image should be about .5 inches wide.

⊕ **EXPLORE** 8. Make sure the photo is still selected and that the Picture Tools Format tab is displayed. In the Arrange group, click the Position button, and then, under With Text Wrapping, click the option in the left column, middle row. This aligns the photo on the left margin, halfway down the page, with the text wrapped around it. You don't need to select an alignment option on the Align menu when you use the Position button.

9. Click in the first paragraph under the heading "Win a Vacation Get-Away," and insert a drop cap that drops two lines into the paragraph. Insert a similar drop cap in the first paragraph after each of the other two headings in the newsletter.

10. Zoom out so you can see the whole page and review your work. Don't be concerned that the newsletter spans more than one page.

11. Add a page border to the newsletter. Select yellow stars as the art for the border. Apply the border to both pages of the newsletter (the entire document).

12. Save your work, submit the finished documents to your instructor, either in printed or electronic form, as requested, and then close any open files.

Challenge | **Case Problem 3**

Explore new techniques as you create the two-sided brochure shown in Figure 4-41.

Data File needed for this Case Problem: Hill.docx

Hill Star Dairy Cooperative   Haley Meskin is the publicity director for Hill Star Dairy Cooperative in Lawrence, Kansas. Local residents pay a membership fee to join the co-op and then receive a 10% discount on purchases of organic dairy products. Many members don't realize that they can take advantage of other benefits, such as free cooking classes and monthly mailings with recipe cards and coupons. To spread the word, Haley would like to create a brochure describing the benefits of joining the co-op. She has already written the text of the brochure. She would like the brochure to consist of one piece of paper folded in three parts, with text on both sides of the paper, as shown in Figure 4-41. (Note: Text you need to type is shown in bold for ease of reference only; do not bold the text unless otherwise instructed.)

Figure 4-41

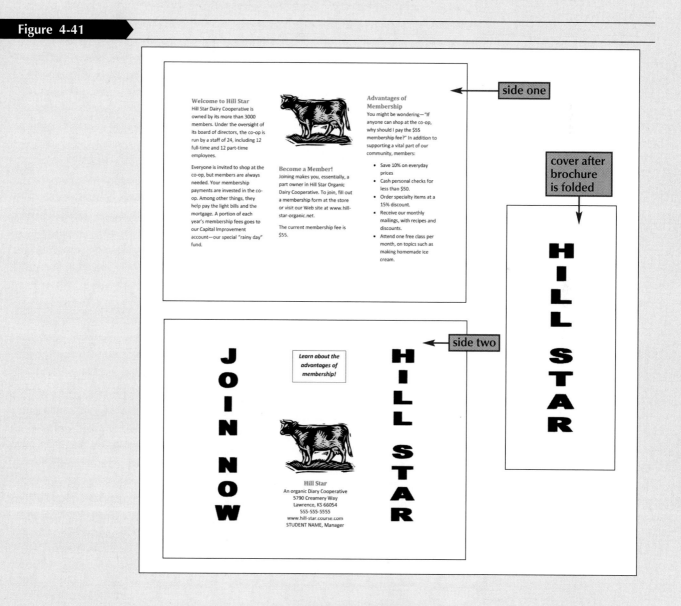

Complete the following:

1. Open the file **Hill** located in the Tutorial.04\Case3 folder included with your Data Files, and then save it as **Hill Star Brochure** in the same folder. This document contains a graphic of a cow. Because no text wrapping has been applied to it, it is an inline graphic. In this case, you want the graphic to remain an inline graphic, because you want it to move with the text as you edit the document.

2. On the second page, below the cow graphic, replace "STUDENT NAME" with your first and last name.

3. Format the entire document in three columns of equal width. Do not include a vertical line between columns. Ignore the page break at the bottom of page 1.

⊕ EXPLORE   4. You are already familiar with adding section breaks and page breaks to a document. You can also add a column break, which forces the text after the insertion point to move to the next column. Click at the beginning of the heading "Become a Member!" (just to the left of the "B"), click the Page Layout tab, and then, in the Page Setup group, click the Breaks button. In the Breaks menu, click Column. Insert another column break before the heading "Advantages of Membership." On the second page, click the second blank paragraph on the page, and then insert another column break. This column break moves the cow graphic and the text below it to the middle column. Press the Ctrl+End keys to move the insertion point to the blank paragraph at the end of the document, and insert another column break; this moves the blank paragraph to the third column on the second page.

5. Zoom out so you can see the whole page and review your work. The document should consist of two pages, with three columns each. The cow graphic and the co-op address should appear in the middle column on the second page.

⊕ EXPLORE   6. Click the cow graphic in the second page, copy the graphic to the Clipboard, click to the left of the heading "Become a Member!", and then insert two blank paragraphs. Click in the first new paragraph (at the top of the column), and then paste the graphic from the Clipboard. The middle column of the first page now contains the cow graphic, with the heading "Become a Member!" below, followed by two paragraphs of text.

7. On page 2, click in the blank paragraph at the top of the left column. Insert a WordArt object. In the WordArt Gallery, select the style in the left column, fourth row down. Use **JOIN NOW** (use uppercase letters) as the text. *Save your work.*

⊕ EXPLORE   8. Select the WordArt object if it is not already selected, and make sure the WordArt Tools Format tab is visible. In the Text group, click the WordArt Vertical Text button. This arranges the letters vertically down the column.

9. Adjust the size of the WordArt object (by dragging a sizing handle), so that it spans the height of the column—do *not* press the Shift key as you drag the handle. When you are finished, the WordArt object should be approximately 6 inches high and 1 inch wide. If you make it too wide, the WordArt will be hard to read. If you increase the height too much, the WordArt will disturb the column breaks, possibly resulting in a third page being added to the document. If that happens, click the Undo button and try again.

⊕ EXPLORE   10. In the WordArt Styles group on the WordArt Tools Format tab, click the Shape Fill button arrow. Click the black square in the top row of the palette. The WordArt changes from a marbleized brown to all black. Save your work.

11. Copy the WordArt object to the Clipboard. Paste a copy of the WordArt in the right column of page 2, select the newly pasted copy, click the Edit Text button in the Text group on the Format tab, and then change the text to **HILL STAR**. When you are finished, page 2 should consist of the JOIN NOW WordArt in the left column, the graphic and address information in the middle column, and the HILL STAR WordArt in the right column. Zoom out so you can see the whole page and examine your work.

12. Use the Center button on the Home tab to center both WordArt objects in their respective columns.

⊕ EXPLORE   13. Click the Page Layout tab, and then, in the Page Setup group, click the Dialog Box Launcher. In the Page Setup dialog box, click the Layout tab, click the Vertical alignment arrow, click Center, and then click the OK button. This centers the text vertically on the page (between the top and bottom margins) and ensures that the brochure will look right when folded. Save your work.

⊕ EXPLORE   14. Change the Zoom setting to 100% and scroll to display the top of the middle column on the second page. Click the top of the middle column, insert five blank paragraphs, click the Insert tab, and then, in the Text group, click the Text Box button. In the Text Box gallery, click Simple Text Box, and then, in the text box inserted in the document, type **Learn about the advantages of membership!**. Select the text in the text box and, using the appropriate tools on the Home tab, format the text in 16-point Calibri, italic, and bold. Center the text in the text box. Place the mouse pointer on the border of the text box, and drag the text box up to position it at the top of the middle column, above the cow. Drag the border of the text box to make the text box narrower than the column, and only as tall as necessary to display all of the text. Zoom out, so you can see the whole page, and adjust the text box size and the position of the graphic as needed, so that the content of the middle column fits nicely on the page. Save your work.

15. To print the brochure, you need to print the first page and then print the second page on the reverse side. Ask your instructor if you should print the brochure before doing so. To print the brochure, click the Office button, click Print, click the Pages option button, type **1**, and then click the OK button. Retrieve the printed page, and then insert it into your printer's paper tray, so that "JOIN NOW" prints on the reverse side of the list of member benefits; likewise, "HILL STAR" should print on the reverse side of the "Welcome to Hill Star" text. Whether you should place the printed page upside down or right-side up depends on your printer. You may have to print a few test pages until you get it right. When you finish, you should be able to turn page 1 (the page with the heading "Welcome to Hill Star") face up, and then fold it inward in thirds, along the two column borders. Fold the brochure, so that the "HILL STAR" column lies on top.

16. Save your work, submit the finished documents to your instructor, either in printed or electronic form, as requested, and then close any open files.

Create | **Case Problem 4**

Create the table shown in Figure 4-42, and then use it as the data source for a mail merge resulting in cover letters and envelopes for your own internship search.

There are no Data Files needed for this Case Problem.

Internship Search Cover Letters You're ready to start looking for an internship, and you plan to use Word to create customized cover letters to accompany your resume. You've decided to use mail merge to customize the letters. You'll start by creating the table shown in Figure 4-42 and filling it with address information for potential internship sponsors. Then you'll create a cover letter to use as a main document, and customize it by inserting the appropriate mail merge fields. (Note: Text you need to type is shown in bold for ease of reference only; do not bold the text unless otherwise instructed.) Complete the following:

1. Open a new, blank document, and then save it as **Intern Data** in the Tutorial.04\ Case4 folder included with your Data Files.

2. Create the table shown in Figure 4-42, and then enter information for three potential internship sponsors. The information can be real or fictitious. For the First Name and Last Name columns, use a fictitious name for an appropriate contact at each company. Use Ms. or Mr. for the Title field. Note that the Title field has to be the column on the far right, or the Address Block merge field won't work correctly. (The Address Block merge field assumes the first seven columns on the left are the fields you want to include in the address.) Save your work and close the document.

Figure 4-42

First Name	Last Name	Company Name	Street Address	City	State	ZIP	Title

3. Open a new, blank document and save it as **Intern Letter** in the Tutorial.04\Case4 folder.

4. Create a cover letter that introduces yourself and describes your experience and education. Instead of an inside address, include the placeholder text **[INSIDE ADDRESS]**. For the salutation, use **Dear [TITLE] [LAST NAME]**. Refer the reader to your resume (even if you don't have one) for more information. Use a proper business letter style for your cover letter. Include a sentence in the cover letter that mentions the company name. Use the placeholder **[COMPANY NAME]** to remind you to insert the appropriate merge field later. Save your work.

5. Save the letter, and open the Mail Merge task pane and follow the steps outlined in it. Use the Intern Letter document as the main document, and select the Intern Data file as the data source.

6. Use the Address block merge field for the inside address (in the "Joshua Randall Jr." format), and verify that the Insert company name check box is selected in the Insert Address Block dialog box. Adjust the paragraph and line spacing for the paragraph containing the Address Block merge field, so the inside address is single spaced.

7. Add a merge field for the title and the last name in the salutation of the letter, and add a merge field to replace the company name placeholder text in the body of the letter. Save your changes to the main document before completing the merge.

8. Preview your letters, and then complete the merge (choosing the Edit individual letters option). Save the merged document as **Merged Intern Letters** in the Tutorial.04\ Case4 folder, close it, and close the Mail Merge task pane.

9. Print your main document, and then close it.

10. Open a new, blank document, and then save it as **Intern Envelopes** in the Tutorial.04\ Case4 folder.

⊕ EXPLORE

11. Open the Mail Merge task pane, click the Envelopes option button under Select document type, and then click Next: Starting document. Click Envelope options, and then click the OK button in the Envelope Options dialog box to select the default settings. The document layout changes to resemble a business size envelope.

12. Continue with the steps in the Mail Merge task pane, selecting the Intern Data file as the data source.

13. Click Next: Arrange your envelope, and notice that the insertion point is positioned in the return address, ready for you to begin typing. Type your name and address as the return address. (Change the Zoom setting if necessary to make the text easier to read.) Click the paragraph mark in the center of the document and insert an Address block merge field in the "Joshua Randall Jr." format. You do not have to adjust the paragraph or line spacing for the Address block field for an envelope. Save your work.

14. Preview the envelopes, and complete the merge (choosing the Edit individual envelopes option). Don't worry about the section break that appears after the return address; the envelopes will print correctly. Save the merged document as **Merged Intern Envelopes** in the Tutorial.04\Case4 folder. If your computer is connected to a printer that is stocked with envelopes, print the main document. Close the Mail Merge task pane and save your changes to the main document.

15. Submit the finished documents to your instructor, either in printed or electronic form, as requested, and then close any open files.

Research		**Internet Assignments**

Go to the Web to find information you can use to create documents.

The purpose of the Internet Assignments is to challenge you to find information on the Internet that you can use to work effectively with this software. The actual assignments are updated and maintained on the Course Technology Web site. Log on to the Internet and use your Web browser to go to the Student Online Companion for New Perspectives Office 2007 at **www.course.com/np/office2007**. Then navigate to the Internet Assignments for this tutorial.

Assess		**SAM Assessment and Training**

SAM

If you have a SAM user profile, you may have access to hands-on instruction, practice, and assessment of the skills covered in this tutorial. Log in to your SAM account (**http://sam2007.course.com**) to launch any assigned training activities or exams that relate to the skills covered in this tutorial.

Session 4.1

1. The document uses multiple fonts; the document incorporates graphics; the document uses typographic symbols; the document uses columns and other special formatting features; the printing is of high quality.
2. Click the WordArt object to select it, click the Edit Text button in the Text group on the WordArt Tools Format tab, edit the text in the Edit WordArt Text dialog box, and then click the OK button.
3. False
4. Text Wrapping button; located in the Arrange group on the WordArt Tools Format tab
5. Columns dialog box
6. BMP, GIF, JPEG, and TIFF
7. Insert tab

Session 4.2

1. Tight
2. True
3. Click the Page Layout tab, and then, in the Page Background group, click the Page Borders button
4. Main document and data source
5. A single row in a data source
6. Select or create a main document. Select or create a data source. Use the Mail Merge task pane to insert merge fields into the main document. Preview the merged document. Merge the data source and the main document.
7. Click the Office button, click New, click New blog post, click the Create button.

Ending Data Files

Tutorial.04 →

Tutorial

Addresses.docx
Cover Letter.docx
Merged Cover Letters.docx
Prevention Newsletter.docx
Sample Blog Post.docx

Review

Addresses.docx
Eating Well.docx
Merged Nutrition Letters.docx
Nutrition Blog.docx
Nutrition Letter.docx

Case1

Audio Books.docx
Audio Books Blog.docx

Case2

Flannery Newsletter.docx

Case3

Hill Star Brochure.docx

Case4

Intern Data.docx
Intern Envelopes.docx
Intern Letter.docx
Merged Intern Envelopes.docx
Merged Intern Letters.docx

Reality Check

You've seen how Microsoft Word 2007 allows you to create polished, professional-looking documents in a variety of business settings. The word-processing skills you've learned will be useful to you in many areas of your life. For example, you could create a Word table to keep track of a guest list for a wedding, or you could use Word's desktop publishing features to create a flyer promoting a garage sale or a concert for a friend's band. In the following exercise, you'll create a number of useful documents of your choosing using the Word skills and features presented in Tutorials 1 through 4.

Using Templates

You can create the documents in this exercise from scratch, or you can use the templates that are available in the New documents dialog box. A **template** is a special Word document that comes with predefined headings, formatting, document controls, and graphical elements. In the New Document dialog box, click Installed Templates, and then click the template you want. To use a template after you've opened it, save it like an ordinary document, and then replace the placeholder text with your own information. If a template includes a sample picture, you can replace the picture with your own JPEG photo file or a clip art image.

Note: Please be sure *not* to include any personal information of a sensitive nature in the documents you create to be submitted to your instructor for this exercise. Later on, you can update the documents with such information for your own personal use.

1. Create a resume that you could use to apply for your ideal job.
2. Create a cover letter to accompany your resume and portfolio. Where appropriate, insert placeholders for merge fields.
3. Create a data source that includes one record for each company or organization you plan to send your resume to.
4. Perform a mail merge, using your cover letter and your data source. Save the merged document.
5. Perform a second mail merge to create the envelopes for your cover letter and resume. In the first step of the Mail Merge task pane, click the Envelopes option button. In the second step, click Envelope options, and then click the OK button to accept the default envelope settings. Continue following the steps in the Mail Merge task pane. Save the merged document.
6. Create a multiple-page report. For the text of the report, you can use a report you have already written for another class or any text of your choosing. Choose an appropriate theme. Include a cover page, header, and footer. Include at least two footnotes or endnotes, and format the headings with appropriate Quick Styles.
7. Use a Word table to design a one-page flyer for an upcoming event. Remember that you can insert graphics into a table cell and that you can format the text in each cell differently. Also, keep in mind that the buttons in the Merge group on the Table Tools Layout tab allow you to combine and divide table cells.
8. Create a newsletter containing information you want to share with friends, family, or colleagues. Include graphics, newspaper-style columns, and other desktop publishing elements, as appropriate, to enhance your newsletter.
9. Save the newsletter as a blog post. Make any changes necessary to make the blog post attractive and easy to read.
10. Review all your documents carefully in Print Preview, and then submit the finished documents to your instructor, either in printed or electronic form, as requested.

Glossary/Index

Note: Boldface entries include definitions.

A

Access. *See* Microsoft Office Access 2007

access keys. *See* KeyTip

aligning text, tab stops, WD 116

alignment The way the text of a paragraph lines up horizontally between the margins. WD 69–71

alignment, graphics, WD 170

anchor To attach a graphic or other object to a paragraph. WD 153

    anchoring WordArt objects to blank paragraphs, WD 156–157

application settings The most common program options. OFF 18

AutoComplete A feature that automatically inserts dates and other regularly used items for you. WD 26–27

AutoCorrect A feature that automatically corrects common typing errors. WD 21–24

B

Backspace key, WD 20–21

balance To make columns of equal length. WD 173

bitmap A type of file that stores an image as a collection of tiny dots, which, when displayed on a computer monitor or printed on a page, make up a picture. WD 161

blank line, inserting, adjusting margins vs. WD 11

blank table, inserting, WD 103–105

blog An online journal available on the World Wide Web; short for "Web log.", WD 185

blog post An addition to a blog, similar to an entry in a journal. WD 185–187

BMP files, WD 161

bold text, WD 78–79

border, inserting around pages, WD 174–176

built-in style, formatting tables, WD 112–115

bullet A heavy dot (or other graphic) before each item in a list. WD 74

    adding, WD 74–76

Bullet Library A panel that offers a variety of bullet styles. WD 75

business letter, WD 2–3

    allowing space for letterhead, WD 68

    beginning, WD 11–12

    entering text, WD 12–15

    proofreading, WD 24–25

    styles, WD 3

button An icon you click to initiate an action. OFF 10–12. *See also specific buttons*

    adding to Quick Access Toolbar, OFF 18

    toggle, WD 78

C

cell The area in a table where a row and column intersect. WD 103

center alignment A type of alignment in which text is centered between the left and right margins and text is ragged along both the left and right margins. WD 69–70

character-level formatting Formatting applied to only a few characters or words. WD 100

clip art A collection of ready made images. WD 160–165

    bitmaps, WD 161

    deleting, WD 164

    finding, WD 160

    inserting into newsletter, WD 161–164

    pasting into documents, WD 164–165

    resizing, WD 165–166

Clipboard A feature that temporarily stores text or graphics until you need them later. WD 57

Clipboard task pane The task pane used for accessing and using the Office Clipboard to copy and paste information from one location to another. WD 57, WD 59–61

closing files, OFF 21

color

    background in document, WD 174

    fonts, WD 99

column

    balancing, WD 183

    newspaper-style, WD 158–160

    table. *See* table column

contextual tab A Ribbon tab that contains commands related to the selected object so you can manipulate, edit, and format that object. OFF 15

copy To place a duplicate of selected text or graphics on the Office Clipboard, leaving the original material in its original location. WD 57

    paragraph formatting with Format Painter, WD 73–74

correcting errors. *See* error correction

cover page

    deleting, WD 135

    inserting, WD 134–137

crop To reduce the size of a graphic by cutting off one or more of its edges. WD 166–167

cut To remove text from a document and place it on the Office Clipboard. WD 57

cut and paste To remove text or graphics from a document and then paste (or insert) it into a document in a new location. WD 57–61

D

data, entering in tables, WD 105–106

data source In a mail merge, a document that contains information, such as names and addresses, which will be inserted into the main document.

    merging main document and data source, WD 184–185

    selecting, WD 179–180

data source in a mail merge A document that contains information, such as names and addresses, which will be inserted into the main document. WD 177

database A collection of related tables stored in the same file. OFF 2

date, inserting with AutoComplete, WD 26–27

Decrease Indent button, WD 72

default A setting that is preset by the operating system or program. OFF 8, WD 9

deleting

    cover pages, WD 135

    graphics, WD 164

    rows and columns from tables, WD 111

    tables, WD 105

    text, WD 52–54

desktop publishing The process of preparing commercial-quality material using a desktop computer system. WD 148–176

    balancing columns, WD 173

    cropping graphics, WD 166–167

    drop caps, WD 170–171

    elements, WD 148–149

    inserting borders around pages, WD 174–176

    inserting graphics, WD 160–165

    moving and aligning graphics, WD 169–170

    newspaper-style columns, WD 158–160

    resizing graphics, WD 165–166

    symbols and special characters, WD 171–172

    WordArt. *See* WordArt

    wrapping text around graphics, WD 168

dialog box A special kind of window where you enter or choose settings for how you want to perform a task. OFF 13–14

Dialog Box Launcher A button you click to open a task pane or dialog box that provides more advanced functionality for a group of tasks. OFF 13

document A collection of data that has a name and is stored in a computer; also called a file. OFF 2

   business letter. *See* business letter
   colored background, WD 174
   entering text, WD 12–15
   formatting. *See* format
   mail merge. *See* mail merge
   merged. *See* merged document
   moving insertion point, WD 18–19
   new, opening, WD 5–6
   opening, WD 84, WD 99
   planning, WD 98–99
   previewing, WD 33–35, WD 84–85
   printing, WD 35, WD 84–85
   proofreading, WD 24–25, WD 52
   reviewing, WD 46–49
   saving, WD 14–15
   saving with new name, WD 49
   scrolling, WD 16–18
   selecting, WD 30
   selecting parts, WD 29–31

document control An on-screen element such as a text box that lets you select settings and other options for a document. WD 129

dot leader A row of dots or other characters separating tabbed text. WD 118

drag and drop To move an item (either text or a graphic) by selecting it and then dragging it with the mouse. WD 54–57

drop cap A large, capital letter that highlights the beginning of the text of a newsletter, chapter, or some other document section. WD 170–171

E

editing WordArt objects, WD 152

endnote An explanatory comment or reference that appears at the end of a document. WD 119–121

envelope, creating, WD 35–37
error correction, WD 21–25
   spelling and grammar errors, WD 21–24, WD 50–53

Excel. *See* Microsoft Office Excel 2007
exiting programs, OFF 28–29

F

field, merge. *See* merge field
file
   closing, OFF 21
   earlier versions of Office, OFF 19
   new, creating, OFF 22
   open, switching between, OFF 5
   opening, OFF 21–22
   printing, OFF 27–28
   saving, OFF 18–21

file extension A three-character code that Office appends to a filename to identify the program in which that file was created. The default file extensions are .docx for Word, .xlsx for Excel, .pptx for PowerPoint, and .accdb for Access. OFF, 19

filename The name you provide when you save a file and the name you associate with that file. OFF 19

Find and Replace dialog box A Word dialog box used to find a word or phrase in a document, replace the word or phrase with other text, or move directly to a specific part of a document. WD 61–64

first column The far-left column in a table. WD 112

floating graphic A graphic that can be moved independently of the surrounding text. WD 153

folder A container for your files. OFF 19

font A set of characters that uses the same typeface, style, and size. WD 9
   changing by changing theme, WD 84
   new, applying, WD 80–82

font color Text color. WD 99

font size Determined by point size, which is a unit of measurement equal approximately to 1/72 of an inch. WD 9, WD 82

footer Text printed at the bottom of every page in a document or at the bottom of every slide in a presentation. WD 128

footer Text printed at the bottom of every page.
   creating for entire document, WD 129–131
   methods for inserting, WD 129

footnote An explanatory comment or reference that appears at the bottom of a page. WD 119–121

format To change the way a document looks. WD 64
   aligning text, WD 69–71
   changing margins, WD 64–68
   character-level formatting, WD 100
   emphasizing text with bold and italics, WD 78–80
   fonts, WD 80–82
   Format Painter, WD 72–74
   formatting documents in sections, WD 122–124
   formatting headings with Quick Styles, WD 99–102
   formatting tables with styles, WD 112–115
   indenting paragraphs, WD 71–72
   lists, bulleted and numbered, WD 74–78
   manually formatting tables, WD 115
   paragraph-level formatting, WD 100
   searching for formatting, WD 64
   themes, WD 80, WD 83–84

Format Painter A button on the Ribbon that you can use to copy all the formatting features of one paragraph to other paragraphs. WD 72–74

G

gallery A grid or menu that shows a visual representation of the options available for a command. OFF 12–13

GIF files, WD 161
grammar error, checking for, WD 50–53

graphic A drawing, painting, photograph, chart, table, design, or designed text such as WordArt. WD 124, WD 160
   aligning, WD 170
   anchored, WD 153
   clip art, WD 160
   cropping, WD 166–167
   desktop publishing. *See* desktop publishing
   detailed view, WD 124
   inline, WD 153
   inserting, WD 160–165
   moving, WD 169–170
   SmartArt, WD 124–128
   wrapping text around, WD 168

gridline Light gray line that defines the rows and columns of a table. WD 103

group A collection of buttons for related commands on the Ribbon. OFF 11

H

handle. *See* sizing handle

hanging indent A type of paragraph indentation in which all lines except the first line of the paragraph are indented from the left margin. WD 71

header Text printed at the top of every page.
   methods for inserting, WD 129
   separating for sections, WD 131–134

header Text that appears at the top of every page in a document or every slide in a presentation. WD 128

Header and Footer view A Word view in which headers and footers are added or modified and the document text is dimmed. WD 128

header column A column on the left of a table that identifies the type of information in each row. WD 103

header row A row at the top of a table that identifies the type of information in each column. WD 103

heading, formatting with Quick Styles, WD 99–102

Help (Office) Information in Office that you can use to find out how to perform a task or obtain more information about a feature. OFF 23–27
   Help window, OFF 23–27
   ScreenTips, OFF 12, OFF 23

Help window A window that provides access to all the Help topics, templates, and training installed on your computer with Office and available on Microsoft Office Online. OFF 23–27

Home tab, Word window, WD 8

I

Increase Indent button, WD 71–72

indent To move a line or paragraph to the right. WD 71–72

indent marker Mark on the horizontal ruler that indicates a paragraph's current indent setting. WD 71

inline graphic A graphic located in a specific position in a specific line of a document. WD 153

insertion point
    moving, WD 18–19
    Word window, WD 4, WD 5

integration The ability to share information between programs. OFF 3

italic type, WD 79

J

JPEG files, WD 161

justified alignment A type of alignment in which full lines of text are spaced between both the left and the right margins and the text is not ragged. WD 69, WD 70–71

K

keyboard shortcut A combination of keys you press to perform a command. OFF 12, WD 79–80

keystroke, moving insertion point, WD 19

KeyTip An on-screen marker that indicates the keyboard shortcut for selecting a button or command; for example, Alt+H selects the Home tab on the Ribbon. WD 80

L

landscape orientation A type of page orientation in which the page is wider than it is tall, so that text spans the widest part of the page. WD 122, WD 123–124

left alignment A type of alignment in which text aligns on the left margin and is ragged on the right. WD 69

letter, business. See business letter

letterhead, allowing space for, WD 68

line
    multiple, selecting, WD 30
    selecting, WD 30

line spacing The amount of vertical space between lines of text. WD 27
    adjusting, WD 33
    adjusting space in inside address, WD 183

list
    aligning text with tab stops, WD 116
    bulleted, WD 74–76
    numbered, WD 76–77

Live Preview An Office feature that shows the results you would achieve in your file, such as the effects of formatting options on a document's appearance, if you click the option to which you are pointing. OFF 13

M

mail merge The process of combining information from two separate documents to create many final documents, each containing customized information. WD 176–184
    adjusting space in inside address, WD 183
    inserting merge fields, WD 180–182
    merging main document and data source, WD 184–185
    previewing merged document, WD 182–183
    selecting data source, WD 179–180

main document In a mail merge, a document that contains the standard text that will remain the same and the merge fields to contain the variable information; sometimes called the starting document. WD 176
    merging main document and data source, WD 184–185

manual page break A page break you insert anywhere on a page. WD 102–103

margin The space between the page content and the edges of the page. WD 11
    adjusting, inserting blank lines vs. WD 11
    changing, WD 64–68
    viewing, WD 65

merge field In a mail merge, placeholder text in a main document that tells Word where to insert information from the data source. WD 176
    inserting, WD 180–182

merged document In a mail merge, a document that is identical to the main document except that the merge fields have been replaced by data from the data source. WD 177
    previewing, WD 182–183

Microsoft Office 2007 A collection of the most popular Microsoft programs: Word, Excel, PowerPoint, Access, and Outlook. OFF 2
    common window elements, OFF 6–10
    contextual tools, OFF 15–17
    files. See file
    Help. See Help
    integrating programs, OFF 3
    Ribbon, OFF 10–14
    starting programs, OFF 3–5
    switching between programs and files, OFF 5
    versions, OFF 19

Microsoft Office Access 2007 A database program you use to enter, organize, display, and retrieve related information. OFF 2

Microsoft Office Excel 2007 A spreadsheet program you use to display, organize, and analyze numerical data. OFF 2

Microsoft Office Help button, OFF 6

Microsoft Office Online A Web site maintained by Microsoft that provides access to the latest information and additional Help resources. OFF 23

Microsoft Office Outlook 2007 An information management program you use to send, receive, and organize e-mail; plan your schedule; arrange meetings; organize contacts; create a to-do list; and jot down notes. You can also use Outlook to print schedules, task lists, phone directories, and other documents. OFF 2

Microsoft Office PowerPoint 2007 A presentation graphics program you use to create a collection of slides that can contain text, charts, and pictures. OFF 2

Microsoft Office Word 2007 A word-processing program you use to create text documents. OFF 2, WD 1

Mini toolbar A toolbar that appears next to the pointer whenever you select text and contains buttons for the most commonly used formatting commands, such as font, font size, styles, color, alignment, and indents that may appear in different groups or tabs on the Ribbon. OFF 15–16

mistake. See error correction

moving
    graphics, WD 169–170
    insertion point, WD 19
    text, See moving text
    WordArt objects, WD 155–156

moving text
    cutting or copying and pasting, WD 57–61
    dragging and dropping, WD 54–57

multiple lines, selecting, WD 30

multiple paragraphs, selecting, WD 30

N

newspaper-style columns Text that is divided into two or more vertical blocks, or columns on a page. WD 158–160

No Spacing Quick Style, adjusting space in inside address, WD 183

nonprinting characters Symbols that can appear on the screen but are not visible on the printed page. WD 8–9

Numbering Library A panel in the Numbering menu that contains a variety of numbered list formats. WD 76–77

O

object Anything that can be manipulated as a whole, such as a chart, table, picture, video, or sound clip. WD 149

   WordArt. *See* WordArt

object Anything that can be manipulated independently as a whole, such as a chart, table, picture, video, or sound clip. OFF 15

Office. *See* Microsoft Office 2007

Office Button A button that provides access to document-level features, such as creating new files, opening existing files, saving files, printing files, and closing files, as well as the most common program options. OFF 18

   Office programs, OFF 6

   Word window, WD 4, WD 5

opening

   dialog boxes, OFF 13–14

   documents, WD 84, WD 99

   files, OFF 21–22

   new documents, WD 5–6

Outlook. *See* Microsoft Office Outlook 2007

P

page break, manual, inserting. *See* format

Page Width A Zoom setting that shows the entire width of a document on your screen. WD 9, WD 10

paragraph Text that ends with a paragraph mark symbol (_) or a single paragraph mark on a single line. WD 27

   blank, anchoring WordArt objects to, WD 156–157

   colored background, WD 174

   indenting, WD 71–72

   inserting border around, WD 174

   keeping together, WD 79

   multiple, selecting, WD 30

   selecting, WD 30

paragraph mark, Word window, WD 4, WD 5, WD 27

paragraph spacing The amount of space before and after a paragraph. WD 27–29

   adjusting, WD 31–32

paragraph-level formatting A format that applies to an entire paragraph. WD 100

paste To transfer a copy of the text or graphics from the Office Clipboard into the document at the insertion point. WD 57

planning documents, WD 98–99

point The unit used to measure the size of the characters in a font. WD 27

portrait orientation A type of page orientation in which the page is taller than it is wide (like a typical business letter). WD 122

positioning. *See* moving

post To publish a document, such as a blog post, on the Web. WD 185

PowerPoint. *See* Microsoft Office PowerPoint 2007

presentation The file you create in PowerPoint. OFF 2

previewing

   documents, WD 84–85

   merged document, WD 182–183

Print Layout view, WD 6–7

Print Preview window A window that shows you what a document will look like when printed. WD∞33–35

printer, shared, WD 35

printing

   documents, WD 35, WD 84–85

   files, OFF 27–28

   shared printers, WD 35

program

   exiting, OFF 28–29

   open, switching between, OFF 5

proofreading, WD 24–25, WD 52

pull quote A brief quotation from the main document. WD 161

Q

Quick Access Toolbar A collection of buttons that provide one-click access to commonly used commands, such as Save, Undo, and Repeat. OFF 18

   Office programs, OFF 6

   Word window, WD 4, WD 5

Quick Style A Word feature that lets you apply an entire set of formatting choices with one click. WD 99–102

R

ragged Uneven text along a margin. WD 69

record A row in a data source. WD 177

Redo button A button on the Quick Access toolbar that you can click to reverse the effects of the Undo button. WD 20

reference marker The superscripted number or symbol that indicates a footnote or endnote applying to the preceding text. WD 119

replacing text, WD 61–64

resizing

   drop caps, WD 171

   graphics, WD 165–166

   window, OFF 6–7

   workspace, OFF 6–7

Ribbon The main set of commands in Office that you click to execute tasks. OFF 10–14

   clicking button icons, OFF 10–12

galleries, OFF 12–13

key tips, OFF 12

keyboard shortcuts, OFF 12

Live Preview, OFF 13

opening dialog boxes and task panes, OFF 13–14

reducing and redisplaying, OFF 10

tabs, OFF 10

Word window, WD 4, WD 5

right alignment A type of alignment in which text aligns on the right margin and is ragged on the left. WD 69

right indent A type of paragraph indentation in which all lines of the paragraph are indented from the right margin. WD 71

rotating WordArt objects, WD 156

row

   changing height, WD 112

   deleting from table, WD 111

   inserting in tables, WD 110

   sorting rows in tables, WD 107–109

rulers

   displaying, WD 7–8

   Word window, WD 4, WD 5

S

saving

   document, with new name, WD 49

   documents, WD 14–15

   files, OFF 18–21

scale To change the size of a graphic to make it fit into a document. WD 165–166

ScreenTip Onscreen text that appears when you position the mouse pointer over certain objects, such as the objects on the taskbar or a toolbar button. ScreenTips tell you the purpose or function of the object to which you are pointing. OFF 12, OFF 23, WD 5

scroll To shift text up or down in a window to display content currently not visible on the screen. WD 16–18

search text The text you want to find using the Find and Replace dialog box. WD 61

section A unit or part of a document that can have its own page orientation, margins, headers, footers, and vertical alignment. WD 122

   formatting documents in sections, WD 122–124

   separating headers for sections, WD 131–134

section break A type of division in a document that divides one section from another. WD 122

   inserting, WD 122–123

select To highlight text or other item in a document or program before changing it in some way (such as deleting or moving it). WD 29 part of a table, WD 106–107

parts of documents, WD 29–31

selection bar The blank space in the left margin area of the Document window. WD 29

sentence, selecting, WD 30

shape, WordArt objects, changing, WD 152–153

shared printer, WD 35

shortcut menu A list of commands directly related to the object that you right-clicked. OFF 17

Show/Hide ** button, Word window, WD 8, WD 47

sizing. *See also* resizing

    WordArt objects, WD 155–156

sizing buttons, Office programs, OFF 6

sizing handle A circle or square on the border of a selected object, such as a graphic, that you can drag to change the graphic's size. WD 126, WD 151

SmartArt A Word feature that allows you to quickly create diagrams and charts. WD 124–128

    adding text to graphics, WD 126–127

    adjusting size of graphic, WD 127–128

    creating graphics, WD 124–126

sort To rearrange information, such as rows in a table, in alphabetical, numerical, or chronological order. WD 107

    sorting rows in tables, WD 107–109

special characters, WD 171–172

Spelling and Grammar checker A feature that checks a document against Word's built-in dictionary and a set of grammar rules. WD 50–52

spelling checker A feature that checks a document against Word's built-in dictionary. WD 21–24

starting Office programs, OFF 3–5

status bar An area at the bottom of the program window that contains information about the open file or the current task on which you are working.

    getting information, OFF 7–8

    Office programs, OFF 6

switching

    between open programs and files, OFF 5

    views, OFF 8

symbols, WD 171–172

T

tab Part of the Ribbon that includes commands related to particular activities. OFF 10

    contextual, OFF 15

    Word window, WD 4, WD 5

tab Space between the left margin and the beginning of the text on a particular line or between the text in one column and the text in another column. WD 115–119

    aligning text, WD 116

    entering text, WD 116–118

    tables vs. WD 119

tab stop The location where the insertion point moves (including any text to the right of it) when you press the Tab key. WD 115

table Information arranged in horizontal rows and vertical columns. WD 103–115

    blank, inserting, WD 103–105

    changing column widths, WD 111–112

    deleting, WD 105

    deleting rows and columns, WD 111

    entering data, WD 105–106

    formatting with styles, WD 112–115

    inserting rows and columns, WD 110

    organizing information, WD 103

    selecting part, WD 106–107

    sorting rows, WD 107–109

    tabs vs. WD 119

table column

    changing width, WD 111–112

    deleting from table, WD 111

    first, WD 112

    inserting in tables, WD 110

table style, formatting tables, WD 112–115

task pane A window that provides access to commands for common tasks you'll perform in Office programs. OFF 13

text

    aligning, WD 69–71

    aligning with tab stops, WD 116

    cutting or copying and pasting, WD 57–61

    deleting, WD 52–54

    dragging and dropping, WD 54–57

    entering, WD 12–15

    finding and replacing, WD 61–64

    selecting, WD 29–31

    wrapping around graphics, WD 168

    wrapping below WordArt objects, WD 153–155

text block, selecting, WD 30

text box A container in a document for text. WD 161

theme A designed collection of formatting options that include colors, graphics, and background images. WD 80

    changing, WD 83–84

    changing font by changing, WD 84

TIFF files, WD 161

title bar, Office programs, OFF 6

toggle button A button (such as the Bold button) that you can click once to turn on, then click again to turn off. WD 78

typographic symbol A special character often used in printed publications. WD 171–172

U

Undo button A button on the Quick Access toolbar that you can click to undo (or reverse) your last action. WD 20

V

view, switching, OFF 8

view button, Word window, WD 5

view shortcuts, Office programs, OFF 6

W

window, resizing, OFF 6–7

window element, common, OFF 6–10

Word. *See* Microsoft Office Word 2007

word, selecting, WD 30

Word window, WD 3–5

    displaying nonprinting characters, WD 8–9

    displaying rulers, WD 7–8

    elements, WD 4–5

    font and font size, WD 9

    Home tab, WD 8

    Print Layout view, WD 6–7

    Zoom setting, WD 9–11

word wrap Automatic line breaking. WD 13

WordArt A Word feature that allows you to insert specially formatted text into a document. WD 149–157

    anchoring WordArt objects to blank paragraphs, WD 156–157

    changing shape of objects, WD 152–153

    creating objects, WD 149–152

    editing WordArt objects, WD 152

    positioning and sizing WordArt objects, WD 155–156

    rotating objects, WD 156

    wrapping text below WordArt objects, WD 153–155

workbook File in which Excel stores an electronic spreadsheet. OFF 2

workspace

    Office programs, OFF 6

    resizing, OFF 6–7

    zooming, OFF 8–10

wrap To flow text around an object. WD 153

    wrapping text around graphics, WD 168

Z

zoom To magnify or shrink your view of a window. OFF 8

    workspace, OFF 8–10

zoom controls, Office programs, OFF 6

Zoom level A setting that controls a document's on-screen magnification. WD 9–11

    viewing margin, WD 65

Task Reference

TASK	PAGE #	RECOMMENDED METHOD
Action, redo	WD 20	Click [icon]
Action, undo	WD 20	Click [icon]
AutoCorrect, set options	WD 21	Click [icon], click Word Options, click Proofing, click AutoCorrect Options
Boldface, add to text	WD 78	Select text, in Font group on Home tab click **B**
Border, insert around page	WD 174	Click Page Layout tab, click Page Borders button in Page Background group, click Page Border tab, click Box
Bullets, add to paragraph	WD 74	Select paragraph, in Paragraph group on Home tab click [icon]
Clip art, crop	WD 166	Click clip art, click Format tab, click Crop button in Size group, drag picture border to crop
Clip art, find	WD 161	Click Insert tab, click Clip Art button in Illustrations group, type search criteria, click Go
Clip art, insert in document	WD 161–164	Click Insert tab, click Clip Art button in Illustrations group, click Organize clips, click picture, click Copy, click in document, press Ctrl+V
Clip art, resize	WD 165	Click clip art, drag sizing handle
Clipboard, use to cut, copy, and paste	WD 57	*See* Reference Window: Cutting (or Copying) and Pasting Text
Clipboard task pane, open	WD 57	In Clipboard group on Home tab, click Clipboard
Column, insert in table	WD 110	Click column, click Layout tab, click Select button in Table group, click Insert Right or Insert Left button in Rows & Columns group
Column width, change in table	WD 112	Double-click or drag border between columns
Columns, balance	WD 173	Click end of rightmost column, click Page Layout tab, click Breaks button in Page Setup group, click Continuous
Columns, format text in	WD 158	Click where you want to insert columns, or select text to divide into columns, click Page Layout tab, click Columns button in Page Setup group, select options, click OK
Date, insert with AutoComplete	WD 25	Start typing date, press Enter
Document, open	WD 46	Click [icon], click Open, select drive and folder, click filename, click Open
Document, open new	WD 5–6	Click [icon], click New
Document, preview	WD 34	Click [icon], point to Print, click Print Preview
Document, save with same name	WD 17	On Quick Access Toolbar, click [icon]
Drop cap, insert	WD 170	Click in paragraph, click Insert tab, click Drop Cap button in Text group, select options
Endnotes, create	WD 119	*See* Reference Window: Working with Footnotes and Endnotes
Envelope, create	WD 36	*See* Reference Window: Creating an Envelope
File, close	OFF 21	Click [icon], click Close
File, open	OFF 22	*See* Reference Window: Opening an Existing File or Creating a New File
File, print	OFF 27	*See* Reference Window: Printing a File
File, save	OFF 18	*See* Reference Window: Saving a File

TASK	PAGE #	RECOMMENDED METHOD
Font, change typeface	WD 81	In Font group on Home tab, click Font arrow, click font
Font size, change	WD 82	In Font group on Home tab, click Font Size arrow, click point size
Footer, add	WD 129	Double-click in bottom margin, type footer text, select options on Header & Footer Tools Design tab
Footnotes, create	WD 119	*See* Reference Window: Working with Footnotes and Endnotes
Format, copy	WD 73	*See* Reference Window: Using the Format Painter
Graphic, crop	WD 166	Click graphic, click Format tab, click Crop button in Size group, drag to crop
Graphic, find	WD 161	Click Insert tab, click Clip Art button in Illustrations group, type search criteria, click Go
Graphic, resize	WD 165	Click graphic, drag sizing handle
Graphic, wrap text around	WD 168	Click graphic, click Format tab, click Text Wrapping button in Arrange group, click text wrapping option
Header, add	WD 129	Double-click top margin, type header text, select options on Header & Footer Tools Design tab
Help task pane, use	OFF 24	*See* Reference Window: Getting Help
Hyperlink, add in document	WD 120	Type e-mail address or URL, press spacebar
Hyperlink, remove	WD 120	Right-click hyperlink, click Remove Hyperlink
Hyperlink, use	WD 120	Press Ctrl and click the hyperlink
Italics, add to text	WD 79	Select text, in Font group on Home tab click *I*
Line spacing, change	WD 32	Select text to change, in Paragraph group on Home tab click spacing option
Margins, change	WD 65	*See* Reference Window: Changing Margins for a Document
Nonprinting characters, show	WD 8	In Paragraph group on Home tab, click ¶
Numbering, add to paragraphs	WD 76	Select paragraphs, in Paragraph group on Home tab click ⊞
Office program, start	OFF 3	*See* Reference Window: Starting Office Programs
Page, view width	WD 10	Click Zoom level, click Page width, click OK
Page break, insert	WD 103	Click where you want to break the page, click Insert tab, click Page Break button in Pages group
Page number, insert	WD 130	Open header or footer, on Header & Footer Tools Design tab, click Page Number button in Header & Footer group
Page orientation, change	WD 123	Click Page Layout tab, click Orientation button in Page Setup group, choose orientation type
Paragraph, decrease indent	WD 72	In Paragraph group on Home tab, click ⊟
Paragraph, increase indent	WD 72	In Paragraph group on Home tab, click ⊟
Print layout view, change to	WD 7	Click ⊞
Program, Office, exit	OFF 28	Click ☒ on the title bar
Programs, Office, open	OFF 3	*See* Reference Window: Starting Office Programs
Row, delete from table	WD 111	Click row, click Delete button in Rows & Columns group on Table Tools Layout tab
Row height, change in table	WD 112	Drag divider between rows; to see measurements, press and hold Alt while dragging
Rulers, display	WD 7	*See* Reference Window: Displaying the Rulers

TASK	PAGE #	RECOMMENDED METHOD
Section, insert in document	WD 122	Click where you want to insert a section break, click Page Layout tab, click Breaks button in Page Setup group, click a section break type
Shading, apply to table	WD 113	Click table, click Design tab, click More button in Table Styles group, click shading style
Special character, insert	WD 172	*See* Reference Window: Inserting Symbols and Special Characters
Spelling, correct individual word	WD 23	Right-click misspelled word (as indicated by a wavy red line), click correctly spelled word
Spelling and grammar, check	WD 50	*See* Reference Window: Checking a Document for Spelling and Grammar Errors
Symbol, insert	WD 172	*See* Reference Window: Inserting Symbols and Special Characters
Tab stop, set	WD 116	*See* Reference Window: Aligning Text with Tab Stops
Table, create in Word	WD 104	Click Insert tab, click Table button in Tables group, drag pointer to select columns and rows
Table, format	WD 113	*See* Reference Window: Formatting a Table with a Built-in Table Style
Table, sort	WD 108	*See* Reference Window: Sorting the Rows of a Table
Text, align	WD 69–71	Select text, click ☰, ☰, ☰, or ☰ on Mini toolbar
Text, copy and paste	WD 57	*See* Reference Window: Cutting (or Copying) and Pasting Text
Text, find and replace	WD 62	*See* Reference Window: Finding and Replacing Text
Text, move by drag and drop	WD 54	*See* Reference Window: Dragging and Dropping Text
Text, select entire document	WD 30	Press Ctrl and click in selection bar
Text, select multiple adjacent lines	WD 30	Click and drag in selection bar
Text, select multiple nonadjacent lines	WD 30	Select text, press and hold Ctrl, select additional lines of text
Text, select multiple paragraphs	WD 30	Click and drag in selection bar
Text, wrap around WordArt	WD 154	Click WordArt, click Format tab, click Text Wrapping button in Arrange group, click text wrap option
Window, close	OFF 6	Click ✖ or click ✖
Window, maximize	OFF 7	Click ▣ or click ▢
Window, minimize	OFF 7	Click ▬ or click ▬
Window, restore	OFF 7	Click ▣ or click ▣
Word, start	WD 3	Click 🟠, click All Programs, click Microsoft Office, click Microsoft Office Word 2007
WordArt, change shape	WD 153	Click WordArt, click 🅰 in WordArt Styles group, click shape
WordArt, edit text	WD 152	Click WordArt, click Format tab, click Edit Text button in Text group, edit text, click OK
WordArt, insert	WD 149	*See* Reference Window: Creating WordArt
WordArt, wrap text	WD 154	Click WordArt, click Format tab, click Text Wrapping button in Arrange group, click text wrap option
Workspace, zoom	OFF 8	*See* Reference Window: Zooming the Workspace
Zoom setting, change	WD 10	Drag Zoom slider